Horton Foote

CASEBOOKS ON MODERN DRAMATISTS
VOLUME 24
GARLAND REFERENCE LIBRARY OF THE HUMANITIES
VOLUME 2038

CASEBOOKS ON MODERN DRAMATISTS

KIMBALL KING, *General Editor*

SAM SHEPARD
A Casebook
edited by Kimball King

CHRISTOPHER HAMPTON
A Casebook
edited by Robert Gross

HOWARD BRENTON
A Casebook
edited by Ann Wilson

DAVID STOREY
A Casebook
edited by William Hutchings

PETER SHAFFER
A Casebook
edited by C.J. Gianakaras

SIMON GRAY
A Casebook
edited by Katherine H. Burkman

JOHN ARDEN AND
MARGARETTA D'ARCY
A Casebook
edited by Jonathan Wike

AUGUST WILSON
A Casebook
edited by Marilyn Elkins

JOHN OSBORNE
A Casebook
edited by Patricia D. Denison

DAVID HARE
A Casebook
edited by Hersh Zeifman

MARSHA NORMAN
A Casebook
edited by Linda Ginter Brown

BRIAN FRIEL
A Casebook
edited by William Kerwin

NEIL SIMON
A Casebook
edited by Gary Konas

TERRENCE MCNALLY
A Casebook
edited by Toby Silverman Zinman

STEPHEN SONDHEIM
A Casebook
edited by Joanne Gordon

HORTON FOOTE
A Casebook
edited by Gerald C. Wood

HORTON FOOTE
A CASEBOOK

EDITED BY
GERALD C. WOOD

GARLAND PUBLISHING, INC.
A MEMBER OF THE TAYLOR & FRANCIS GROUP
NEW YORK AND LONDON
1998

Library of Congress Cataloging-in-Publication Data

Horton Foote : a casebook / edited by Gerald C. Wood.
        p.   cm. — (Garland reference library of the humanities ; v. 2038.
Casebooks on modern dramatists ; v. 24)
   Includes bibliographical references and index.
   ISBN 0-8153-2544-4 (alk. paper)
   1. Foote, Horton—Criticism and interpretation.   2. Texas—In
literature.   I. Wood, Gerald C.   II. Series: Garland reference library of the
humanities ; vol. 2038.   III. Series: Garland reference library of the
humanities.   Casebooks on modern dramatists ; vol. 24.
PS3511.0344Z69   1998
812'.54—dc21   97-31399
                                        CIP

Cover photograph of Horton Foote courtesy of Eric H. Antoniou.

Printed on acid-free, 250-year-life paper
Manufactured in the United States of America

For Tim and Sarah

Table of Contents

General Editor's Note

Horton Foote, who has won the Pulitzer Prize for Drama, the William Inge Lifetime Achievement Award, the Lucille Lortel Award, two Academy Awards for his screenplays, and numerous Writers Guild Awards, considers himself primarily a playwright, although he is equally well known for his television and film work. A major interpreter of American experience, he is famous for his realistic portrayals of life in rural Texas. Like Faulkner, who drew upon the legends and history of his native Mississippi and who blended actual events with fictitious characters in his mythical Yoknapatawpha County, Foote has populated his hometown of Wharton, Texas (renamed Harrison) with a large cast of characters, who appear in both major and minor roles in a cycle of semi-autobiographical dramas. Often referred to as the "American Chekhov" because of his dark humor and his compassion for flawed characters, Foote locates the small victories and defeats of everyday life in a spiritual and historical context.

The editor of this volume, Gerald Wood, has interviewed Horton Foote several times and has edited a selection of his one-act plays for Southern Methodist University Press. He has also written critical essays on Foote for *Christianity and Literature* and for the *Journal of American Drama and Theatre*. Wood is currently completing a book-length study of Foote for the Louisiana State University Press. He is professor and chair of English at Carson-Newman College.

Kimball King

Acknowledgments

I began this project while studying collateral material on Foote under a John Stephenson Fellowship with the Appalachian College Association. I want to thank that organization and its director, Alice Brown, for continuing support of my research and writing. These opportunities and many others were made possible by the leadership of Larry Osborne, then Dean of Academic Special Programs, Mike Carter, Provost, and Cordell Maddox, President—all of Carson-Newman College.

I also want to thank Horton Foote for offering early and generous access to his personal papers, when they were still in his guest house in Wharton, Texas. The other contributors and I appreciate his gracious permission to study those manuscripts at the DeGolyer Library, Southern Methodist University and to use material from that collection—with care and discretion—in this volume.

Attendance at the Signature Theater Company's series of Foote plays inspired many of the essays in this casebook.

Angela Ellis Roberts, at Carson-Newman, was responsible for much of the correspondence, proofing, and organization in preparation of this manuscript. Kimball King and Phyllis Korper have been most encouraging and supportive throughout the process.

Introduction

Horton Foote began writing plays when he was an actor in (and co-founder of) the American Actors Company in the late 1930s. Since then, more than 85 of his dramas have been produced for theater, television, and film. He has received two Academy Awards for his screenwriting: the first for his adaptation of Harper Lee's novel *To Kill a Mockingbird* (1962) and the second for his original screenplay for *Tender Mercies* (1983). His adaptation of his own stageplay and teleplay *The Trip to Bountiful* was also nominated by the Academy, and other Foote screenplays are recognized as major achievements in American independent filmmaking: *Tomorrow* (1972), *1918* (1985), and *Courtship* (1987), for example. For these contributions to the art of film Foote has been honored by the Writers Guild, both East and West.

But Horton Foote's primary allegiance has always been to the theater. During the 1950s, when Foote was writing successfully for television, he considered himself a playwright using the new medium to showcase his work for the stage. Barely 20 of his works have been shown on TV, only half of that number being original productions. Despite many excursions into film and television, Foote has continually returned to the theater even when there were few financial incentives for his many homecomings. After almost 40 years in the theater and turning sixty years old, he began his most ambitious dramatic work—the nine-play cycle *The Orphans' Home*. The production of those plays throughout the United States was eventually followed by the Signature Theatre Company 1994–95 series of four Foote plays. For one of his original works in that program—*The Young Man from Atlanta*—the writer received the 1995 Pulitzer Prize for Drama. And yet, this two-time Academy Award winner, recipient of the Lucille Lortel Award, and Pulitzer dramatist is often considered a relatively obscure figure, a secret of the contemporary American stage.

Because Foote is less well known than writers with similar careers (for example, Sam Shepard and David Mamet), this casebook begins by establishing the biographical, theatrical, and critical contexts for his work. The first essay, Marion Castleberry's "Remembering Wharton, Texas," describes the influence of the writer's East Texas past on his early work for the American Actors Company. Castleberry argues that Foote, though not an autobiographical writer, learned to fashion the history and stories of his region—coastal southeast Texas—into plays with both personal and universal resonance. After experimenting with various dramatic forms throughout the 1940s, including a more abstract style heavily influenced by music and modern dance, Foote had returned to his initial impulses to write a personal brand of historical/psychological realism. This style, realized most definitively in *The Chase*, also led Foote to the new medium of television, which in its golden age was, as Terry Barr shows in "Horton Foote's TV Women," well suited to Horton Foote's intimate stories. Most interesting, Barr writes, is how the writer used television to examine the political and psychological issues of women facing social changes in modern America. Simultaneous with this success on television, Foote enjoyed the first production of one of his screenplays—*Storm Fear*—released in 1956. Though not as noteworthy as subsequent work, especially *To Kill a Mockingbird* at the beginning of the 60s, this film began the writer's series of film adaptations of literary works with, in Rebecca Briley's words, "Southern Accents." Though often considered the American Chekhov, Horton Foote is better understood, Briley explains, as part of the Southern tradition of Flannery O'Connor, William Faulkner, and Katherine Anne Porter, whose work inspired Foote's becoming a reluctant but effective adaptor of the region's literature. Foote's distinction, she says, is his ability to recreate authentic Southern voices without denying his own distinctive style and themes.

The essays in the middle section of this casebook continue this focus on characteristics unique to Horton Foote's dramas. As Tim Wright explains in "More Real Than Realism," one source of Foote's achievement is his recognition and integration of both objective and subjective truths. In all his mature work, Wright argues, the writer insists on historical accuracy even as he embraces the subjectivity of narrative art; Foote writes a personal form of literary impressionism. Like Wright, Crystal Brian and Laurin Porter believe the rigorously realistic surfaces of Foote's work are deceiving. For Brian, in "'To Be Quiet and Listen,'" the key is the influence of music, especially that of Charles Ives, made explicit in *The Orphans' Home*. The found art of both the playwright and the composer, while evoking a particular historical place, weaves personal obsession into a tapestry of theme and variation more akin to religious meditation than the structures of traditional dramatic art. Implicated, according to Porter in "Subtext as Text," is Foote's use of language which requires audiences capable of compassionate, empathetic, and imaginative collaboration. Kimball King, in his review of *The Death of Papa*, the concluding play in *The Orphans' Home* cycle, explores how such a mediative theater should be represented in artistic performance. Finally, S. Dixon McDowell discovers in "Film Aesthetic" that Foote uses his training and experience in theater to create a discernible film style in the tradition of American independent film and international cinema.

The last critical section of the casebook focuses on the Signature Theatre Company's series during 1994-95. More than the previous essays, these final pieces study individual plays, offering more in-depth analysis of the complexities of Horton Foote's methods and ideas. Using *Talking Pictures* as a paradigm, Susan Underwood demonstrates that texture in Horton Foote's plays is a matter of subtext. The writer, she finds, freezes traditional plot in the interest of his psychological and religious subjects; all the physical terror in the plays is finally subsumed to an implicit assertion in this play, as in all his work, of a spiritual perspective that redeems and lends humor to the linear action. The catalysts for this spirituality, I argue in my essay on *Night Seasons*, are the nurturing women present in many of Horton Foote's works. Unfortunately, in this play the ideal is inverted; Laura Lee embodies the unnatural darkness created when the loving female will, and its deep ties to selfhood and generation, is paralyzed by the-family-turned-inward. There is more health—and hope—in *The Young Man from Atlanta*, where intimacy is reestablished between Lily Dale and Will. The stimulus for this healing lies in the characters' recognition of a profound sense of mystery, which fosters humility, honest need, and even responsible language. Finally, in his study of *Laura Dennis*, Dean Mendell returns to the issue of dramatic construction, finding (like others in the book) that Horton Foote is the master of calm surfaces that hide intense subtexts. In a world where every character has his or her own good reasons, the drama resides in the search, by both Foote and his audiences, for motive and character.

Despite the wide divergence in the subjects of this casebook, the contributors share a recognition that Horton Foote utilizes the found art of a regional writer, in his case the voices, characters, and stories of coastal southeast Texas. But each essayist also contends, at least implicitly, that these plays—whether for stage, television, or film—are not merely historical and literal; the most arresting quality is the rich and complex subtext of Foote's stories. The texture, as he has called it, of his plays is fashioned from transparent plots designed to reveal psychological and religious issues which the writer believes essential to all life and art. Horton Foote's distinctive style and his unique contribution to contemporary American theater are created by the tension between these humanistic values and the disarmingly simple, almost photographically real, texts they serve. While willing to betray all the tenets of the well-made play, Foote reacts against the deconstruction of language and demands an audience willing to preserve both subjectivity and empathy. He implicitly calls for a return to a more humane and healing theater.

Thus these essays argue that Horton Foote should be placed—with some qualification and much care—in the American tradition of dramatic realism. His work is regionalist like that of E. P. Conkle, Lynn Riggs, Paul Green, or Thornton Wilder, but the religious resonance in Foote's writing is closer to Southern prose writers like Flannery O'Connor or Katherine Anne Porter. Like Tennessee Williams, Foote dramatizes the endless search for identity, but Foote's people are more capable and courageous, even when they fail, than Williams' studies in beautiful paralysis and death. Foote's plays are political like those of Arthur Miller and David Mamet; they deal with similar economic, racial, and sexual injustices. But the private worlds of Foote's characters are more pressing and finally carry more weight than his public ones. While Horton Foote's mental theater is close to that of Eugene O'Neill, Foote is much more faithful to the speech and mythology of his particular place than O'Neill. His search for roots is similar to that of Lorraine Hansberry or August Wilson. And yet his experimentation with dramatic form leads Foote far from the classical tradition of the well-made play in Europe or the United States.

One the one hand, Horton Foote's dramas claim the strict realism of found art. They embrace the power of language and stories used by real people living in historical moments. Since this world of nature must be recreated with accuracy and fidelity, Foote's dramatic space is flawed, broken, confusing, and ineluctably mysterious. At every point it requires a radical dedramatization, a disruption in the artificial order of art, especially the false comforts of the formulaic and theatrical. And yet the texture and subtext of the plays establishes a more poetic, essentially religious, vision which asserts the healing power of loving connection to bring peace in the face of death. In their eternal struggles with fear, Foote's characters gain courage when they choose to believe, with William Blake, that eternity is in love with the productions of time.

A Christian humanist who wants to see the world with a cold, clear eye, Horton Foote writes in reaction to the spiritual wasteland of the twentieth century. But this opposition is understated, hidden in plays driven more by questions than answers, qualification than assertion. And while his stories recognize all forms of violence and death, the writer believes in the power of love, like that between Horace and Elizabeth in *The Orphans' Home*, to bring order to the chaos of the orphaned, placeless world Foote sees around him. All his characters, whether they recognize it or not, are driven by the need for connection to something beyond themselves, to a sense of the transcendence born of life's many cultures—natural, familial, social, or religious. Throughout his work, though rarely understood or articulated by the characters, is Foote's drama of intimacy. His most content characters recognize their needs for nurturance, individuation and responsibility, and final sacrifice to divine mystery. His saddest, his weakest people never understand the power of benign attachments. They end in violent despair.

But Foote is not a rhetorical writer. His plays typically explore their subjects with compassion, not judgment. The search for intimacy—in individual plays as well as the whole Foote canon —is studied in quiet but profoundly dramatic moments of rising emotional awareness and choice. Like the hard circular stairs in Yeats' tower, the themes and variations in an Ives score, or the slow unwinding of an Ozu film, the patterns of conflict and freedom flow through Foote's theater with the power of a personal myth. Usually without awareness on their part, the Foote characters are called to self-awareness and the courage to face death. Such drama rarely informs the dialogue in the plays, and it never is fully revealed or resolved in the conclusions. However, it is implied in all the language used by the characters, whether clumsy or quietly poetic.

Thus, while not holding Horton Foote's work up as a standard or defending its psychological and religious humanism, this casebook seeks to describe the ethos of his plays. Foote is a Southern writer with affinities to Faulkner, Porter, and O'Connor. Within this tradition, his work is essentially dramatic, following a dialectical pattern of theme and variation; this is his Chekhovian temper and method. But Foote's work is most engaging when he moves beyond these influences to test the boundaries of realism, creating hyperrealistic texts which dedramatize theatrical form in unconventional ways. Beneath the surface of each play lies Foote's preoccupation with the loss of history, community, and religious sensibility in twentieth-century American life. Within the public worlds of theater and film, he continues his personal study of the sources and nature of courageous responses to such loss.

Foote Chronology

March 14, 1916   Born in Wharton, Texas, the first of three boys, to Albert Horton and Hallie Brooks Foote.

1933–35   Studied acting at Pasadena Playhouse in California.

1936–44   Worked as an actor in New York City area (1936–42), training at Tamara Daykarhanova school (1937–39).

First plays written for American Actors Company under direction of Mary Hunter: *Wharton Dance* (1939–40), *Texas Town* (1940–41), *Out of My House* (1942), *Only the Heart* (1943, also produced on Broadway, 1944).

Brief experience as writer for Universal Studios in Hollywood (1944).

Wrote *Daisy Lee* (1944), a dance play choreographed and performed by Valerie Bettis.

For Neighborhood Playhouse wrote *Miss Lou, The Lonely* (a dance play choreographed by Martha Graham) and *Goodbye to Richmond* (all 1944).

June 4, 1945   Married Lillian Vallish.

1945–49   Moved to Washington, DC, where he wrote and directed *Homecoming, People in the Show, Themes and Variations,* and *Goodbye to Richmond.*

1949   Returned from Washington, DC, to New York City.

1951–54   Wrote for television, including *The Gabby Hayes Show* (also called *The Quaker Oats Show*) (1950–51), *Ludie Brooks* (1951), *The Travelers* (1952), *Expectant Relations* (1953), *The Trip to Bountiful*

(1953), *A Young Lady of Property* (1953), and *The Shadow of Willie Greer* (1954).

Wrote ballet-with-words for Jerome Robbins musical *Two's Company* (1953).

Wrote for stage: *The Chase* (1952), *The Trip to Bountiful* (1953), *The Traveling Lady* (1954).

1955–65   Continuing work in television, mostly commissioned: *The Roads to Home* (1955), *Flight* (1956), *Drugstore, Sunday Noon* (1956), *A Member of the Family* (1957), *Old Man* (1960), *Tomorrow* (1960), *The Shape of the River* (1960), *The Night of the Storm* (1961), *The Gambling Heart* (1964).

Moved from New York City to Nyack, New York, in 1956.

First screenplay: *Storm Fear* (1956).

Academy Award and Writers Guild of America Award for adaptation of Harper Lee's novel *To Kill a Mockingbird* (1962).

Screenplay for *Baby, the Rain Must Fall* (1964), from his play *The Traveling Lady*.

Moved from Nyack, New York, to New Hampshire (1966).

1966–77   Commissioned work in film adaptation: *Hurry Sundown* (1966), *The Chase* (1966), revisions for Lillian Hellman screenplay, *The Stalking Moon* (1969).

HB Playwrights Foundation production of *Tomorrow*, adapted from a short story by William Faulkner, in New York City (1968).

Adaptation of *Gone with the Wind* as stage musical in London and Los Angeles (1971–73).

Film production of *Tomorrow* (1972).

Wrote *The Orphans' Home Cycle* (1974–77).

HB Playwrights Foundation production of *A Young Lady of Property* (1976).

1977–81   Adaptations for PBS of Flannery O'Connor's short story "The Displaced Person" (1977) and Faulkner's short story "Barn Burning" (1980).

Worked with Herbert Berghof at HB Playwrights Foundation. Taught acting at HB Studio, 1978–79. Productions of *Night Seasons* (1977), *In a Coffin in Egypt* (1980), *Arrival and Departure* (1981). Directed three plays of *The Orphans' Home Cycle—Courtship* (1978), *1918* (1979), *Valentine's Day* (1980).

1982–89   *The Roads to Home* (Manhattan Punch Line Theater, 1982).

The Widow Claire (off-Broadway, 1982).

The Old Friends (HB Playwrights Foundation, 1982).

Academy Award, Writers Guild of America award and Christopher Award for original screenplay of *Tender Mercies* (1983).

Keeping On: A Drama of Life in a Mill Town, teleplay for PBS American Playhouse, 1983.

Blind Date, The Prisoner's Song, The One-Armed Man (HB Playwrights Foundation, 1985).

The Road to the Graveyard (Ensemble Studio Theatre, 1985).

Ensemble Studio Theatre Founders Award (1985).

Academy Award nomination for screenplay of *The Trip to Bountiful* (1985). Also, Independent Film Award and Luminas Award.

Blind Date (Ensemble Studio Theatre, 1986).

Beginning of independent film production: *1918* (1985), *On Valentine's Day* (1986), *Courtship* (1987). The three films re-edited and shown on PBS as *The Story of a Marriage* (1987).

Off-Broadway productions of *The Widow Claire* and *Lily Dale* (1986–87).

The Man Who Climbed the Pecan Trees and *The Land of the Astronauts* produced by Ensemble Studio Theatre (both 1988).

Directed first production of *The Habitation of Dragons*, Pittsburgh Public Theater (September–October 1988).

Compostela Award (1988).

Dividing the Estate (McCarter Theatre, Princeton, New Jersey, 1989).

William Inge Lifetime Achievement Award (1989).

Evelyn Burkey Award, Writers Guild East (1989).

Since 1990   *Convicts*, film of *Orphans' Home* play, released starring Robert Duvall and James Earl Jones (1990).

Talking Pictures (Asolo Performing Arts Center, Sarasota, Florida, 1990).

Great Lakes Theater Festival of Foote works for theater, film, and television, including production of *Dividing the Estate* (1990).

Of Mice and Men, film adaptation of John Steinbeck novel, released starring Gary Sinise and John Malkovich (1991).

Habitation of Dragons, TNT teleplay for Steven Spielberg Productions, Spring 1992.

The Roads to Home (Lambs Theatre, New York City, 1992).

A.C.T. Theatre (San Francisco) productions of *Convicts, Courtship*, and *1918* (1992).

August, 1992: Death of Lillian Vallish Foote.

Night Seasons (American Stage Company, Teaneck, New Jersey, 1993).

Laurel Award, Writers Guild West (1993).

1994–95 Signature Theatre Series: *Talking Pictures* (September 1994), *Night Seasons* (November 1994), *The Young Man from Atlanta* (January 1995), and *Laura Dennis* (March 1995).

Brigham Young University Festival of his films and plays (Provo, Utah, Spring 1995).

Lucille Lortel Award (1995).

Pulitzer Prize for Drama (1995).

Outer Critics Circle—Special Achievement Award (1995).

Lily Dale, film version of his play from *Orphans' Home* cycle, on Showtime, June 9, 1996, starring Mary Stuart Masterson, Sam Shepard, and Stockard Channing.

Induction into Theatre Hall of Fame (1996).

The Young Man from Atlanta restaged: Alley Theatre, Houston; Goodman Theatre, Chicago, Illinois (January 1997); and The Longacre Theatre, New York City (March 1997).

The Death of Papa, Playmakers Repertory Theatre, Chapel Hill, North Carolina, dir. Michael Wilson, and starring Ellen Burstyn, Matthew Broderick, Hallie Foote, Ray Virta, and Polly Holliday (1997).

Old Man, CBS Hallmark Hall of Fame, February 9, 1997, starring Jeanne Tripplehorn and Arliss Howard.

Alone, original teleplay, Showtime, 1997, starring Hume Cronyn, James Earl Jones, and Piper Laurie.

Remembering Wharton, Texas
Marion Castleberry

> When I was growing up in Wharton, I had no idea of becoming a writer; I was determined to be an actor. And yet, now, looking back, I can see that in some subtle, mysterious way, my talent...was being nurtured for my future work.
>
> —Horton Foote, "Why I Remember" 9

The first-born son of Albert Horton Foote, Sr., and Harriet Gautier (Brooks) Foote, Albert Horton Foote is descended from two of the oldest and best-known families in Texas.

His maternal great-grandfather was John Brooks, whose aristocratic ancestors immigrated to America from Gloucester, England, in the 1600s, where they had been affluent merchants, doctors, and lawyers. His maternal great-grandmother was Harriet Gautier Brooks, whose parents (Peter William and Elizabeth Gautier) were among the first settlers of the Texas Gulf Coast as well as the region's most prominent land-owning family. Although John Brooks, a businessman and community leader, prospered until the Civil War, the post-war drop in cotton prices threw him into bankruptcy. He died on October 4, 1870, leaving his wife and five children alone and penniless. Fortunately, Harriet Brooks was a strong matriarch who kept her children fed and instilled in them a deep respect for their familial heritage. Her courage and resourcefulness became legend in the family stories passed down to Horton Foote.

Born on May 10, 1865, Tom Brooks—Foote's maternal grandfather—was only five when his father John died. But his mother's firm guidance tempered the young Brooks' mathematical mind with moral steadfastness. He was concerned for the "welfare of his family," ready to "help the less fortunate," and respected as a community leader (Outlar Interview). After graduating from Texas A&M University, Tom moved—in 1886—to the rural community of Wharton, Texas, to work in the merchandising business with his cousin John Smith. While serving as a clerk for the firm, Tom met and fell in love with Daisy Phelps Speed.

Daisy Speed was one of ten children born to Virginia Yerby and John Speed. Virtually self-educated, Daisy was an intelligent young woman. After serving as a governess on a large plantation, she became, according to family stories, the first secretary in Wharton. Miss Daisy was a "fierce aristocrat with a capacity for deep, unfaltering devotion to those she loved" (Foote, Interview 18 Nov. 1988).

Daisy Speed and Tom Brooks were married on January 11, 1893, and to this union were born eight children; six lived to maturity. They were Harriet Gautier (Hallie, the mother of Horton Foote), Laura Lee, Rosa Vaughn, Thomas Harry, John Speed, and William Smith. All the children were born and raised in the family's impressive home on Richmond Road, where they lived in Southern elegance and adhered to the Victorian morality of their parents. Unfortunately, as much as the Brooks clan was upheld by aristocratic pride and familial devotion, the writer's paternal ancestors—the Footes—were nearly overwhelmed by lost inheritance and personal rejection.

Albert Clinton Horton—the playwright's namesake and great-great-grandfather—moved from Alabama to Texas in 1834, quickly rising to economic and political prominence. At the outbreak of Texas' war for independence from Mexico, Horton joined his fellow statesmen in their struggle for autonomy, fighting at the Battles of Goliad and San Jacinto. Later, after Texas joined the Union in 1845, he became the state's first elected Lieutenant Governor. But the Civil War served Horton no better than it had John Brooks; by 1865 Horton had lost his fortune, and later that same year he died at his summer home in Matagorda. In the story of Albert Clinton Horton his great-great-grandson discovered a compelling theme: the need for courage in the face of deprivation and loss (Freedman 50).

Following the death of his father, Robert Horton (Horton Foote's great-grandfather) tried to build a new life for himself, but with little success. Robert apparently received nothing from his father's estate and was cheated out of his inheritance by his brother-in-law (Foote, Interview 18 Nov. 1988). He tried to make a living as a merchant, but economic conditions in Wharton during Reconstruction were prohibitive. He worked as a lighthouse operator on Matagorda Bay until 1886, when a Gulf Coast hurricane devastated the area and left his family homeless. Robert and his wife, Mary Hawes, finally returned to Wharton, where they built a small home, raised six children, and survived on a meager income. Deprived of social position and wealth, the Horton family struggled in a world that often seemed perilous and unjust.

Corella Horton, Foote's paternal grandmother, married Albert Foote in 1889. Albert's family had moved to Texas from Virginia during the 1840s, bringing its own proud aristocratic history. His mother was Elizabeth Robedaux Foote (whose American heritage reached as far back as the Revolutionary War), and his father, John Foote, had been a wealthy Galveston cotton broker who owned his own fleet of ships. By the time Albert and Corrie married, the family had lost their fortune, and they lived in a small house in Wharton, with Albert as their sole provider.

As the descendants understand it, the emotional and financial demands of the larger Foote family soured the otherwise promising marriage (Foote, Interview 18 Nov. 1988). Corrie, who cooked the meals and cared for the children, began to feel put upon, her resentment often leading to quarrels with her proud mother-in-law. The wife and mother grew distant and remote, and after the birth of her second child, Lilyan Dale, Corrie returned to her mother and father. Albert began to drink heavily and died in 1902, only thirty-six years old. A year later, Corrie married P. E. Cleveland, a railroad engineer, and moved to Houston, abandoning her young son, Albert Horton (the playwright's father).

These harsh realities weighed heavily upon the Foote children. Albert was twelve and Lilyan Dale ten when their father died. Neither was mature enough to understand the circumstances surrounding their parents' estrangement or their father's death. Lilyan Dale remained close to her mother and with time grew bitter towards her father and paternal family (Foote, Interview 18 Nov. 1988). Albert Horton was devoted to his father; neither time nor family scrutiny would diminish the love and respect he had for him. As the writer explains, the death of Albert Foote senior haunted Albert Horton:

> I often questioned my father about the day my grandfather died, but he wouldn't say much except that it was a sad time, and his father was considered a brilliant lawyer....When my Grandfather Foote died there was not enough money to buy a tombstone for his grave, and so it

> was unmarked until my father, when he was twenty-seven,
> married and with a child of his own, took his first savings
> and bought the tombstone for his father's grave. (Foote,
> Interview 18 Nov. 1988)

Horton Foote was obviously impressed by his father's longing for a
lost father; it became a central issue in *The Orphans' Home Cycle*.

Albert's relationship with his mother was further threatened when
his stepfather, Mr. Cleveland, refused to care for him. Cleveland offered
to rear Lilyan Dale as his own child, but he would not allow Albert to
live in his home and even resented the child's occasional visits. Corrie
appears to have done little to soothe her son's growing hatred of his
stepfather, nor did she stop the humiliation to which he was sub-
jected. The most revealing example of Corrie's failure with her son
was expressed by her grandson, Horton Foote:

> The classic story is that my father couldn't live with her,
> but she would give him breakfast each morning. My fa-
> ther had to be out of the house each morning by five. He
> never put all this together until one morning he arrived
> by seven and his mother met him at the door.... My fa-
> ther thought she was unusually nervous and he looked
> over his shoulder and there sat Mr. Cleveland. His mother
> was not able to tell him the truth or to invite him inside.
> (Foote, Interview 18 Nov. 1988)

As a consequence of this betrayal and rejection, Albert Horton's childhood was spent in pursuit of a single dream—"to belong to a family"
(Foote, Interview 18 Nov. 1988). Years later (1974–1976), Horton
Foote would faithfully reconstruct his father's quest in plays like *Roots
in a Parched Ground* and *Convicts* from *The Orphans' Home Cycle*.

Albert Horton Foote's story continues, as does his son's cycle,
with the tall, handsome, good-natured lad opening a small cleaning
and pressing shop in Wharton during 1914. About the same time, he
began courting Hallie Brooks. Having searched for true companionship all his life, Albert proposed, and Hallie accepted. However, Hallie's
father did not favor the match, partly because her chosen mate had
earned the reputation of a "hell-raiser" and partly because Mr. Brooks
thought no man "worthy of his daughter's hand in marriage" (Outlar
Interview). But Hallie's devotion to Albert Horton was undeniable;
on Valentine's Day, 1915, Hallie Brooks eloped with Albert Horton

Foote, but the stakes of their marriage were high. Mr. Brooks severed all ties with his daughter for over a year, and the strained relationship between the proud father and his son-in-law was never fully repaired. Sixty years later the events leading to Hallie's elopement became the subject of her son's play *Courtship*.

Although the details of the early married life of Albert and Hallie Foote will never be known, he clearly was devoted to her, and she adored him. The Footes were, and would always be, a very private pair. Relatives and friends recall that Hallie and Albert Horton were "totally absorbed in each other, and in all the years of their marriage they were never separated for longer than one day" (Foote, Interview 18 Nov. 1988).

On March 14, 1916, Hallie gave birth to their first son, Albert Horton Foote, Jr., and from then on she dedicated her life to being a wife and mother. Horton Foote's birth was an important event for his family because it motivated the reconciliation between his mother and her father, dramatized in *Valentine's Day* from *The Orphans' Home Cycle*. The high-minded Mr. Brooks apologized to his daughter and son-in-law after the child was born, thereby mending the emotional scars left from the previous year. In addition, as a peace offering Mr. Brooks built the young family a house next to his own. Although Albert Horton never claimed ownership of the property, he did move his family to that house on North Houston Street in 1917, when the writer was one year old. The small house and the surrounding land became a source of security and adventure. It was, as Foote remembers, "my garden, my Eden as it were—and I spent most of my early waking days when not in school roaming its confines" (Foote, "Seeing" 1–3). The freedom he felt as a child on Houston Street became a norm sought by all the characters in Foote's dramas.

At the center of this seemingly stable world were the writer's maternal grandparents, especially his Grandmother Brooks. She was, in his words, "very feminine, fiercely aristocratic to her toenails," a woman with "an enormous sense of pride" (Foote, Interview 18 Nov. 1988). Although she was not demonstrative in her affections, the boy adored her; and since it was only a short distance to her house, he visited her every day. His grandmother made him feel special, and he grew up knowing that this woman would respond to his every request. Foote admits that "she offered an enormous sense of security. I always knew if I ever needed anything, I could call on her. Time after time her generosity saved me" (Foote, Interview 18 Nov. 1988).

Horton's feelings for his grandfather were not as clear; they fluctuated between devotion and awe. Tom Brooks was a devoted family man, but he was also a man of great power who expected much from his children. He had risen from the poverty of his youth to become Wharton's most prestigious citizen, setting an example few could ever hope to match. He had served the township in a number of capacities: he was a successful merchant, a county treasurer, a financier, and a real estate investor. He was also an imaginative speculator who, in the 1920s, embarked upon a business venture that would make his family rich and change the face of Wharton forever. Realizing the financial potential in post–World War I Wharton, Mr. Brooks acquired old plantations which he subdivided and sold to immigrant families. Through the efforts of Brooks and other entrepreneurs, the town began to experience "the erosion of tradition and identity" which "resounds" through work by Horton Foote (Freedman 50).

The unexpected death of grandfather Brooks on March 3, 1925, was devastating for Horton Foote, and it would have a profound effect upon him. "The event that always stuck with me," he admits, "the event I've been groping toward as a writer, was the day my grandfather died. Until then, life was magic. I never felt so secure in my life as sitting on the porch swing and knowing I was the grandson of one of the richest families in town and my grandfather was the most respected man in town" (Freedman 51). Foote was only nine at the time, but he can still recall that

> in mid-March of my ninth year I came home from school...and slowly walked into my grandparents' back yard. Eliza, who cooked for my grandparents, and her sister Sarah were there. I went up to them as Eliza was saying, "I knew someone in that house would die today when I saw a dove, a mourning dove, light on the roof of the house".... I started slowly toward the house when my mother appeared at the back door.... She was crying and she took me in her arms and asked if I wanted to see my grandmother. I said I did, still not knowing what had happened.... Mother led me to my grandparents' room and I saw my grandfather, his eyes closed lying on a couch and my grandmother sitting beside him. My mother said, "Little Horton's here, Mama," and my grandmother turned to me, and I saw she was crying and she held out

her arms to me and I went to her and she began to sob
and held me as I looked at my grandfather and I realized
that he was dead. (Foote, "Seeing" 14–16)

Mr. Brooks' death brought enormous grief and hardship to the
family. Miss Daisy mourned the loss of her husband for over two
years. Every afternoon she would visit his grave, Horton often going
with her. He remembers that she always dressed in black, carried
flowers, and sometimes would sit and cry for hours. By observing his
grandmother's daily ritual, the boy discovered that mourning was a
vital part of the healing process and that grief is a subject for all times:
"When I was growing up, the dead were almost as alive as the living.
People talked about them, remembered, reminisced....now everything
is so anonymous" (Darnton 22). For Foote as a child there was no
escaping or ignoring the unpleasant phenomenon of death; as a writer
he has repeatedly explored its mystery and challenges.

Miss Daisy, a remarkably strong, resilient, and faithful woman,
had one unremittent source of sorrow and shame. "The one thing my
grandmother could never understand," Foote has said, "was what went
wrong with her sons" (Foote, Interview 18 Nov. 1988). The three
Brooks boys (Tom, Speed, and Billy) had been reared in an atmosphere of respectability. Friends and relatives recall that they were extremely bright and likeable, but none was blessed with their father's
ambition. As young men, they began to drink heavily, and within a
few years, the three brothers developed into chronic alcoholics.

After their father died, the boys were tortured by one failure after
another. Tom, the oldest son, inherited one of his father's farms, but
in less than a year, he had mortgaged it so heavily that his mother had
to pay off the debt to recover the property. He left Wharton soon
after and for a time wandered around the world as a merchant sea-
man. He died at age fifty, a drunkard, picking fruit on an Arizona
ranch. The younger brothers experienced much the same fate and
were eventually forced to live off the charity of their mother, who
tried, unsuccessfully, to rescue them from their own destruction.
Horton Foote would later explore the seeming futility of his uncles'
lives in numerous plays and screenplays. He today believes "there was
no meaning to the boys' lives. Unless you were a doctor, a lawyer, or a
merchant there was nothing for you to do in Wharton....They thought
of themselves as rich boys but they weren't....There was simply no

order to their lives, it had all been broken up, along with the plantations" (Foote, Interview 18 Nov. 1988).

Fortunately, Horton Foote and his brothers did not have to endure the same hardships as their uncles. Foote was exceptionally close
to his mother whom he describes as a "woman of great dignity." She
was a perceptive and responsible citizen of Wharton, and she could
make people of any social background feel at home. She dressed quietly, was soft-spoken, knew first hand the perils of the world, yet "never
complained or burdened anyone with her fears or grief" (Foote, Interview 18 Nov. 1988). She was honest with her children and revealed through her actions that courage was one of life's most valu-
able virtues. In many ways, Foote characterized his mother when he
commented on the type of women who populate his plays:

> I'm struck by these women who have very little in posses-
> sions but have great dignity, even though they've married
> young and often have to raise children alone. I write them
> from a sense of appreciation and admiration. They can
> be very confident, though they've certainly been given
> more than their share of difficult problems to work out.
> (Sterritt 38)

Remembered as a loving but stern mother, Hallie taught her children the importance of fine manners, respect for elders, and devotion
to family. Horton adored listening to the sounds of his mother's music, and, with her guidance, he learned to sing scores of popular songs
and religious hymns at a young age. He also enjoyed hearing his mother
read aloud, and under her tutelage, he became an avid reader by the
age of six. Hallie, who had grown up in a family of devout Method-
ists, later became a dedicated Christian Scientist. From her and from
their shared church experience, young Horton heard and cherished
the biblical stories. At an early age he was taught to respect the Bible
as "a wonderful storytelling device that explains much about the family" (Foote, Interview 12 Mar. 1988). Foote maintains a "deeply religious" (Wood and Barr 232) but understated practice of Christian
Science, emphasizing self-reliance and discipline. Through his mother's
quiet faith, Foote learned the moral and spiritual principles that remain a dominant part of his character and writings.

In his early years Horton Foote could not be as close to his father
as he was to his mother. His father's clothing business kept him away

from home as many as twelve hours each day, but the writer apparently never felt abandoned by his father:

> Growing up without a father was a constant experience
> in my family. I think it was almost a fear for me and I
> always wondered what it would be like if I had lived
> through the hardships that my father experienced as a
> child.... No, I never felt neglected... I always felt very
> nurtured by him. (Foote, Interview 18 Nov. 1988)

During his teenage years Horton Foote moved closer to his father and to the public world of Wharton. When the young man began to spend Saturdays and summers working at his father's haberdashery,

> I saw all kinds of people in my daddy's store. I saw coun-
> try people and lost people. I saw blacks who were unable
> to write their name or unable to pay more than $1.50
> down for a suit....They took me into an entirely different
> world than I was used to..., listening to their country
> speech and voices and stories of weather and crops, of
> illnesses or hard times their friends were undergoing or
> their personal tragedies. There was laughter, too, teasing
> and joking. I learned to love these people, to look for-
> ward to Saturdays and to hear their accents so different
> from my family's and to listen to their stories. (Foote,
> Interview 18 Nov. 1988)

The bond between Horton and his father strengthened during this time as the youth began to realize the many demands of his father's job and the kindness he showed to other, less fortunate people.

From his father, as well as the other members of his extended family in Wharton, Texas, Foote inherited his homeplace's greatest resource: storytelling. A quiet and polite child, he intently observed everything around him, especially narratives about the past: "My father loved to speculate about the past, what might have happened if this had happened or why did this happen this way. I know that's where I got my own curiosity and speculative nature" (Foote, Interview 18 Nov. 1988). No truth or speculation, he remembers, was withheld from him: "I was never told to leave the room no matter how gruesome or unhappy the tale and so early on I learned to accept the tragic events as part of life. I heard in lurid detail of feuds, hurt feelings, suicide, jealousies, passions, scoundrels of all kinds and descriptions" (Foote, "Seeing" 10–11). Beyond the stories themselves, Foote was fascinated with how the events of the past were constantly being reorganized and shaped by the storyteller's imagination: "I've learned that you can hear the same story told by six or seven people, and even though they think it's the same story, it's not. Every version is personal, subjective and all of them are telling the truth as they see it" (Foote, Interview 18 Nov. 1988). In such multiple narratives Foote discovered a way to reveal the inner lives of his characters and the drama between speakers.

Foote claims that the one thing he missed during childhood was sufficient time to spend with his younger brothers. When he left home at the age of sixteen, to pursue an acting career, Tom was only ten years old and John, eight. While Horton enjoyed listening to his family's endless talk or reading books, his brothers found excitement in sports or country-western music. Since Horton felt quite comfortable as the center of his family's attention and intended to remain the favorite nephew and grandson, there was what he calls a "terrible sibling problem" (Foote, Interview 18 Nov. 1988). It was the kind of hidden competition he would recreate in, for example, *Roots in a Parched Ground* and *Lily Dale*.

Horton Foote's favorite childhood pastime was movie-going; he attended the Queen Theatre to watch the movie stars whenever he could. The boy's fascination with cinema grew until at age twelve he awoke one morning and decided to be an actor. He remembers the feeling as akin to a religious calling; at twelve he "just awakened one day with the sure knowledge that I wanted to be an actor; more, that I was going to be. Of that I hadn't the slightest doubt (Foote, "Seeing" 19). After graduating from high school in early summer of 1932, Foote pleaded with his parents to let him go to New York to pursue training as an actor. Since he was only sixteen years old, the parents argued that he should attend college for two years. Horton refused. And so they compromised. His father told him that he could attend California's famed Pasadena Playhouse: "Pasadena, they felt, would be a more wholesome atmosphere for a young man away from his family for the first time" (Foote, "Seeing" 24). It was September 1933.

While the next six years were times of great personal and financial sacrifice for the family, they tolerated and even encouraged the young actor's going away (Foote, Interview 18 Nov. 1988). Memories of

Wharton, of the rich personal and regional past he had left behind would sometimes leave Horton Foote sad in Pasadena:

> On Saturday night as I sat in my small room at the Y, I thought of my father's store always busy, even in Depression times. I thought of the black and white farmers who would be coming into the store, always cheerful these Saturday nights, even when there was little money. It was also the time when cotton pickers and their families flooded the country and swelled the always crowded Saturday night streets. But lonely or not, I knew somehow I would never fully go back to that life again. (Foote, "Seeing" 32)

He was crossing a threshold that in some ways was taking him forever away from his homeplace. This lesson was most poignantly taught him when he was told that if he expected to become a successful actor, he would have to correct his Southern accent: "I soon learned that I came from a part of the world that was looked down on by more sophisticated people. I became ashamed of where I came from and I began to learn to speak the English language" (Foote, Interview 18 Nov. 1988). Even as Foote moved away from Wharton—emotionally as well as physically—this elitism seemed prejudicial, an attack on his past and identity.

As secondary as they had become, Horton Foote did keep his connections to Wharton, Texas. His mother wrote him letters every day, often relating the events of a complete day in the life of his family and friends, and in his lonely hours Foote would "read them over and over" (Foote, Interview 18 Nov. 1988). His grandmother Brooks came to visit him, and in the spring of 1934, she took him to Eva Le Gallienne's performances of Ibsen's *Hedda Gabler* and *The Master Builder* at the Biltmore Theatre in Los Angeles, which he now recognizes were crucial to his choosing a more realistic and poetic theatre as both an actor and, later, writer (Foote, "Pasadena" 38). Later he successfully played a young black boy in Paul Green's *No' Count Boy* in summer stock on Martha's Vineyard which, though it had little effect on his aspirations as an actor, kept him in touch with regional subjects and genuine American dialogue, like that he would rediscover as a writer remembering Wharton, Texas (Foote, "Pasadena" 42–43).

Still, in the fall of 1935 when Horton Foote moved to New York as an actor, Wharton was not part of his everyday life. At first, though he wanted to be a "Broadway star by the age of twenty-two," he found only an occasional job as a scissors grinder in an industrial film or a prop boy for a musical review at the Provincetown Playhouse (Foote, Interview 18 Nov. 1988). Luckily, in the winter of 1936 he became reacquainted with Rosamond Pinchot, who was studying acting with Tamara Daykarhanova, Vera Soloviova, and Andrius Jilinski (distinguished protégées of Konstantin Stanislavsky) at their School for the Stage and needed an acting partner. Foote jumped at the chance to learn more about his craft. Through Andrius Jilinsky, an early pioneer in the "Stanislavsky method" of acting, and others Foote was introduced to the new and revolutionary emphasis on psychological truthfulness, inner feelings, and true-to-life movement (Foote, "Pasadena" 54). Foote's subsequent training at the School for the Stage gave him confidence that authentic emotions and speech could be made integral to a new American theatre. But this all seemed to have little, if anything, to do with life back in Wharton, Texas.

From 1937 to 1939, Foote secured more acting jobs: he was cast as a supernumerary in Max Reinhardt's dramatic spectacle *The Eternal Road* and Ernest Hemingway's *The Fifth Column*. He was hired by the Maverick Theatre in Woodstock, New York, to perform eight roles, and he toured in a patriotic musical, *Yankee Doodle Comes to Town*. He was also cast in three one-act pieces for the One-Act Repertory Company at the Hudson Theatre: *The Coggerers* by Paul Vincent Carroll, *The Red Velvet Coat* by Josephine Nigli, and *Mr. Banks of Birmingham* by Jean Giraudoux. Unfortunately, these productions were quickly dismissed by critics like Brooks Atkinson of the *New York Times*, who cited them as examples of "prolixity, careless workmanship and bad acting" (Atkinson, "Program of Three Dramas" 16:6). Foote admits that he became very discouraged and expected "this to be the pattern of the rest of [his] life" (Foote, "Pasadena" 60).

What changed that pattern was Foote's association with Mary Hunter and the American Actors Company. Hunter was a student at the School for the Stage when Foote enrolled there in 1936. By 1938 both Foote and Hunter had become dissatisfied with the practices of the New York theatres. Foote explains: "we were all at Daykarhanova's being indoctrinated with the ideal of group acting. We were taught, and believed, that Broadway with its dependence on stars was ruinous to any real creativity. The Group Theatre was about to disband, but all of us at our studio felt that the group ideal was the correct one and that the failure of the Group Theatre had to do with Broadway economics as much as anything" (Foote, "Pasadena" 61).

In 1938, Mary Hunter embarked upon a project that would give young talents a chance to work in New York and lead them out of the wilderness of commerce into the promised land of art. That spring she drew up plans for the creation of a permanent acting troupe, the American Actors Company, using her friends and colleagues as its nucleus. The original members included such notables as Agnes DeMille, Jerome Robbins, Mildred Dunnock, Valerie Bettis, June Walker, Lucy Kroll, Joseph Anthony—and Horton Foote. Under Mary Hunter's direction the AAC would, as she explains in her foreword to Foote's first published play, *Only the Heart,* "uncover" its members' "own cultural roots, and since the members of the company represented almost a regional survey of the U.S., the sources were rich and varied" (5). In its small space over a garage on West 69th Street, the Company began rehearsing plays by established American writers such as E. P. Conkle, Paul Green, and Lynn Riggs—writers whose works represented characteristic aspects of American life. In 1939, the troupe also began work on "American Legend," a folk venue which was to feature group improvisations and the choreography of Agnes DeMille. During their rehearsals, Mary Hunter encouraged the actors to draw on their regional diversity and pool their experiences to arrive at a meaning of "American." The cast was asked to mine their memories and evoke the characters they found there, improvising dialogues between them. They wrote scenes and monologues based on real situations, dramatizing but not fabricating. The goal was realism, not entertainment.

It was in these sessions—searching for authentic American voices and dramatic material—that Horton Foote began his return to Wharton, as actor and then as a writer. Initially he performed an improvisation, which instantly gained the approval of Agnes DeMille. After his performance, DeMille casually asked, "you seem to be in touch with some interesting theatrical material. Did you ever think of writing a play?" As her suggestion took root, he began to write down his memories of Texas:

> I got in touch with material that was…for lack of a better
> word, regional material…. I really believe this material

> chose me more that I chose it…it is amazing to me how
> many of these themes keep repeating themselves, or atti-
> tudes, or approaches to character. I don't know if I ever
> consciously worked on this, but I think I worked at what-
> ever instincts I had matured, and I hope they got better
> and stronger. (Edgerton 4)

Horton Foote's imagination, which had never completely abandoned
Wharton, was home again.

Foote called his first play *Wharton Dance*, and in the fall of 1940,
the American Actors Company staged the piece along with one-acts
by Paul Green and Thornton Wilder. Set in Wharton on a Saturday
night, *Wharton Dance* depicts the tender relationships between a group
of teenagers attending a community dance. While trying to protect
the reputation of two friends who defy their parents' wishes by dating
each other, the youths are made privy to the secret conversations of
their elders, whose lives have grown cold and lonely. Foote admits
that *Wharton Dance* was largely reportage, even using real names, in
which he mistakenly thought he was honoring his homeplace: "My
memory of it is that it too was very improvisational in form, based on
a real situation, and used the names of the boys and girls in what was
known back in high school as 'our crowd'" (Foote, "Pasadena" 64).
Wharton Dance is unquestionably the work of a beginning playwright,
but already he is revealing his command of the language and atmosphere of a small Texas town, the dreams and frustrations of young
people, and the tension between the innocence of youth and the fallen
world of their parents.

Horton Foote recalls that Robert Coleman, a dramatic critic for
the *New York Mirror*, wrote favorably of *Wharton Dance*. "Noel Coward acting in his own plays was the vogue then," Foote remembers,
"and because of Coleman's review, I was interviewed by another re-
porter who wrote of my potential as a Texas Noel Coward. That was
far from my mind, but I did want to act and I'm sure I thought that
one way to get good parts was to write them for myself" (Foote, "Pasadena" 64). Suddenly, Foote found himself being hailed as a promising
new playwright even though he knew little about writing plays. When
the American Actors Company requested that he write a three-act
play, he began to feel "a certain security" about accomplishing the
task before him, a security he had never felt as an actor (Foote, "Pasadena" 65). So in the winter of 1940, Foote boarded the bus in New

York and headed for Wharton to write a new play.

When Foote arrived in Texas, he discovered a number of changes in his hometown. His Grandmother Brooks was living permanently in Houston, and his Grandmother Cleveland had recently been diagnosed as having a terminal illness. The news of her declining health was unsettling to Foote as was the realization that his uncles—Tom, Billy, and Speed—had become hopeless derelicts. His brothers had also changed; they were no longer "little boys, but young men" with the same questions about their futures as he had faced six years earlier (Foote, "Learning" 66).

Responding to the familial changes that confronted him that winter, Horton Foote wrote *Texas Town*, which the AAC performed at the Humphrey-Weidman Studio Theatre in New York during the spring of 1941. Set in a small-town drugstore, *Texas Town* tells the story of two friends, Maner and Ray, who are in love with the same girl. Maner, the proprietor of the drug store, wants to stay in the town, marry Carrie, and lead a conventional life. Ray, who has been victimized by a manipulative mother and mean-spirited brother, finds small-town life stifling and wants badly to leave. Through the gentle coaxing of the town doctor, Ray is able to break free from his mother's clutches and walk away from the town he despises. Carrie realizes the depth of her love for Ray and breaks off her engagement to Maner; however, the moment she decides to follow Ray, news comes that he has been killed in an automobile accident. Carrie and Maner are left alone to deal with their loss. They do so with courage and dignity.

Horton Foote's accurate portrayal of Wharton was acknowledged in its positive reviews. Brooks Atkinson, for example, in his *New York Times* review of the play, felt the authenticity of *Texas Town*: "it is impossible not to believe absolutely in the reality of his characters. The melancholy doctor who drinks in the back room, the hearty judge and his cronies, the bored wife who is looking for excitement, the chattering girls, the bumptious boys, the sharp edges of bad feeling that cut through the neighborhood leisure, the quick impulses of emotion, the sense of drifting without purpose of direction—these are truths of small-town life that Mr. Foote has not invented" (22:3). The play's small-town setting, its fixed values pitted against an ever-changing world, its array of simple but spiritually bankrupt people, and its characters' need for a sense of order and stability in their lives are themes that Foote would continue to explore throughout his career.

After the success of *Texas Town*, Foote completed (in the spring of 1941) four one-act plays, which the Company presented as a single bill under the title *Out of My House*, set in Wharton in the 1920s. In the initial play, *Night after Night*, Clara, a strong and compassionate Bohemian, is torn between returning home to her family, where she will spend her life as a field laborer, or continuing to work as a waitress at Ted Miller's restaurant, where she is forced to cope with insults and cultural prejudices. More than anything else, she wants a truck driver to marry her and rescue her from her lonely world. At play's end, Clara peers out the window, waiting for her lover and attending to the customers who drink their lives away.

In *Celebration*, the second play in *Out of My House*, Sonny and Babe Mavis return after a year at college to a party thrown by their older sister, Red. The joyous celebration soon turns tragic when it is revealed that Red has been ostracized from the family because of her drinking problem. But Red sees her alcoholism as merely a symptom of the changes that threaten her once-proud family: "Grandpa was an aristocrat," she explains. "We were born different....We're all that's left of the old.... But Mama, whispering her fears and her poisons, tried to make us forget it" (8). When Ellen Belle Croy, the neighborhood snob, disrupts the party by questioning the social status of the Mavis family, Red becomes enraged. She forces Sonny, who has a heart condition, to drink in order to prove his manliness. Sadly, the indulgence causes Sonny's death.

The third play, *The Girls*, provides a humorous glimpse at two spinster sisters, Nora and Sue Anthony, who have spent over thirty years trying to insure an inheritance from their rich Aunt Lizzie. Their dreams come to naught when their new sister-in-law, in a fit of religious fervor, tells the sisters in Aunt Lizzie's presence that they should confess their deceit and ask for forgiveness. Ironically, their disinheritance actually frees the women from the emotional stress of their pretense.

The fourth and last play, *Behold a Cry*, centers around two brothers sharply divided by their fears and ideals. One brother is trying to re-establish his family economically by adopting a servile attitude toward the influential people of the town, while the other brother thinks deference more odious than poverty. The brothers' anger finally explodes as Ford, the climber, verbally attacks Jack's alcoholism and manhood and Jack harshly condemns Ford as a hypocritical "bastard" who cares for nobody except himself (15). Finally, Jack turns to Grandpa Robedaux who renews the young man's hope for a better life: "All around they are ready for you, the hopeless, the confused, the lost.... Make them see that men cannot live divided and hating, envious and greedy, that together they must find their strength" (21). Jack courageously exits into the dark night believing that he can make a difference in the world.

Even though *Out of My House* shows Horton Foote struggling with problems of dramatic form, the plays once again use his Wharton past to study, with compassion, society's unfortunates. Present are fully developed character types who will later dominate Foote's dramatic landscape. There are youth who are physically and emotionally orphaned, young men who are haunted by feelings of futility and hopelessness, and adults who are dislocated and forlorn. There are also many interesting women: the strong-willed and heroic, those cowed by society or victimized by their family, others in the full bloom of their beauty. Emerging, too, is his talent for creating accurate and thought-provoking dialogue, for interpreting the darker aspects of family life, and for depicting the tragic consequences of alcoholism, death, racism, and greed. Taken together, the four plays return to themes he has always found in Wharton: a sense of place, the inevitability of change, and the resilience of the human spirit.

Among the players cast for the production of *Out of My House* was Tom Foote, who had followed his older brother to New York to pursue an acting career. According to the writer, through the shared experience the two grew closer than in the recent past. Then in the spring of 1942, after the bombing of Pearl Harbor, Tom Brooks Foote was drafted by the Army as a radio pilot on fighter planes. On February 22, 1944, while fighting in the skies over Belgium, Tom's plane was shot down. The Foote family was left in limbo for months because military authorities couldn't verify his status. Foote recalls that it was not until after the war "when I met the man who had been his pilot that my brother's death was finally confirmed. Tom's body had been so disfigured by the crash that he had been buried in a military cemetery in Belgium" (Foote, Interview 18 Nov. 1988).

The news of Tom's death was very hard on his parents:

> My father put all of my brother's belongings in the attic
> and then said to me "Someday when the pain and the
> hurt are gone, you and your children can have them." It

> must have been very rough for him. I don't think my
> mother ever got over it; she was never able to talk about
> it. I know it haunted her the rest of her life. (Foote, In-
> terview 18 Nov. 1988)

The writer's acceptance of his brother's death is reflected in his writings where meaningful lives are often inspired by unexpected and
undeserved losses. Many of his plays, from *Ludie Brooks* to *The Young
Man from Atlanta*, focus on grief's temptations and opportunities. As
Reynolds Price suggests, Horton Foote's plays remind us that "suffering
(to the point of devastation) is the central human condition and our
most unavoidable mystery. Yet we can survive it and sing in its face"
(Introduction, *Courtship* xii).

In spite of the sadness that must have accompanied returning to
Wharton, even in his imagination, the war years continued to be very
productive ones for the playwright. In the autumn of 1943, he finished
a new three-act play, *Mamie Borden*, and submitted it to Mary Hunter
and the American Actors Company for approval. Retitled *Only the
Heart* in order to please the Hollywood actress Hilda Vaughn, who
played the lead role (Foote, "Learning" 82), it was produced by the
American Actors Company at the Provincetown Playhouse in December 1943. The play is set in September 1921, and Wharton has
become a small Texas Gulf Coast town called Richmond, where the
discontent of the war years has been replaced by a new order that
values money and professional success. The play centers around Mamie
Borden, a wealthy businesswoman whose obsessive drive for affluence
leads to her tragic downfall. Mamie's flaw is her deep need to control
and manipulate others so that they grow to depend on her, thus giving her power and security rather than loving relationships. For years,
Mamie has forbidden her sister India to marry Jack Turner because
she feels his habits are not steady enough. She has also ruined her
own marriage by demanding that Mr. Borden meet her high standards of living, thus motivating him to take a Bohemian mistress.
Over the years she has turned to work as a sedative for her pain and
adopted the philosophy that "as long as a person has work to do, you
can get by.... Get busy...then nothing can hurt you for long" (71).
Now Mamie has begun manipulating her daughter Julia into marrying Albert, a young man whom Mamie believes she can control. Problems emerge when Albert becomes totally absorbed in his work as

Mamie's business partner and Julia begins to feel neglected and un-loved. Julia must ultimately choose between her mother's wishes and her own needs.

Only the Heart is a powerful indictment of parental manipula-tion and personal greed, but it is also political and universal. The play considers not just one Wharton/Richmond family; it implies the fact and consequences of alienation in a materialistic post-war world. The tragedy of Mamie Borden is also the tragedy of many people follow-ing the war who, like her, believed that, "there's gonna be more happy people in this country than was ever known before.... Rich and happy" (32). Foote clearly demonstrates that affluence, proclaimed as a vir-tue, leaves one disconnected not only from family but from human-ity as a whole. The writer's studies of Wharton are becoming more personal and plastic in *Only the Heart*; his regional stories are gaining the resonance, the texture that he will return to in the 1950s.

By 1945, the American Actors Company had begun to disband, leaving Horton Foote without a familiar theatre for his plays. He admits, "It was a lonely feeling" (Foote, "Learning" 88). Then the war ended, and the actors, directors, and writers who had been in the army returned home with news of a new kind of avant-garde theatre much different from Broadway. Foote recalls that compared to the works of such French writers as Sartre, Camus, and Anouilh, "the New York theatre seemed grim and uninspired" (Foote, "Learning" 89). For a time, Foote tried to ignore the changes taking place in the American theatre, but he eventually followed Valerie Bettis' advice to concentrate on writing works for a non-realistic, lyric theatre. "Valerie was very much against what she considered the realistic theatre," Foote explains, "and she wanted to see created a theatre that used more boldly the elements of dance, words, and music" (Foote, "Learning" 80). Of course, Foote had been interested in music and dance since his early days with the American Actors Company. But after the war his experimentation with the new possibilities for a choreographic drama would lead Foote into, for him, a radical experimentation with dramatic form. It was the answer to his dissatisfaction with reportage, and his interest in Wharton would never again be so literal and im-personal.

At the end of the war, Horton Foote had been a playwright for more than five years. He had seen his dreams of becoming a Broad-way actor give way to the truth that his genius came from writing,

not acting. He had written a half dozen plays, most of them produced in Off-Broadway theatres, and he had begun experimentation
with various theatrical forms. Over the years, he had learned his craft
from varied and unexpected sources—from his Russian acting teach-
ers, from Mary Hunter and the American Actors Company, from
great choreographers like Agnes DeMille, Martha Graham, and Valerie
Bettis, from other writers, and from productions of his own plays.
Each of his experiences played an important part in his early career
and influenced all his subsequent writing.

Yet no matter how diverse his writing has become, the source of
his creativity has always been Wharton, Texas. Foote was fascinated at
an early age by the people around him—living and dead—how they
lived and died, loved and lost, prevailed and endured. The dramatic
tension between their inner lives and their appearance of decorum
and calm made profound impressions on him. Today, his home place
still inspires his writing. The cotton fields, the pecan trees, the front
porch swings, the cemeteries, the dwindling towns—images of his
youth—move poignantly through his plays. They testify to the brutality, beauty, and mystery of life, to the universals discovered in the
particular reality of a small Texas town and its people.

∾

Works Cited

Atkinson, Brooks. "American Actors Company Produces Horton
    Foote's 'Texas Town' in Sixteenth Street." *New York Times* 30
    April 1941: 22:3.

———. "Program of Three Dramas." *New York Times* 18 Jan. 1939:
    16:6.

Darnton, Nina. "Horton Foote Celebrates a Bygone America in
    '1918.'" *New York Times* 21 April 1985, Sun. ed.: 17, 22.

Edgerton, Gary. "A Visit to the Imaginary Landscape of Harrison
    Texas: Sketching the Film Career of Horton Foote." *Literature/
    Film Quarterly* 17.1 (Winter 1989): 2–12.

Foote, Horton. "Horton Foote: 'Why I Remember.'" *A Walk Through
    Wharton County.* Special ed. *Wharton County Journal Spectator*

[Wharton, TX] 24 Sept. 1989: 9.

——. "Learning to Write." Unpublished manuscript. From Horton Foote's private collection.

——. Introduction. *Selected One-Act Plays of Horton Foote*. Ed. Gerald C. Wood. Dallas: Southern Methodist UP, 1987: xiii–xxii.

——. *Only the Heart*. New York: Dramatists Play Service, 1944.

——. *Out of My House*. Unpublished typescript. From Horton Foote's private collection.

——. Personal interview. 12 March 1988.

——. Personal interview. 18 November 1988.

——. "Pasadena and Beyond." Unpublished manuscript. Horton Foote Collection. Southern Methodist University.

——. "Seeing and Imagining." Unpublished manuscript. Horton Foote Collection. Southern Methodist University

——. *Texas Town*. Unpublished typescript. Horton Foote Collection. Southern Methodist University.

——. *Wharton Dance*. Unpublished typescript. Horton Foote's Collection. Southern Methodist University.

Freedman, Samuel G. "From the Heart of Texas." *New York Times Magazine*, 30 Feb. 1986: 30, 50, 61–63, 73.

Hunter, Mary. Foreword. *Only the Heart*. By Horton Foote. New York: Dramatists Play Service, 1944.

Outlar, Nan. Personal interview. 8 November 1988.

Price, Reynolds. Introduction. *Courtship, Valentine's Day, 1918: Three Plays from the Orphan's Home Cycle*. By Horton Foote. New York: Grove Press, 1986: ix–xiii.

Sterritt, David. "Let's Hear It for the Human Being." *Saturday Evening Post*, Oct. 1983: 36–38.

Wood, Gerald C., and Terry Barr. "A Certain Kind of Writer: An Interview with Horton Foote." *Literature/Film Quarterly* 14.4 (1986): 226–37.

Horton Foote's TV Women

The Richest Part of a Golden Age
Terry Barr

> It was a play in which the writer closed in on one hour, one day, one week in someone's life and in doing so implied a neighborhood, a community, a world.
> —Ned Hoopes (Kaufman 12)

> I'm a foolish old woman, I know, but I don't want to sell my house and be forced to live on a pittance every month.
> — "Fannie Jackson," in *Expectant Relations*, first aired on the *Goodyear Television Playhouse*, 21 June 1953 (Foote, *Harrison, Texas* 125)

There are significant hurdles for historians and critics who would evaluate Horton Foote's teleplays written during TV's "Golden Age," the 1950s. In the first place, due to neglect and the technological deficiencies of that era of TV, only a few of his original teleplays have been preserved. While most of Foote's original plays for TV are available in print, the extant scripts are often not the final ones used in the production. And since, as Gerald Wood has observed, Horton Foote "did not write specifically for television...[it] was just one more place to present his plays" (*Selected One-Acts* xiv), there are questions of his commitment to the medium itself, even when many TV producers of this period considered the writers to be the "stars."

Despite these qualifications, live TV drama, mirroring the more established visual and performing arts, often reflected the significant tensions, transitions, and turmoil of the 1950s. During the brief time that Horton Foote worked actively in TV, the new medium began imagining the ordinary person trying to cope with life's normal problems. And, as much as the technology would allow, the perspectives of these regular people were being captured by an innovative camera, experimenting with, for example, point of view. From time to time TV would even risk examination of controversial (and to some, subversive) subjects and themes. While 50s television had its technical weaknesses, genuine failures, and eventual compromises with commercial interests, remarkable young playwrights—like Horton Foote, Gore Vidal, and Paddy Chayefsky—wrote simply and eloquently of the complexities of everyday life.

In the case of Horton Foote, the roads that led him, his characters, and his many collaborators to TV screen/homes were long and sometimes rather difficult. By examining the rise and fall of live TV drama in the 1950s, Foote's transition from stage to small screen, and a number of his plays of this period, a viewer can understand how for a few years the new medium transcended its expectations to offer a penetrating and accurate view of American life. For Horton Foote the key public support came from producer Fred Coe, while in his private world he was inspired by his wife, Lillian. From these two influences he learned to focus on the lives of women, creating the vibrant, active, and complex females who became his greatest contribution to the golden age of TV drama. He, more than any other writer, focused attention on middle-class women who found themselves struggling in their small towns for a place in twentieth-century American society.

The Rise of Live Network TV Drama

Today's television seems to be allergic to reality. Many shows are either sadomasochistic or silly, and the most creative ones, like "Northern Exposure" and "The X-Files," remove the viewer from reality, establishing arresting alternate worlds. "Reality TV," anything from "C.O.P.S." to "America's Most Wanted" to "ER," thrives on a hyperreality that is extremely distorted. With such escapism and luridness in TV today, it may be hard to imagine a time when the networks offered eighteen weekly or monthly live TV dramas as they did in 1952–53 (Cantor 49). Yet in the early 1950s the powers-that-be in TV allowed their writers to focus on serious issues without resorting to gimmickry. Of course, such artistic freedoms were not based on the altruism and integrity of the corporate executives who controlled the medium.

In the beginning, network TV was trying to find its entertainment niche—to catch some viewers and to find a formula to expand its viewer base. And while there were various types of programming—musical-variety, comedy, religious, genre-drama—realistic drama was popular for a number of reasons. First of all, the audience was largely "the wealthier, better-educated part of the public, the part best able to afford a television set" (Brown 154). They expected original drama or adaptations of literary masterworks. Live network TV drama was also centered in New York and often modeled itself on Broadway. The performances, though often flawed, could also be "electrifying" one-shot affairs in which the producers took stylistic and thematic risks. Unlike the Hollywood dramas, which were designed for syndication, New York teleplays were mostly experimental one-shot productions (Castleman and Podrazik 78). And New York TV used the anthology format—where the artists worked on a relatively autonomous project—rather than the Hollywood episodic series which "invited writers to compose…defined…scripts for specific actors and often for a particular sponsor, who was inclined to think of a play as a setting for his commercials" (Barnouw 25).

Unlike the episodes, the New York anthology series, for which Horton Foote wrote, had no specifications other than length and space (Castleman and Podrazik 25). And since the anthology dramas grew out of a theatrical tradition, as opposed to the episodic series' radio-influenced tradition, its "stars" were often Broadway and off-Broadway regulars and ingenues: Lee Strasberg, Paul Newman, Joanne Woodward, Kim Stanley, Sidney Poitier, and Arthur Penn, for example. Most importantly, these anthologies (often named for their corporate sponsor: Dupont, Goodyear, Philco, Lux, Gulf, Kraft) were very respectful of the writers. These actors and writers, often under the leadership of innovative New York directors and producers, gained significant artistic control. As producer Fred Coe remembered, "Good or bad it was *our* [the artists'] responsibility…they [the networks and executives] couldn't control the show once the subject matter had been chosen, because we were running things" (Wilk 135).

The key to the success of these shows was not just the politics of the productions, however. As Paddy Chayefsky, one of live TV's prominent writers, has explained, live network TV drama reflected the lives of its audiences:

> all of us then were writing about our audience, and say-
> ing to the people, "This is your life, This is what's going

on, and this is one shred of understanding about that
life." (Wilk 136)

The subjects, as Chayefsky again explains, were as real and relevant as
the people portrayed:

> There is far more exciting drama in the reasons why a
> man gets married than in why he murders someone. I am
> just becoming aware of the marvelous world of the ordi-
> nary. (Barnouw 32)

His interest in the "marvelous world of the ordinary," a world which
included teleplays by Horton Foote, inspired such award-winning
productions as *Marty*.

As TV audiences expanded and became more middle and working class, they grew increasingly disenchanted with viewing their own
lives week after week. They grew to prefer programs that removed
them from immediate problems, and thus episodic series like "Drag-
net," "Medic," "Cheyenne," or variety shows like "Texaco Star Theatre" ("Uncle Miltie") and "The Ed Sullivan Show" won the day. The
ratings for the anthology shows declined in proportion to the rise of
the episodic series, and the live dramas were finally judged too expensive (Castleman and Podrazik 98). Finally exposure to commercials,
which ask us to believe that any problem can be fixed in thirty sec-
onds, set the standard rather than quality programming written by
dramatists like Foote or Chayefsky.[1] But before advertising saturated
the screen, live TV gave Horton Foote a stage where he refined his
craft.

Fred Coe: The Writer's Producer

Though the national artistic interest in the ordinary person was
inspired by playwright Arthur Miller's essay "Tragedy and the Common Man," which accompanied Miller's most famous work *Death of
a Salesman*, its success on TV in the 1950s is attributable to "Philco/
Goodyear Television Playhouse." Its producer, Fred Coe, fought for
his writers' freedom to create original human dramas. He gave many
unproduced playwrights, often working outside traditional commercial theater, the opportunity to submit original material. Rather than
making formula pieces like those from Hollywood, Coe asked his
writers for "extended character sketches, taking one or two people

and placing them in engrossing, life-like situations" (Castleman and Podrazik 78).

One of Coe's first discoveries was Horton Foote. Foote was introduced to Coe very early in the 50s by Vincent J. Donehue, himself a producer/director. At that first meeting, Coe asked Foote if he had any material to offer him. Foote gave the producer *The Rocking Chair*, a play Coe liked but didn't have a place for at the time. The writer went on to work for a children's television show ("The Gabby Hayes Show") for more than a year. By 1952, when the producer and writer discussed working together, Coe accepted the Foote play *The Travellers*, which appeared on "The Philco Television Playhouse" on 27 April 1952 (Interview, 18 July 1985). That telecast began a partnership which lasted through 1956, producing seventeen plays on live TV, ten in 1953 alone.

As Horton Foote remembers, Coe explained that since he had no money to pay big stars, he would make stars out of the writers (Interview, 18 July 1985). In fact, as Foote explains in his Preface to *Harrison, Texas*, his 1956 collected edition of teleplays, Coe

> believes deeply in writers, and his belief, in turn, gives the writer a feeling of confidence in himself, his talent, and his craft...in nearly all instances...problems were kept away [by Coe] from the writer and he was left free to do his job as best he could. (viii)

Eventually, despite Fred Coe's support and encouragement to make personal statements about common people, the pace became too taxing for Horton Foote. By 1956 Foote felt the medium was on the verge of asking him to "churn out" plays indefinitely. Even his friend and collaborator Coe, in asking the writer to complete a teleplay every three months, didn't recognize that some plays took "years of thought and worry" (Interview, 18 July 1985). By the end of the decade Horton Foote returned to his artistic home: theater.

The Women in His World

> There's a kind of woman my father always writes—gentle but very strong. Often, they seem dependent on the man, but they exhibit this strength. These women survive and they do it with dignity.... And that's how my mother is. She believes so completely in my father and his talent. It's

almost like she had a plan for him. She's the rock.
—Hallie Foote (Freedman 62)

Horton Foote was raised by strong and nurturant women. He felt close to his grandmothers, aunts, and especially his mother. They supported him, told him stories, and inspired his work. Foote and his wife Lillian met when Horton was working in a New York bookstore, and they were married within a year, on June 4, 1945. Within another year the young couple moved to Washington, DC, where Foote wrote and directed several plays and managed a semi-professional theatre (Interview, 18 July 1985). Until her death in 1992, Lillian Foote was the most influential person in his writing career. According to Foote, Alan J. Pakula, producer of Foote's screen adaptation of *To Kill a Mockingbird*, believes that Foote's most resourceful women are based on Lillian Foote (Interview, 18 July 1985).

Such closeness and sympathy with women, especially his wife, led Horton Foote to explore in his teleplays the roles of women in society. Although the place-specific and understated style he developed in this period was itself personal, Foote was exceptional in capturing women's internal and external struggles to find their identity in American culture. In his mid-50s live TV dramas Horton Foote demonstrated his conviction that the plight of women is a subject worthy of deliberation in drama.

Foote's choice of subject seems especially courageous when compared with the view of women in other episodic TV. His work was written when the most recognizable role models for women were "Gunsmoke's" "Miss Kitty" and "Perry Mason's" "Della Street." Interesting for their "supporting" roles to their principal male characters, these characters were not dynamic. Women in 1950s and 60s TV comedies fared no better, being either domestic goddesses like "Donna Stone" (Reed) or "June Cleaver," childish clowns like "Lucy Ricardo"; or fantasy/aliens like "Jeannie," "Samantha," and "My Living Doll." Of course "Julia" and "Mary Richards" partially broke the mold for ethnic and working women, but 1970s "dramas" re-established women as objects of male fantasy: see "The Bionic Woman," "Wonder Woman," and "Charlie's Angels." In the 1980s "Cagney and Lacey" and "Kate and Allie" were popular for a time. Yet equally attractive were the babe-vixens from "Dallas" and "Dynasty." Compared to this tradition of one-dimensional female characters, Horton

Foote's rounded and often unforgettable women are remarkable.

While female characters in each of Horton Foote's 50s teleplays exhibit complexity,[2] five plays feature women who are unusually strong for their time: *The Trip to Bountiful* (1953), *A Young Lady of Property* (1953), *The Tears of My Sister* (1953), *The Midnight Caller* (1953), and *Flight* (1956). Three of these plays concern unrequited love, but the plays also focus on other universal issues, such as coping with death, finding/establishing a "home," raising and letting go of children, and finding the courage to face adversity.

The Trip to Bountiful, originally aired on "The Goodyear Playhouse" on Sunday evening, 1 March 1953, starred Lillian Gish as Carrie Watts, Eva Marie Saint as Carrie's young acquaintance Thelma, and John Beal as Carrie's son Ludie. The teleplay concerns Carrie's quest to return to her hometown of Bountiful, Texas, where she spent most of her life farming her father's and then her husband's land. Carrie has grown old, is widowed, and for the past few years has been living with her son and daughter-in-law in a two-room apartment in Houston. Carrie has tried repeatedly to escape the inertia and suspicion imposed on her by her daughter-in-law, Jessie Mae, by returning to Bountiful to see her homeplace once more.

Most of the play describes her successful escape from Houston to Bountiful, during which she meets Thelma, with whom she shares her life story. She confesses that she neither married the man she loved nor loved the man she married. She had children who died; she struggled to make a living on her farm. When Carrie does get to Bountiful, almost nothing remains; her old house, ramshackle now, is as dried up as the town. At the end of the play, Carrie is retrieved by Ludie and Jessie Mae, but the conclusion is bittersweet. She returns to a safe place and offers a spirit of compromise to her daughter-in-law, but Bountiful can only be a memory.

For Carrie Watts, then, life was always a series of difficult decisions. At times she wonders if God is punishing her for marrying a man she didn't love, but she never asks why she lost the farm, the place she gave most of her life to making a home. While the dramas of this period often describe the ambitions, sacrifices, and struggles of male characters, *The Trip to Bountiful* focuses on Carrie, a woman who dreamed of and tried hard to get the life she wanted, failed, and yet was never broken by her failure to do so. And she did get home, though it wasn't the place she remembered. In the life of this ordinary woman, Horton Foote discovers the universal drama of going away and coming home again.

The pain of Carrie Watts' decisions is equaled by that of Wilma Thompson in Foote's *A Young Lady of Property*, which aired on NBC's "Philco Playhouse" on 5 April, 1953. Kim Stanley played Wilma, a young woman living in 1925-era Harrison, Texas, whose fondest desire is to travel to Hollywood and become an actress. Wilma's family and hometown, of course, seek to undermine her fantasies. However, Wilma's desire is further complicated by her mother's death and her father's remarriage. Though her mother willed their house to Wilma, her father tries to sell it without consulting her. Wilma, now living with an aunt, must decide whether to stay in Harrison and fight for the house and her mother's legacy or to abandon her mother's dreams and follow her own out to Hollywood. As she contemplates this choice, she is flooded by bittersweet memories:

> I love to swing in my front yard. Mama and I used to come out here and swing together. Some nights when Daddy was out all night gambling I'd wake up and hear her out swinging away. Sometimes she'd let me come and sit beside her. We'd swing until three or four in the morning. (Foote, *Harrison, Texas* 21)

Wilma ultimately decides to forego her acting in order to live in her mother's house and perhaps to raise a family there some day. Fortunately, her father's new wife convinces him to return the house to Wilma so the young woman's inheritance can be realized.

But, typical of Horton Foote's desire to keep art close to life, to the complex and unresolved tensions within human experience, *A Young Lady of Property* ends with an unpleasant memory that clouds Wilma's new-found tranquillity in the house that has become hers:

> I used to sleep in there. I had a white iron bed. I remember one night Aunt Gert woke me up. It was just turning light out, she was crying. I'm taking you home to live with me, she said. Why? I said. Because your Mama's gone to Heaven, she said.... I can't remember my Mama's face anymore. I can hear her voice sometimes calling far off: Wilma, Wilma, come home. Far off. But I can't remember her face. I try and try, but finally I have to go to the bureau drawer and take out her picture and look to

> remember....Oh....It isn't only the house I wanted. It's
> the life in the house. My Mama and me and even my
> Daddy coming in at four in the morning. (Foote,
> *Harrison, Texas* 39)

Even while the play celebrates Wilma's decision, it demonstrates the
sense of loss in any choosing. There is poignancy and pathos as well as
joy in Wilma's decision to live the dreams she shared with her mother.
In *A Young Lady of Property* a young woman takes an active role in
deciding her fate, and yet she also must confront the consequences
and responsibilities of choice. Horton Foote's drama, like the life he
describes, has little closure; life and memory go on.

Later in 1953, Foote experimented stylistically with two teleplays:
The Death of the Old Man, first aired on the "Gulf Playhouse" on 17
July, and more importantly for this study, *The Tears of My Sister*, first
presented on the "Gulf Playhouse" on 14 August. These two plays,
produced by Fred Coe and directed by Arthur Penn, use a subjective
camera. *Tears* is told from the perspective of Cecilia Monroe, played
by Kim Stanley, who narrates the story of her sister Bessie, who is
marrying for the family's security, not love. Bessie's true love, Syd,
tries to convince her to run away with him, but her mother discovers
the plot and threatens to call the police.

Using the camera as the perspective of Cecilia, Horton Foote
filters the action through her consciousness. She loses some of her
innocence as her mother's words explain motives and even implicate
Cecilia herself:

> All right honey. Cry. Get it all out. It hurts now, but some
> day you're gonna be glad. We have to be practical in this
> world, honey....Try not to cry, honey. It upsets your sis-
> ter to hear you cry. She's too young to understand. (Foote,
> *Harrison, Texas* 92)

While Cecilia doesn't fully understand all the implications, she does
feel subterranean drama:

> I love my sister, Mama, and I'm sorry for my sister and
> I'm sorry for you.... And maybe I don't know why, but
> I'm cryin' too Mama. Cryin' for my sister and cryin' for
> you. (93)

Though her words are not heard by her mother or sister, Cecilia's
tears indicate the pain of a woman's abandoning her dream for a life

she didn't choose, doesn't desire.

How many American women, Foote seems to be asking, had to make such compromises in an age when only men were free to choose their life's companions? Unable to gain control of their own lives through active choosing, the women remain the objects of the men they follow, as Cecilia explains through her mother's voice,

> Mama says men understand not a thing about the sorrows of women. She says it just scares them. She says all men want women to be regular doll babies all the time. Happy and good-natured and with no troubles. (*Selected One Acts* 161)

As Gerald Wood explains, *Tears of My Sister*, by imagining marriage as "little more than a business deal," is "one of Horton Foote's darkest representations of the lives of women early in this century—and to some extent even to this day" (*Selected One-Acts* 149–50).

An even darker examination of faded and abandoned love is Foote's *The Midnight Caller*, produced by Fred Coe, directed by Vincent J. Donehue, and first aired on the "Philco Playhouse" on 13 December 1953. Unlike *The Trip to Bountiful* and *A Young Lady of Property*, which were crowd-pleasers, *The Midnight Caller* was a "neurotic" play according to the public and to media reviewers. Furthermore, according to Foote, Catholic priests strongly objected to the play and wanted it censored because of its inference of premarital sex (Interview, 18 July 1985). It centers on a group of people living in a boarding house in Harrison, Texas. The main character, Helen Crews, has not been able to marry the man she loves, Harvey Weems. Because Helen's mother, a widow with little money, doesn't want to lose Helen and her sister, Helen has to sneak out at night to meet Harvey. Things are made worse by Harvey's excessive drinking and his mother's disdain for Helen. Though Helen keeps reassuring Harvey that everything will work out, the obstacles against them are ultimately too formidable. In order to survive emotionally, she has to leave Harvey, and every midnight Harvey drunkenly "calls" on her at the boarding house for all the town to hear.

Harvey's nocturnal visits lead many of the other residents to consider Helen a "fallen woman." And there, of course, lay the objections of many of the play's viewers. Though it is never made explicit whether Helen and Harvey consummated their love, the implication made

The Midnight Caller unsuitable for a 50s prime-time audience according to some reviewers. But sex is not the issue in the teleplay; obsession is. Though by the end of the play Helen has agreed to marry Ralph Johnston, a stable man who stays at the boarding house, she will most likely be haunted by memories of "the midnight caller." This is the price she must pay for finding the courage to rebel against her family's control and local gossip in the pursuit of healthy attachments.

The most penetrating portrayal and analysis of the plight of women in Foote's literary world to this point is his *Flight*, produced by Fred Coe on NBC's "Playwrights '56" (28 February 1956) directed by Vincent J. Donehue, and starring Kim Stanley. This teleplay was based on Foote's mother's defiance of her parents to nearly marry a man of whom they vehemently disapproved: "It was probably fortunate that she didn't," Foote says, although "She later did marry a man that her parents didn't really approve of" (the subject of *Courtship* from *The Orphans' Home Cycle*) (Interview, 18 July 1985). *Flight*, set in 1915 in Harrison, Texas, concerns a young woman, Martha, who loves, elopes with, and is later abandoned by a young man who cannot stand the strain of their secret—a secret which both realize will devastate Martha's parents. By the time her parents learn about the marriage, it is too late for them to approve, disapprove, or openly recognize it. Upon realizing that her husband has left her, Martha doesn't wallow in her misery or submit to her parents' judgment; she follows a childhood dream by hopping a train to San Antonio to start a new life—alone.

The time frame—1915—is extremely important to its theme, as Foote observed, since it was uncommon at that time for a young woman to leave home and pursue an independent life:

> [1915] was a time when many of the fixed and settled values in American life were changing or being re-examined and when the whole concept of family life and family responsibility was being altered.... A crisis occurs in [Martha's] life and [her parents] are prepared to shelter and protect her, to help in whatever way they can to repair any wrong or damage that has been done to her. She refuses them and chooses to go away to a city alone. Hers is an exodus, a flight that was unusual for a girl of her background and environment then. Today, for good or bad, it is constant. (Burack 148–49)

For her time Martha is a liberated woman; she stares down her husband's rejection and moves on, wanting help from no one. No compromiser, Martha has the resilience and resourcefulness that anticipates other strong Foote female characters, particularly Rosa Lee in the 1982 film *Tender Mercies*.

Unfortunately, the history of TV suggests that Horton Foote's female characters during the live era had little lasting influence on the view of women in American popular culture. But Foote has always been a personal writer who, despite commissioned work and successful adaptations, has stubbornly maintained and pursued his own vision. Inspired by the women in his past, his wife, and creative collaborators like Fred Coe, he examined women's struggles, their very human journeys, as an integral part of his world view. As early as the mid-50s, Horton Foote demonstrated his belief that the subject of drama is *all* of humanity.

ல்

Notes

1.   For more on the demise of live TV drama, see George Terry Barr, *The Ordinary World of Horton Foote* (Diss., U of Tennessee, 1987), 96-100.

2.   See Gerald C. Wood, ed., *Selected One-Act Plays of Horton Foote* (Dallas: Southern Methodist UP, 1989); Horton Foote, *Harrison, Texas: Eight Television Plays* (NY: Harcourt Brace, 1956); and George Terry Barr, *The Ordinary World of Horton Foote* (Diss., U of Tennessee, 1987).

Works Cited

Barnouw, Erik. *The Image Empire: A History of Broadcasting in the U.S.* Vol. 3. New York: Oxford UP, 1970.

Brown, Les. *Television: The Business Behind the Box*. New York: Harcourt Brace, 1971.

Burack, Abraham, Ed. *Television Plays for Writers: Eight Television Plays with Comment and Analysis by the Authors*. Boston: The Writer, 1957.

Cantor, Muriel G. *Prime-Time Television: Content and Control.* Beverly Hills: Sage, 1980.

Castleman, Harry, and W.J. Podrazik. *Watching TV: Four Decades of American Television.* New York: McGraw-Hill, 1982.

Foote, Horton. *Harrison, Texas: Eight Television Plays.* New York: Harcourt Brace, 1956.

———. Interview. 18 July 1985.

Freedman, Samuel G. "From the Heart of Texas." *New York Times Magazine* 9 Feb. 1986: 31, 50, 61, 63, 73.

Kaufman, William I., Ed. *Great TV Plays.* New York: Dell, 1969.

Miller, Arthur. "Tragedy and the Common Man." *New York Times* 27 Feb. 1949, sec. 2: 1, 3. Rpt. in *American Playwrights on Drama.* Ed. Horst Frenz. NY: Hill & Wang, 1965. 79–83.

Wilk, Max. *The Golden Age of Television: Notes from the Survivors.* New York: Delacorte, 1976.

Wood, Gerald C, Ed. *Selected One-Act Plays of Horton Foote.* Dallas: Southern Methodist UP, 1989.

Southern Accents
Horton Foote's Adaptations of William Faulkner, Harper Lee, and Flannery O'Connor
Rebecca Briley

In his seminal study of Southern literature, *Southern Renascence: The Literature of the Modern South* (1953), Louis D. Rubin identifies five common denominators among Southern authors: emphasis on the past, appreciation of family, attachment to place, a sense of the concrete, and awareness of the impact of religion. While useful for identifying the nature of Southern literature itself, Rubin's categories also demonstrate that Horton Foote, often considered an American Chekhov, writes within the tradition described in *Southern Renascence*. As Foote has explained, from his initial writing for the stage, "I got in touch with material that was...for the lack of a better word, regional material" (Edgerton 4). In fact, it was a subject that he feels was given to him: "I did not choose this task, this place, or these people to write about so much as they chose me, and I try to write of them with honesty" (Locher 210). And his Southern place in all of his personal writing has been Wharton, Texas, and coastal southeast Texas.

Like many of his Southern colleagues, Foote relies on the personal voices and stories from his region. One of his tasks as a writer is to be the "recorder" of his family's history, based on the stories he heard growing up; he cherishes his heritage and its impact on his creation production (Foote, Interview 14 Nov. 1987). Acknowledging the "strong oral tradition" of the South and the family legends passed from one generation to another (Edgerton 4), Foote proudly takes his place among similar Southern storytellers, citing Katherine Anne Porter, James Agee, Eudora Welty, Flannery O'Connor, and William Faulkner as influential authors whose works he admires (Wood and Barr 226). Like these Southern writers, Foote discovers universal patterns in his regional material. Marian Burkhart, writing for *Commonweal*, points out that "even if Foote's plays are based upon events in the life of his own family, his work turns outward to a world

Americans know, an unexaggerated, uninflated world where most of us live" (110). Foote concurs, explaining that his interest in family and history is both personal and universal, extending his definition of "family" to include the larger community (Foote, Interview 14 Nov. 1987).

While his ability to make the regional universal has led to Foote's growth as an original playwright and screenwriter, he also has been an award-winning adaptor of material by other writers, particularly Southern writers. His sympathies for the characters created by other Southern storytellers and his understanding of their settings and sensibilities is demonstrated in his translations to the screen of works by William Faulkner, Harper Lee, and Flannery O'Connor. Although Foote prefers personal writing, his success in adapting these writers relies on his recognition of similar regional accents. And then, like the writers themselves, he transforms those place-specific stories into universal experiences of love, loss, and reconciliation.

Adaptation requires "taking on someone else's identity and submerging yourself in it," Foote explains. "While you don't have to feel it's great literature, you do have to be sympathetic toward it" (Interview 14 Nov. 1987). At first Foote was reluctant to attempt such literary role-playing, afraid of losing his writing identity or failing to find common ground with the work itself as in the case of Clinton Seeley's novel *Storm Fear* in 1956. With William Faulkner, things were different. Claiming Faulkner as his greatest literary influence (Interview 14 Nov. 1987), Foote could identify with the Southern terrain of arguably the region's most significant contributor to literature. The same common ground was eventually established between Horton Foote and Harper Lee and Flannery O'Connor.

These authors all share Louis Rubin's characteristics of Southern writing, but each writer emphasizes one or two of these in his or her work. While Foote maintains the writer's Southern spirit, he tends to shift the focus toward family issues, father-child relationships in particular. In each piece, Foote deals compassionately with the borrowed characters, suspending the plot to linger on their development and sometimes offering them a more healthy society than they had in the original.

Horton Foote recalls being impressed with William Faulkner's work as early as the 1940s; when it was relatively unknown Foote was "in some measure a student of his then existing work" ("On First

Dramatizing Faulkner" 50). After wisely side-stepping a request to dramatize *The Sound and the Fury*, feeling "the unique qualities of the work" could not be preserved on television, Foote agreed in 1958 to adapt Faulkner's "Old Man" for Fred Coe's "Playhouse 90." "Very wary to get involved" because of early television's limited locations, Foote nevertheless carefully adhered to Faulkner's plot, mostly giving order to the story's chaotic journey. The novella describes a convict's rescue of a pregnant woman from a flooding Mississippi River and his safe, but unjust, return to prison.

The characters in the rural Southern setting, not unlike those in his own East Texas world, attracted Foote to the project. Here were simple people speaking a subtle language Foote recognized. The writer was particularly fascinated by the character of the woman: "I never tired thinking of the woman," Foote muses. "She was always (and remains so) a delight to me… I wanted as soon as possible to establish a specific character for the woman. I made her a talker and gave her a detailed history" ("On First Dramatizing Faulkner" 54–55). While Faulkner narrates the journey of the convict through interior mono-logue, giving little attention to the other characters, Foote expands the woman's role, shifting the perspective from the male character to his relationship with the pregnant woman. Unlike in Faulkner's story, the two create a surrogate family which nurtures both of them.

The result is a more humane story. Through his narrative, Faulkner's convict reveals a desperate desire to escape from the real world, first into the "birth canal" of the flooding river and finally back to the protective "womb" of the penitentiary. He gratefully ac-cepts the additional ten-years' punishment for his mistaken escape since in prison he'll be "without no female companionship" (Faulkner, "Old Man" 579). Foote's convict, on the other hand, cares for his new-found female partner, anticipating a life with her and the child. He resents his premature capture and the additional confinement, while the woman, eager to establish family ties, is willing to wait for the convict's release. In line with this clearer sense of family, Foote erases derogatory or suggestive language from Faulkner's coarser text, giving the teleplay a more gentlemanly tone. While Faulkner's "Old Man" is more psychological, darker, and comical, Foote's version develops more intimacy between characters and offers a more hopeful conclusion.

The teleplay "Old Man" won an Emmy nomination and William Faulkner's own endorsement, but Horton Foote's second Faulkner adaptation, "Tomorrow," appeared successfully in three media: television (1960), stage (1963), and film (1972). One of the stories in the detective collection *Knight's Gambit, Tomorrow* investigates cotton-farmer/jurist Jackson Fentry's reasons for refusing to acquit the killer of ruffian Buck Thorpe. As with "Old Man," Foote re-creates Faulkner's rural setting and characters, but while Faulkner focuses on the details of Gavin Stevens's investigation of Fentry's motives, Foote concentrates on the relationship between Fentry and the woman Faulkner only describes as "black complected," the dying mother mentioned in only three paragraphs of the original story. As in the previous adaptation from Faulkner, Foote recalls it was "the character of the woman [that] became alive to me, even though Faulkner gives only a few paragraphs to her" ("Tomorrow: The Genesis of a Screenplay" 149–50). "I called her Sarah, although Faulkner never names her" (153), Foote continues, admitting that "what I had written was monstrously out of proportion to the rest of the story" (154). A substantially different story emerged because, as Foote explains, "the more completely I dramatized the relationship between Fentry and Sarah, the less room it left for the dramatizing of the other elements of the story" ("Tomorrow: The Genesis of a Screenplay" 157). Once again, even as Foote used the accent of his collaborator, his own voice proved stronger and in the end justified the reshaping of Faulkner's characters.

Under Foote's rewriting, the detective element at the core of Faulkner's study nearly vanishes while the love story blossoms. It becomes a study of Fentry's growing compassion for the woman he finds outside his house and her child. As he attempts to nurse the woman back to health, Fentry gives her every consideration, even promising to build her the house she always wanted. Foote allows this woman to be a "talker" like the one he developed in "Old Man," and the quiet Fentry listens as she relates the history of her estranged family and the hopes for her child. Fentry, who has enjoyed a distant but congenial relationship with his own father, is undaunted by Sarah's cold and bitter past; he asks to become her husband and the child's father. When Sarah dies on the heels of their hasty marriage, Fentry is determined to bring up her child "like he was my own" (Foote, *Tomorrow* 83). Although the child is the offspring of a man who rejected it,

Fentry's commitment to his "son"—whom he names Jackson and Longstreet—is strong, illustrating Foote's belief that love, rather than blood, creates the human bond. Horton Foote's version of "Tomorrow," like his adaptation of "Old Man," demonstrates the power of unconditional love; unlike Faulkner, Foote focuses on the need for reconciliation within the family.

In the second half of Foote's *Tomorrow*, the study of family values shifts from husband-wife to father-son. The film fleshes out Faulkner's scant description of the relationship between the child and Fentry in a series of silent scenes which visualize the bond between the two. When Bruce Kawin finds it "unfortunate that the relationship between Fentry and his 'son' is so hurriedly summarized" (65), he clearly misses the message so deeply etched in Foote's montage, what Jack Barbera calls a "delight of the film" (194). For although more film time is spent on Fentry and Sarah, the deep love between the father and son—also Foote's contribution to the story—is more explicitly developed (Yellin and Connors, "Faulkner" 12). It is true that, being "flesh and blood kin," the Thorpes legally and forcefully remove Jackson and Longstreet from his new-found family to rear him as Buck Thorpe. But even fifteen years later, Fentry "can't vote Bookwright free" because "there still remained...at least the memory of that little boy...even though the man the boy had become didn't know it and only Fentry did" (Faulkner, "Tomorrow" 51–52). According to Foote, Fentry's "capacity for love" (Foote, *Tomorrow* 159) toward his adopted son is what finally "endures...tomorrow and tomorrow and tomorrow" (Faulkner, "Tomorrow" 52).

Although co-producer Paul Roebling disagreed with Foote's interpretation of "what Mr. Faulkner wrote and...what I wanted to put on the screen" (Yellin and Connors, "Conversations" 171), director Joseph Anthony felt Foote's writing "was truly relevant to the basic story" (178). Robert Duvall, who claims his film role as Fentry is still one of his favorite parts, applauds Foote's rewriting: "I didn't read [the Faulkner story] until after I made the movie," Duvall explains. "Horton had put in much of his own material and it was great. He knows the area and the people" (173). Foote admits that Faulkner's story "is separate and equal and powerful" but also believes that his film version is "the most complete, on its own, as an experience" (165). Realizing there comes "a selfish moment" in adaptation when "you take it over" (Foote, Interview 14 Nov. 1987), Foote maintains, "I wouldn't have known how to do 'Tomorrow' except the way that I did it, and although I'm not close in form, I feel I'm close in essence to Faulkner's story" (Yellin and Connors, "Faulkner" 21).

Successful on television, *Tomorrow* gained additional popularity by appearing on stage and as a significant independent film. Faulkner was so pleased, Horton Foote says, with the television and screen renditions that he insisted Foote share the copyright with him (Interview, 14 Nov. 1987). Many critics agree that Foote's *Tomorrow* is "one of the best screen adaptations of a Faulkner work" (Millichap 104), and Bruce Kawin calls it "simply one of the best independent productions in the recent history of American narrative film" (65). It certainly is one of the best examples of a work in harmony with the original material while at the same time remaining true to the individual voice of the adaptor.

Foote's final (to date) Faulkner adaptation, *Barn Burning*, was written for the PBS American Short Story Series in 1980. From the beginning, the production company was determined "to keep the film as faithful as possible to William Faulkner's plot" (Skaggs 6). In another typically rural setting with similar country characters, Faulkner's much-studied story portrays firebrand Abner Snopes through the eyes of his son Sarty, whose desperate pride in his father finally dies when the son can no longer justify his father's lawlessness. Merrill Skaggs, the wife of the producer, believes the film transforms "Sarty Snopes' struggle to forge an acceptable identity" into the story of "Ab Snopes, the father," reasoning that Tommy Lee Jones, who plays that role, "steals the show because he has the most talent to begin with" (8). She goes on to assume that it is Ab's story because he totally controls the family and "most often delivers the lines which explain the actions" (12).

While performance cannot be overlooked when determining the emphasis of a film, Skaggs' thesis is irrelevant to the primary focus of *Barn Burning*. Both Faulkner and Foote write of a father *and* son relationship in which the son is bullied and confused by his father's twisted convictions. The theme for both writers is summed up in the elder Snopes' warning to his son, who is tempted to report the father to the authorities: "You've got to learn," he tells Sarty, "to stick to your own blood or you ain't going to have any blood to stick to you" (Faulkner, "Barn Burning" 1496). Sarty initially comprehends this conflict in simpler terms: "our enemy...ourn! Mine and hisn both!

He's my father" (1493). But as the boy's eyes are opened to his father's dangerous narrowness, the conflict intensifies. Once he realizes that his father has no intention of warning the deSpains before spitefully burning their barn, Sarty grasps that though blood may be thicker than water, it cannot be thicker than truth. When the father's example can no longer be followed, Sarty runs to the other side, first to warn the deSpains and then to strike out on his own, forging a new way of life for himself.

Horton Foote retains this conflict of blood explicitly in his script. Sarty goes from acquiescing to his father's instruction that blood is blood to denying that blood's power to keep him from doing the right thing. But the important difference between the two versions occurs in the endings. In Faulkner's story, when Sarty hears shots and cries "Pap! Pap!" (Faulkner, "Barn Burning" 1506) and thereafter thinks of his father in the past tense: "My father...he *was* brave!... He *was*! He was in the war!" (1507, my emphasis), it is easy to assume Snopes is dead. Although Faulkner, using the complexity of stream of consciousness, leaves the ending somewhat ambiguous, Sarty may be running from the rest of the family, thinking he is responsible for his own father's death. In any case, Abner Snopes, according to William Faulkner, is at least *metaphorically* dead; the son can no longer defend the blood of the father.

When Foote depicts Snopes leaving with his family in the wagon silhouetted against the fire and Sarty running in the opposite direction, the boy's choosing against his father is made explicit. Foote himself has expressed displeasure in the conclusion, admitting that "Barn Burning" was hard to adapt because of the ending's interior monologue. "The film's end was lame," he laments, "and didn't stand up to Faulkner's at all" (Foote, Interview 14 Nov. 1987). While the mystery and poignancy of Faulkner's ending certainly are diminished, Foote's resolution is still psychologically real. But the film's closure, following a scene in which Sarty overhears the truth about his father's unscrupulous war record, does tip the scales; Foote's *Barn Burning* prefers Sarty's responsibility to society over his commitment to his father.

Because of the popularity of his film translations of Faulkner's stories, and perhaps also due to the few good stage or screen adaptations of the Nobel Prize–winning author's work, Foote is often approached for advice on dramatizing Faulkner. "Hollywood has so often failed with him," Foote suggests, "because they insist on improving on him—for whatever reasons." He advises: "I think it would be well for any dramatist to give up this approach. He can be dramatized: he can't be improved" ("On First Dramatizing Faulkner" 65). And yet Foote's adaptations of Faulkner reveal the times when fidelity to the original has to be replaced by Foote's own chemistry. The key is the degree of shared chemistry between the two writers. Horton Foote says he writes from deep belief in the human spirit ("Horton Foote," CBY 147); Faulkner describes his art as a "life's work in the agony and sweat of the human spirit" (Faulkner, "Address" 723). When Foote says he admires people's "grace to meet what comes their way and find strength to survive" (Neff 30), he echoes Faulkner's Nobel Prize acceptance speech: "I believe that man will not merely endure; he will prevail...because he has a soul, a spirit capable of compassion and sacrifice and endurance" ("Address" 724). Though they write in different forms, both Foote and Faulkner speak with the same "poet's voice" (Faulkner, "Address" 724).

"A certain kinship" is required when an author adapts another's work because, as Horton Foote explains, "you're trying to get under the skin of a person" (Hachem 41). Not surprisingly, Foote's words echo those of Atticus Finch in Harper Lee's novel *To Kill a Mockingbird*: "You never really understand a person until you consider things from his point of view...until you climb into his skin and walk around in it" (Lee 36). Foote established his kinship with Lee and her Southern world when he adapted her Pulitzer Prize–winning bestseller for Robert Mulligan's film in 1962, which won both the Best Screenplay Oscar and the Writer's Guild Award. When producer Alan J. Pakula first approached him, Foote was reluctant to commit to the "backbreaking job," complaining the novel "sprawls all over" (Barr 149). Pakula assured Foote that the novelist, who had declined the assignment, specifically requested Foote take her place. Finally he agreed to meet Lee, and, as he says, "I just loved her.... And I thought, 'Well, I'll enjoy this, if no more than getting to know her'" (Barr 149).

Foote soon felt he had known Lee all his life; the similarity between his own Southern heritage and the "tree houses, small towns, black cooks, and people like Boo Radley" of Lee's fictionalized world quickly enabled him to make *To Kill a Mockingbird* his own (Interview 14 Nov. 1987). Harper Lee acknowledged the sympathy between her work and Foote's in her foreword to the published film script:

The complaints of novelists whose work has been trans-
ferred to screen are so numerous and so often justified
that I sometimes wonder if I am a minority of one when
I examine my own feeling about the film *To Kill a Mockingbird*.... For me, Maycomb is there, its people are there:
in two short hours one lives a childhood and lives it with
Atticus Finch, whose view of life was the heart of the novel.
("A Word" v)

The shared penchant for detailed storytelling, as well as the concerns
for history and place, were there; Foote felt very much at home with
her small-town, Depression-era setting, affectionately peopled with a
cross-section of Southern "kinfolks" from the educated to the illiter-
ate, the elderly to the eccentric. But the screenwriter most identified
with Atticus Finch's family dealing with loss and reconciliation.

Budget and time restrictions forced Foote to condense the two-
year span of the novel to a little more than a year and reduce many of
its scenes and characters. His tightening focuses the novel's winding
narrative on major characters and the immediate family. Omitting
historical background on Maycomb and the Finch family, Foote emphasizes Atticus as the ideal father-figure. The script immediately establishes Atticus' honorable dealings with the impoverished
Cunninghams, his small-town neighbors (congenial and otherwise),
the dignified black cook Calpurnia, the town officials, and, most importantly, his own children, Jem and Scout. As Terry Barr rightly
asserts, "in many ways Lee's Atticus Finch is Horton Foote's kind of
character: the head of a broken family; a relentless dreamer and be-
liever in the basic honor and dignity of all living characters" (152–
53). While Foote's male characters rarely are as near-infallible as Lee's
protagonist, the need for a hero of Atticus' stature is evident throughout Foote's canon.

Atticus Finch is a single parent since the death of his beloved
young wife and a "liberal" lawyer in a conservative small Southern
town. While the novel tends to give more attention to Atticus the
public servant, the screenplay describes him as both mother and father to his children. Foote undoubtedly shares Lee's concerns for the
civil rights issues and is equally as compassionate with the gracefully
drawn black characters. But he focuses on father-child relationships,
adding to Lee's story a poignant scene in which the children discuss
the absent mother. Drawing on his own past in which he "used to lie

in bed at night and listen to the grown-ups talking outside" (Barr 157), Horton Foote develops the children's curiosity and insecurities and Atticus' silent but brooding presence.

Because Lee and Foote share a common Southern voice, it is often difficult to tell where one leaves off and the other begins. Generally, though, as in all his adaptation work, Foote's more charitable characterizations tend to be softer, rounding off the sharper edges of Scout's sometimes sarcastic narration in the novel. But, as with Faulkner, his changes "blended so delicately with the original" they seem—at least to Harper Lee—part of her own script:

> Horton Foote's screenplay is a work of such quiet and unobtrusive excellence that many people have commented on the fact that the film's dialogue was lifted chapter and verse from the novel. This is simply not so. Scenes humorous, scenes tender, scenes terrifying, each with a definite purpose and value, blended so delicately with the original, created the illusion that these were Harper Lee's words. ("A Word" v)

Once inside Harper Lee's skin, Horton Foote creates a "quiet and unobtrusive" re-creation of her Maycomb.

As in his other adaptations of Southern literature, Horton Foote revises in the interest of family. He omits scenes from the Lee text partly for economy. But dropping characters like Mr. Link Deas and Mr. Dolphus Raymond, for example, and omitting the fire and much of Mrs. Dubose's story shift the focus from the community as a whole to the Finches in particular. On the other hand, Foote includes the scene about the rabid dog, not for dramatic spectacle but because it allows the children to see Atticus in a new light. Thereafter, they know they can count on their father in more dangerous circumstances.

The real test of a father's influence comes when his children respond positively to his instruction. When Atticus agrees to defend Tom Robinson, the black man falsely accused of raping Mayella Ewell, the father becomes for many townspeople a "nigger-lover." Atticus goes to great pains to explain to his children his reasons for defending a black man against the prejudice of the white community. "If I didn't," he tells Scout, "I couldn't hold my head up in this town. I couldn't even tell you and Jem not to do somethin' again" (Foote, *To Kill a Mockingbird* 61; Lee, *To Kill a Mockingbird* 83). In spite of the difficulty the family may experience because of his stance, Atticus realizes he must stand by his principles not only in support of social justice but also to be a healthy role model for his children. In fact, since the story is Scout's, the novel and film describe Atticus' continuing influence on his daughter; her memory inspires the story.

Like Harper Lee, Horton Foote uses other characters as points of comparison with Atticus and the Finch family. The father held in sharpest contrast is, of course, Bob Ewell, the parent of the alleged rape victim. Lee describes the Ewell family as filthy, ignorant, and mean and the father of this family as "a man [who] spends his relief checks on green whiskey [while] his children [cry] from hunger pains" (*Mockingbird* 37). Foote is a bit more generous, omitting much of Lee's derogatory description of Bob Ewell, though the images carry equal meaning. His rendering of Mayella, however, elicits the pity of the children, and thus the audience. Similarly, while Lee allows the children's morbid curiosity about Boo Radley to ramble through her narrative, Foote cuts through the sensationalism of local gossip to emphasize his role as a substitute father for "his children" (Lee, *Mockingbird* 294). Despite the children's fears, Boo is another incarnation of Atticus: he gives them soap dolls and other gifts, mends Jem's pants, risks his life to save the children from Bob Ewell. Likely it is the longing for loving family relationships missing from his own life that motivates Boo to keep a watchful, caring eye on the Finch children, and although Jem and Scout shower their affection on their own father, even as they openly dramatize misconceived and offensive notions about Boo himself, Boo does not hesitate when the opportunity arises to demonstrate his concern for them. In some odd way, his actions on their behalf seem to atone for the lack of love he himself has known in his own family.

As in other scenes, Foote summarizes the trial for the film, characteristically modifying Lee's coarser language and its implications. The novel's description of the rape is more explicit, and Lee implies Mayella has been sexually abused by her father as well as beaten. Foote seems reluctant to allude to such specific atrocities and is careful, too, to curtail the use of the word "nigger," using it only when unavoidable, either because of his own sensibilities or that of his 1960s audience. After the trial, the screenwriter quickly refocuses on the father when the blacks in the balcony stand in honor of Atticus, his compassion and courage. The significance is both public and private as Jem and Scout are urged by the black Reverend Sykes to "Stand up. Your father's passin" (Foote, *Mockingbird* 101). For Foote, more than Lee, the private acts can sometimes redeem public injustice.

The ending to the film *To Kill a Mockingbird* remains controversial. Perhaps it is the potentially confusing shift in perspective that led Foote to omit the powerful lines which conclude Harper Lee's book:

> It was summertime, and two children scampered down the sidewalk toward a man approaching in the distance.... It was fall, and his children...trotted to and fro around the corner, the day's woes and triumphs on their faces.... Summer, and he watched his children's heart break. Autumn again, and Boo's children needed him. (293–94)

Instead, maintaining Scout's narrative voice, Foote inserts: "Boo was our neighbor. He gave us two soap dolls, a broken watch and chain, a knife, and our lives" (116). The differences are subtle but substantial, and Foote again feels, as with *Barn Burning*, the film's ending does not sustain that of the novel. As Terry Barr writes, "Foote's ending...simply does not carry the weight that Lee's ending does...and clearly shows the problems of adapting one work to another" (160). However, by giving Scout the final lines—"Atticus said you never really knew a man until you stood in his shoes and walked around in them. Just standin' on the Radley porch was enough" (Foote, *Mockingbird* 116)—he returns the story to the daughter and father. The final emphasis in the film is Atticus and his "view of life," making it nearly impossible for the audience to forget the "heart" of their story. As *New York Times* film critic Bosley Crowther correctly summarized, the "crucial" focus of the film is "the relationship between Atticus and his children" (10:2).

These additions and modifications, while reflecting Horton Foote's belief in the powers of love and family, re-create the intention and ideals of Harper Lee's work as she recognizes in the foreword to the published script:

> If the integrity of a film adaptation is measured by the degree to which the novelist's intent is preserved, Mr. Foote's screenplay should be studied as a classic...its producers, its screenwriter, and its actors have kept faith with a novel, for better or worse, and the result is a film that has a life of its own as a work of art. (v)

It is as though Foote did climb into Lee's skin and walk around, but the footprints he left behind are deepened by the weight of his own interest, style, and purpose.

Although Foote achieved much success and acclaim for *To Kill a Mockingbird*, he was afraid of "getting into the nature of adapting" lest he lose his identity (Wood and Barr 228). Still, in order to support his growing family, he agreed in 1966 to join producer-director Otto Preminger in bringing K. B. Gilden's best-selling novel, *Hurry Sundown*, to the screen. Its Texas setting and timely racial theme may have initially enticed Foote to the project, but he abandoned the screenplay when he and Preminger quarreled over the script's content. Though the director insisted Foote share screenwriting credit with Thomas Ryan, who completed the adaptation, Foote confesses embarrassment over the film which he has never seen (Wood and Barr 228). Foote also agreed in 1969 to work again with director Robert Mulligan and producer Alan J. Pakula on an adaptation of *The Stalking Moon*, a Western novel by Theodore V. Olsen. Not surprisingly, since Foote's Southern themes have little in common with the Western genre, Foote disagreed with the progress of the piece and withdrew from the assignment, leaving Alvin Sargent and Wendell Mayes to receive the credit for the screenplay.

Foote followed these unhappy experiences with another adaptation of Southern literature when in 1972 he reworked Margaret Mitchell's world-renowned *Gone with the Wind* for musical theatre. Despite the universal popularity of the novel and movie, Foote could not corral Mitchell's sprawling Southern saga into a believable stage drama, and though the production even appeared in London, England, Foote was not surprised when the theatrical "soap opera" fell into oblivion after a brief run (Barr 165–66). By then the pattern was painfully clear to the writer. "Everyone thought I was a Southern specialist," Foote complains, "Hollywood, being the copycat that it often is, any time there was a third-rate, or fourth-rate, or a fifth-rate Southern novel, they'd call me up" (Edgerton 5). Wanting to keep his own identity as a writer while avoiding such poor material, Foote was willing to shun adaptations of even Southern material.

Then in 1977 PBS asked him to translate Flannery O'Connor's short story "The Displaced Person" for the "American Short Story" Series. Here again was his familiar Southern milieu but in short-story form, not a long-winded novel. Besides, it was an O'Connor story, a single, clear, and brilliant note in the symphony of modern Southern literature, a heritage Foote inherited and claimed. Of the Southern characteristics identified by Louis Rubin, religion is the province of Flannery O'Connor. Although her Catholicism wasn't exactly his own, there was much Foote could agree with: "I'm almost like one of those crazy Protestants she writes about!" (Wood and Barr 229). For although he is quick to deny that he writes from a religious point of view, Foote openly admits he is a "deeply religious" man, confessing that religion is "deeply rooted in my makeup" (Wood and Barr 231). Acknowledging that spirituality sustains many Southerners, including some characters in his own plays, Foote adds, "I think there is a lot of strength in the Southern Protestant religion...[and I have an] abiding deep respect for it" (Wood, SBTS).

Foote follows the general outline of O'Connor's thesis in *The Displaced Person*. O'Connor "does believe that most Christians are kind of sentimental and do-gooders, and she's not interested in all that," Foote explains (Barr 171). And so in his screenplay, Foote champions her exposé of the hypocrisy-riddled Bible Belt. He also accepts and articulates her belief that "religion does break and distort us and transcend us. And remakes us" (Barr 171). In *The Displaced Person*, a widowed Mrs. McIntyre, facing ruination by white-trash tenants, turns for her salvation to the hard-working Mr. Guizac, a Pole expelled from his homeland by Nazis. When he offends her racist philosophy, she allows a preventable accident to eliminate his Christ-like exposure of her prejudices. Neglected by everyone at the end, the unredeemed, bedridden Mrs. McIntyre is as displaced as all the rest.

Partly because he shares much of O'Connor's outlook and heritage and also because her tightly-constructed story leaves little room for modification, Foote stayed close to O'Connor's text. But he does highlight the areas of his deepest sympathy: the Southern appreciation for family graveyards, the characters' attachment to place, and the primacy of family. Throughout this adaptation, he also adheres, as much as the visual nature of film will allow, to O'Connor's spiritual allegory. As in the literary text, Mr. Guizac is a Christ figure, and both displaced persons—the Pole and Christ himself—without being aware of their influence, still distort, transcend, and remake those around them. In both the story and the film, the spiritual inflicts itself on a self-satisfied, selfish world.

Foote has dedicated his energies since his work for PBS to bringing his original work to the stage and screen. Following the success of both his award-winning *Trip to Bountiful* and *Tender Mercies*, he has focused primarily on producing *The Orphans' Home Cycle*, nine plays based on his father's family. He has adapted John Steinbeck's *Of Mice and Men* for Gary Sinise, but he hasn't, unfortunately, adapted any other works by Southern writers like Faulkner, Lee, and O'Connor, who always require the kind of sensitivity Foote offers their work. In *Old Man*, *To Kill a Mockingbird*, *Tomorrow*, *Barn Burning*, and *Displaced Person*, Foote brought to the screen authentic Southern voices whose dialect, both literal and metaphorical, harmonizes with his own. This Southern accent, regional in tone and universal in implication, is one of Horton Foote's many contributions to the history of American filmmaking.

❧

Works Cited

Barbera, Jack. "Tomorrow and Tomorrow and *Tomorrow*." *Southern Quarterly* 19.3–4 (Spring/Summer 1981): 183–97.

Barn Burning. Writ. William Faulkner. Adapt. Horton Foote. American Short Story Series. PBS, 1980.

Barr, George Terry. "The Ordinary World of Horton Foote." Diss. U of Tennessee, 1987.

Briley, Rebecca L. *You Can Go Home Again: The Focus on Family in the Works of Horton Foote*. New York: Peter Lang, 1993. [Much of the material in this article first appeared in some form here. The material is used by permission of the publisher.]

Burkhart, Marian. "Horton Foote's Many Roads Home: An American Playwright and His Characters." *Commonweal* 115.4 (26 February 1988): 110–15.

Crowther, Bosley. "To Kill a Mockingbird." *New York Times*. 15 February 1963, late ed.: 10:2.

The Displaced Person. Writ. Flannery O'Connor. Adapt. Horton Foote. American Short Story Series. PBS, 1977.

Edgerton, Gary. "A Visit to the Imaginary Landscape of Harrison, Texas: Sketching the Film Career of Horton Foote." *Literature/ Film Quarterly* 17.1 (January 1989): 2–12.

Faulkner, William. "Address upon Receiving the Nobel Prize for Literature." *The Portable Faulkner*. Ed. Malcolm Cowley. New York: Viking, 1974. 723–24.

———. "Barn Burning." *The Norton Anthology of American Literature*. 2nd ed. Vol. 1. Ed. Nina Maym, et al. New York: Norton, 1979. 1492–1507.

———. "Tomorrow." *Knight's Gambit*. NY: New American Library, 1956. 59–73.

———. "Old Man." *The Portable Faulkner*. 481–581.

———. "Tomorrow." *Tomorrow and Tomorrow and Tomorrow*. Eds. David G. Yellin and Marie Connors. Jackson, MS: UP of Mississippi, 1985. 33–52.

Foote, Horton. "Old Man." *Three Plays*. New York: Harcourt, Brace, and World, 1962. 3–47.

———. "On First Dramatizing Faulkner." *Faulkner, Modernism, and Film: Faulkner and Yoknapatawpha, 1978*. Eds. Evans Harrington and Ann J. Abadie. Jackson, MS: UP of Mississippi, 1979. 49–65.

———. Interview. 14 November 1987.

———. *To Kill a Mockingbird* [the screenplay]. New York: Brentwood, 1964.

———. *Tomorrow* [play]. New York: Dramatists Play Service, 1963.

———. "Tomorrow." *Tomorrow and Tomorrow*. 53–106.

———. "Tomorrow: The Genesis of a Screenplay." *Faulkner, Modernism, and Film*. 149–62.

Hachem, Samir. "Foote-work." *Horizon* 29.3 (April 1986): 39–41.

"Horton Foote." *Current Biography Yearbook* 47 (1986): 143–47. [Referred to as *CBY*.]

Kawin, Bruce. *Faulkner and Film*. New York: Frederick Ungar, 1977.

Lee, Harper. *To Kill a Mockingbird*. New York: J. B. Lippincott, 1960.

———. "A Word." Foreword. *To Kill a Mockingbird*. Screenplay by Horton Foote. New York: Brentwood, 1964.

Locher, Frances Carol, Ed. *Contemporary Authors*. Vols. 73–76, 1978.

Millichap, Joseph R. "Horton Foote." *Dictionary of Literary Biography* 26 (1984): 101–4.

Neff, David. "Going Home to a Hidden God." *Christianity Today* 30.6 (4 April 1986): 30–31.

O'Connor, Flannery. "The Displaced Person." *The Complete Stories*. New York: Farrar, Straus, and Giroux, 1982.

Rubin, Louis D. *Southern Renascence: The Literature of the Modern South*. Baltimore: Johns Hopkins, 1953.

Skaggs, Merrill Maquire. "The Story and Film of *Barn Burning*." *Southern Quarterly* 21.2 (Winter 1983): 5–15.

Wood, Gerald C. "Keynote Address." Southern Baptist Theological Seminary First Annual Conference on Religion and the Arts. Louisville, KY: 14 Sept. 1989. [Referred to as SBTS.]

——— and Terry Barr. "'A Certain Kind of Writer': An Interview with Horton Foote." *Literature/Film Quarterly* 14.4 (1986): 226–37.

Yellin, David, and Marie Connors. "Conversations with the Film's Creators." *Tomorrow and Tomorrow*. Eds. David Yellin and Marie Connors. Jackson, MS: UP of Mississippi, 1985. 163–84.

———. "Faulkner and Foote and Chemistry." *Tomorrow and Tomorrow*. Eds. David Yellin and Marie Connors. Jackson, MS: UP of Mississippi, 1985. 3–31.

More Real Than Realism
Horton Foote's Impressionism
Tim Wright

Many critics regard Horton Foote's plays and screenplays as expressions of dramatic "realism." And for good reason. His stories seem to reflect the reality experienced by most people. There are no artificial scenarios that strain plausibility—no "they-lived-happily-ever-after" twists to placate an audience or to fulfill preconceived expectations (Barr 40). His work seems very "real" to us. And yet there is another aspect of Foote's writing—something deeper, more intriguing—that extends beyond flat realism. Foote's work, despite its familiar surface, continually rejects realism's "corrected chronicle" of reality (Kirschke 140), offering instead Foote's distinctive brand of American impressionism. It is a dramatic wold in which the material world is at every moment interpreted, shaped, and hopefully redeemed by the consciousness of the writer, characters, and audience.

Impressionism, especially in drama, can often be mistaken for realism. As a matter of fact, it has been suggested that impressionism is actually more "true to life" than the "realistic" art that preceded it (Kirschke 206). In *Theatrical Style: A Visual Approach to the Theater*, for example, Douglas Russell points out that impressionism "will at times be accepted as reality" (20), and Albert Aurier considered impressionism "merely a kind of realism, a refined, spiritualized realism" (qtd. in Courthion 17). Such misinterpretation probably reflects the historical growth of impressionism out of realism: "The impressionist painters had begun as realists and then felt that they were deepening their realism through underlining nature's or people's moods" (Russell, *Stage* 392). However, as it developed its own style impressionism added to realism "a level of abstraction, with a strong element of subtle, intuitive emotionalism and a weak or vague compositional form"[1] (*Theatrical Style* 20). Impressionism stops short, however, of the radical subjectivity of symbolism and expressionism, remaining "nature-bound and reality-affirming" in its basic presentation (Shiff 44; Hauser 229).

Impressionism is distinguished from both realism and expressionism by insistence that objectivity be integrated with, but not replaced by, subjectivity. Believing that viewing an object dramatically shapes one's perception of that object, the impressionists allowed their focus to be determined by the conditions surrounding an object—rather than the actual physical traits of the object itself. Although impressionism is most commonly associated with the hazy application and mixture of colors of impressionist painters, it actually is a way of experiencing the world which varies according to the media and forms. In painting, for example, the central focus is almost exclusively the visual experience while in literature, film,[2] and drama traditional elements such as dialogue, plot, and character are implicated. But, while the styles are various, the impressionists—in whatever form—try to synthesize objective and subjective experience.

Impressionism is essentially an attempt to offer an artistic "objectification" of subjective phenomenon, as William Harms, in his dissertation *Impressionism as a Literary Style*, explains:

> Impressions are the fragmented parts of some presumed whole, not quite definitive, loosely arranged, sensually perceived and emotionally acknowledged—the very antithesis of scientific fact-mongering and mimetic rationality. The art of Impressionism, whether in painting or in literature, attests not only to an overwhelming belief that human existence is essentially made up of these myriads of impressions (instead of the linear accumulation of empirical facts and events), but it also attempts to establish a correspondingly appropriate medium which will itself become an objectification of the way it seems to feel inside oneself when one receives and forms these impressions. (133)

While many techniques of the impressionists vary with the media, the need for "objectification" creates identifiable traits across the disciplines, including literature and drama. These include: (1) a preference for atmosphere over subject or plot; (2) the deliberate use of ambiguity; (3) the appearance of being unfinished or fragmentary; (4) focus on the mundane and non-dramatic (in the traditional sense); (5) muted and subtle expression; (6) emphasis on the transient and impermanent; and (7) the presence of spiritual elements. Of course, these attributes do not operate in isolation; they are purposely integrated into a seemingly spontaneous gestalt.

Emphasis on Mood and Atmosphere

In most conventional works, the subject or plot is primary. Impressionism, however, shifts its focus to the ambiance generated by the creation of a specific work. As Georges Rivière points out, impressionist painting is distinguished by its "treatment of a subject for the sake of the tones, and not for the sake of the subject itself" (qtd. in Hauser 171). Similarly in dramatic impressionism the subjective experience of the "process" becomes the focal point, leaving the plot a means to an end rather than an end in itself. With this shift away from what happens, or might or should happen, impressionist drama is free to explore the subjective, subtextual concerns of the characters. Their conflicts, both physical and emotional ones, become more intriguing and meaningful than the action in the story.

This artistic emphasis is found repeatedly throughout Horton Foote's writing. As Samuel Freedman notes, the "major events [in Foote's stories]...do not propel the plot as much as they create a mood" (50). Like poetry, the concrete but resonant details in Foote's dramas dominate the story line; as one reviewer has noted, "I don't think it's the overall plot that grabs me, but the details—character's faces, their conversations, the discussion of a little lamb on the child's tombstone. Those are the things that haunt me" (Davis 300). In *The Trip to Bountiful*, for example, although the plot concerns whether Carrie Watts will return to her childhood home, Bountiful, Texas, the heart of the drama are her reflections during the journey. The completion of her physical journey is only peripheral; Mrs. Watts' quiet but determined recapturing of her dignity seizes the audience's attention. Little "happens" in the traditional sense of theatrical construction; the atmosphere of longing and the subtle revelation of character drive the work. "For Horton Foote, it's not only how the journey ends that matters, but what we perceive along the way" (Smith 27).

Mood and atmosphere similarly dominate *Convicts*, the second play in *The Orphans' Home Cycle*. Young Horace Robedaux is a clerk on a remote cane plantation worked by convicts. His employer and the overseer of the prisoner-workers, Soll Gautier, is an elderly alcoholic tyrant who ruthlessly governs his charge and evades paying him.

Soll's frequent drunken rantings create an intense mood of potential danger and general chaos. Although violence surrounds the action of *Convicts*, the play focuses on the slow and sometimes comic sliding of Soll towards death. The real subject is Horace's vulnerability after the death of his father and his gradual development of a sense of distance, autonomy, and judgment about the injustice and disorder around him. Horton Foote's impressionism describes Horace's mood and predicament, showing little interest in what happens to him or what he can do in the physical world.

Deliberate Ambiguity

Impressionism also practices a "surrender to the uncertain, to the undefined" (Courthion 23, 26). Believing subjectivity makes universal interpretation impossible, impressionists create a style which embraces complexity and uncertainty:

> [The impressionists'] stylistic qualities emerged from the realization that since they lived in a prismatically impressionistic world, they must recreate that world of individualized sensory perception, epistemological indeterminacy, relativism, ambiguity, fragmentation, and surfaces. (Stowell 15–16)

Impressionism focuses on particulars in an atmosphere of relativism which discourages any definitive interpretation. Impressionistic art does not construct a solid representation of reality; it is filled with ambiguity and creative possibility. As Hurbert Muller summarizes, literary impressionists

> have…substituted the creation of atmosphere for inventory or set picture, subtle evocation for analysis or comment. They have discarded formal chronological narratives, with a definite beginning, middle and end, in favor of retrospective, discontinuous, or unfinished actions, streams of association canalized by emotion and the logic of the unconscious, of some kind of proliferous growth more nearly corresponding to the way in which we experience life—life, as Conrad insisted, does not *narrate*. They have broken up the relatively simple, trim patterns of characterization, presenting figures who have no shape to speak of and who defy simple summary or category. In general they have destroyed the solidity and rigidity of

> life as traditionally represented, blurred the contours and,
> like the painters, have sacrificed symmetry and neatness
> to intensity and expressiveness. Hence the mysterious-
> ness in much impressionistic fiction, the shadows deep-
> ened by the very brilliance of its illuminations. (qtd. in
> Stowell 20)

By inserting such "shadows" into a work of art, impressionism encourages the integration of subjective participation in the creation of
meaning. It invites the onlooker to engage the work and to enter
more deeply into the imaginary world created by the impressionistic
artist; "The comparative absence of articulation forces the viewer to
'put the painting together' himself" (Kirschke 9).

This is one way in which Horton Foote's work is Chekhovian.[3]
As Peter Stowell notes, Chekhov crafted his plays toward a stimulat-
ing ambivalence:

> Chekhov has structured his plays so that every reaction is
> set against an obliquely conflicting reaction; we are meant
> to feel ambivalent toward every character, every line of
> dialogue, every human response, every scene and act, and
> finally, of course, toward everything in the play—even
> the play itself. (159)

Similarly, Foote engages his audience with a troubling but provocative sense of mystery. For example, who is this young man from
Atlanta who never appears in Foote's Pulitzer Prize-winning play? What
causes the transformation experienced by Carrie Watts at the end of
The Trip to Bountiful? In *Tender Mercies*, why does Mac tell his daughter
he can't remember "On the Wings of a Snow White Dove" but then
softly sing it to himself as she drives away? Apparently there is more
to this man, and to all men and women, than can be described by the
play.

The Unfinished and Fragmentary

Susanna de Vries-Evans notes that when the early impressionist
painters first exhibited their work, "most collectors jeered at what
they regarded as unfinished sketches" (9). Those collectors were responding to the sense of things happening beyond the boundaries of
the work itself. It is impressionism's rejection of the artificial closure
which dominates most realism, leaving "the way open for further
possibilities" (Courthion 25). Seeking an art rigorously close to the

reality of everyday experience, as Arnold Hauser notes, the "impressionistic vision transforms nature into a process of growth and decay. Everything stable and coherent is dissolved into metamorphosis and assumes the character of the unfinished and fragmentary" (169). Borrowing from the artistic methods of the Japanese, this technique creates the illusion of a moment in time, that which Norma Broude finds in Manet's "Boating" (1874):

> the natural movement of contemporary life is...here—
> the "slice-of-life" captured, monumentalized, and contrived to appear uncontrived, as the boat and its passengers, viewed up close and radically cropped by the frame in the manner of the Japanese print, threaten to drift away beyond our field of vision. (28)

In search of a realism that would include the fragmentary nature of much human experience, impressionism, in the words of Heinrich Wölfflin, employs incomplete "clarity of form and...depreciated component parts" (227).

Like other impressionists, Horton Foote is most comfortable with incompleteness. In an almost pointillistic fashion, Foote often constructs his plays and screenplays with truncated scenes and abbreviated dialogue; studying an implied world "beyond the picture-frame," Foote tells inconclusive stories which defy traditional closure. In *Tender Mercies*, for example, the courtship between Mac and Rosa Lee is executed in brief scenes of minimal dialogue:

> MAC and ROSA LEE in the garden; he is digging with a hoe and she is weeding.
>
> MAC: I haven't had a drink in two months. I think my drinking is behind me.
>
> ROSA LEE: Do you? I'm glad. I don't think it gets you anywhere.
>
> MAC: You ever thought about marrying again?
>
> ROSA LEE: Yes, I have. Have you?
>
> MAC: I thought about it, lately. I guess it's no secret how I feel about you. A blind man could see that. (Leaning on hoe.) Would you think about marrying me?
>
> ROSA LEE: Yes, I will.
>
> (MAC resumes his gardening, and so does ROSA LEE.)
> (*Three Screenplays*, 96–97)

Later Mac's grief over his daughter's sudden death is expressed in a single speech by Mac to Rosa Lee, again in their garden. There are no tears, no heightened displays of anguish:

> I was almost killed once in a car accident. I was drunk and I ran off the side of the road and I turned over four times. They took me out of that car for dead, but I lived. And I prayed last night to know why I lived and she died, but I got no answer to my prayers. I still don't know why she died and I lived. I don't know the answer to nothing. Not a blessed thing. I don't know why I wandered out to this part of Texas drunk and you took me in and pitied me and helped me to straighten out and married me. Why, why did this happen? Is there a reason that happened? And Sonny's daddy died in the war. (Pause) My daughter killed in an automobile accident. Why? You see, I don't trust happiness. I never did, I never will. (*Three Screenplays* 144–45)

The film ends shortly afterwards with an inconclusive scene showing Mac and Sonny passing a football as Rosa Lee watches from a distance with no comment. As Terry Barr notes:

> [Foote's] world is presented as is, for to understand how and why people make the crucial decisions that potentially decide the rest of their lives, the artist must allow his audience to see life in open-ended fashion, since rarely are our lives tied up in neat little packages. (*The Ordinary World* 4)

The open world of impressionism is integral to Foote's dramatic construction.

The Ordinary and the Mundane

Impressionistic art is typically centered on the ordinary; "The subject matter of Impressionism is often casual, everyday life, captured with an immediacy enhanced by transient effects of light and atmosphere" (Gerdts 29). It celebrates the quiet circumstances and events that comprise the majority of our everyday experience.

> Often [Impressionists] simply painted people doing "nothing," enjoying themselves at concerts and dances in the park or picnicking or rowing on a holiday. In contrast to

the most renowned painters who worked before them,
the Impressionists treated mundane, everyday, non-dramatic, non-message subjects. (Kirschke 13)

Like the early impressionist artist Degas, who refused to "idealize or
condemn" through his artistry, the tradition seeks to maintain a non-
critical stance toward its subjects (de Vries-Evans 34). "The impressionist attempts to capture the feel, texture, and consciousness of the
phenomenological *tabula rasa* or, as Muller notes in the impressionist
lexicon, 'the innocence of the eye'" (Stowell 24). Resisting the temp-
tation to be didactic or moralistic, the impressionistic artist strives to
record the world as he or she perceives it, hiding no evil and exalting
no virtue:

> In his essay on "Impressionistic Writing" [Walter] Symons
> more directly champions the cause of Impressionism when
> he states that of all of the qualities necessary to be an
> Impressionist writer, "the first thing is to see, and with an
> eye which sees all, and as if one's only business were to
> see; and then to write from a selecting memory." (Kirschke
> 116)

This radical acceptance of his characters and their world is fundamental to Foote's approach to writing. As the writer himself asserts,
"I honestly do want to cast a cold eye, if you will.... An unsentimental eye. But no sense of superiority and no sense of condemnation"
(qtd. in Davis 313). His work is filled with guileless observations of
the quiet struggles of ordinary men and women. Foote does not mor-
alize or pontificate; he merely looks on with an intensely focused
interest. As Gerald Wood points out, Foote "writes to discover, not to
preach. Rather than lecture his readers, he investigates with them the
'great mystery' about the sources of courage and personhood"
(*Selected One-Acts* xix).

The fruit of this perspective is a subtle, understated drama about
seemingly very ordinary people who live relatively quiet lives. By stay-
ing close to real, lived experience Foote endows his characters with a
pervasive sense of authenticity; he "is a master craftsman at shaping
parables from gentle folk tales. His characters talk like real people and
act like real people. Nothing really happens to them; their lives just
unfold" (Brown A1). As Terry Barr summarizes, Foote's characters are
not "glamorous, sophisticated, and highly educated people"; they are

"ordinary, middle-class men and women who struggle from day to day paying their bills, dealing with familial problems, and simply coping with the [*sic*] life's difficulties" (*Ordinary World* 3). In Al Reinert's words,

> They are no more clever or muscular or beautiful or villainous than the rest of us. Like us, they are only trying to cope with the indignities of the human experience, weary sinners yearning for a call to come home. (110)

Rebecca Briley asserts that Foote's commitment to presenting his characters in this manner is perhaps one of his most remarkable traits as a playwright.

> What does distinguish Foote from his contemporaries...is the demonstrated determination to concentrate on the development of character over the other elements of play writing and his compassionate approach to characterization. Almost without exception, Foote depicts his characters as human beings, complete with flaws and virtues alike, providing insight into their misdirected lives to elicit the sympathy of his audience. (Briley 2)

But Horton Foote "is no Norman Rockwell" (Freedman 61); he uses neither saccharine-sweet characters nor nostalgia. His stories "seem gentle and full of decency; yet they have a dark side that drives them and that vibrates through all the action" (Anderson 26). Alcoholism, madness, stillbirth, parental abuse, and an assortment of other iniquities inhabit Foote's pages, stages and screens. He doesn't condemn those characters who manifest these weaknesses, however. As reviewer John Simon notes, "Everyone in [Foote's plays]—however ornery, meddlesome, mean-spirited, crazy, or just plain dull—somehow ends up likable" (115). This is a result of Foote's immense understanding and compassion for his characters. "I really do believe," states Foote, "that if you knew everything about the most evil person in the world, you would bring some understanding to him. But there are all kinds of antagonists; it needn't be just a character" (qtd. in "Dialogue on Film" 16). Even Jessie Mae, the churlish daughter-in-law in *The Trip to Bountiful,* has her strengths and virtues according to the author:

> I think that you have to be very careful that you don't caricature her. That's not my intention. Jessie Mae exists.

> I see her all the time. It's easy to feel superior to Jessie
> Mae, but they do endure, don't they? And in some ways
> they're very practical and pragmatic. (qtd. in Davis 308)

Foote's work is non-judgmental; rather than criticize or indoctrinate, he asks his audience to "see" theater and, ideally, their own lives, in new, more compassionate ways.

Subtle Expression

While impressionism stays close to clear and hard realities, it re-designs the distinct lines and shapes of naturalism into a more "painterly" technique of blended forms. This style, as described by Heinrich Wölfflin in *Principles of Art History: The Problem of the Development of Style in Later Art*, transforms the more "linear" techniques of earlier artistic methods into impressionism's diaphanous atmosphere in which objects often appear to "dissolve into the air" (Rapetti 9). Impression-ism is, by definition, translucent:

> Impressionism meant also the suppression of line and of
> chiaroscuro, the objects no longer being separated from
> their setting, but enveloped by atmosphere and height-
> ened by reflections. No longer was the drawing fixed or
> the outline sharp. Instead all was undefined, following
> the variation of time, light, and taste. (Courthion 22)

Such diffusion, as in the case of ambiguity, makes subjectivity—for the artist and audience—both possible and necessary.

The muteness of his literary impressionism liberates Horton Foote from the excesses of melodrama. According to the writer, producers tend to "over-theatricalize" (Foote, Interview 9 Nov. 1995) his work, often leaving them—like many films—"visually conceived," "thinned out," without "substance" (Davis 314–15). What Foote prefers, and wise producers embrace, is a distinctive imaginary landscape in which everything "is suggested, little is demonstrated" (Kanfer 23). It is, as Rebecca Briley notes, an essentially understated drama:

> Foote's "taste" is one of understatement. A student of the
> "less is more" principle, Foote claims there is too much
> "real drama" for fiction, meaning that incidents from life
> do not need embellishment to create interesting theatre.
> (12)

Despite the muted expression, there is a rich sense of drama in Foote's work. But the conflicts are emotional, not physical; "[a] great deal happens, though much of it happens deep inside the characters" (Sarris 39). Foote refuses to cater to modern theatrical appetites by inserting a false sense of "dramatic action" that violates his artistic conscience:

> Our loud and violent times are not particularly hospi-
> table to retiring creatures like these [Foote's characters].
> We like crackups on the stage, car crashes on the screen
> and brash characters who will at least go down swinging.
> Mr. Foote's gentleness will be viewed by some as torpor.
> Admittedly, his roads to home are little byways—not even
> paved, I suspect, and doubtless no wider than a Model T.
> But they lead someplace humane and caring, where heart-
> break doesn't have to be desperate and noisy to merit our
> concern. (Richards 5)

Since loss and change are constant and universal in Foote's imaginary world, he studies "reaction," not just "the events themselves," as Gary Edgerton explains:

> Each case exhibits his [Foote's] preference for portraying
> the reaction of lead characters to tragic happenings, rather
> than graphically showing the events themselves. This tech-
> nique is important because it foregoes plot cliches for
> deeper resonances. Primary attention is forcefully shifted
> away from the more immediate, melodramatic potential
> of presenting a mother dying in childbirth; a newborn
> stricken with influenza; or a teenaged daughter being killed
> in a drink-driving [*sic*] accident; to scenes of reflection
> and understatement which suggest meanings well beyond
> the simple actions and words on-screen. (11)

As a literary impressionist, Horton Foote explores the subtle and com-plex reactions in which his characters reveal their true selves.

Mutability

The early impressionist artists were obsessed with capturing the fleeting impressions created by the shifting light and atmospheric conditions. In Diane Kelder's words, they were "uniquely conscious of and responsive to the ever-shifting physical reality of the moment"

(13). Typically these artists returned to the same subject again and again in an attempt to discover and record the various effects generated by the changing conditions. Eventually impressionistic art became less interested in permanence and stability than in change and uncertainty:

> The dominion of the moment over permanence and continuity, the feeling that every phenomenon is a fleeting and never-to-be-repeated constellation, a wave gliding away on the river of time, the river into which "one cannot step twice," is the simplest formula to which impressionism can be reduced. The whole method of impressionism, with all its artistic expedients and tricks, is bent, above all, on giving expression to this Heraclitean outlook and on stressing that reality is not a being but a becoming, not a condition but a process. (Hauser 169)

The result was a characteristic "apprehension of the world as a shifting semblance" (Wölfflin 27).

Once again Horton Foote is within the impressionist tradition, for change is "at the center of [Foote's] literary world" (Barr 277). This is partly because his subject is his native American South, "a community in transition" (Lawrence n.p.). His first full-length play, *Texas Town*, revolved around what critic Brooks Atkinson called "a real and languid impression of a town changing in its relation to the world" (Atkinson, Rev. of *Texas Town* n.p.). By keeping Wharton/ Richmond/Harrison as his primary subject, Foote has also maintained that change is "the one dramatic certainty in Horton Foote's fictional world" (Edgerton 6). More recently the nine plays of *The Orphans' Home Cycle* are structured by what Foote himself named "change, unexpected, unasked for, unwanted, but to be faced and dealt with" (Introduction, *Four Plays* xii).

But this theme transcends a particular place; "Foote is preoccupied with change, with the erosion of tradition and identity" (Freedman 61) as a universal antagonist and opportunity. "I feel that finally there is something tragic about human life," states Foote, "as exciting as it is. It's finite. There's always that sense of loss, sense of change" (qtd. in Pacheco 5). And he asks his characters to grapple with this aspect of reality; for example, "When Elizabeth Robedaux says in *On Valentine's Day*, 'I want everything to stay the way it is,' she is uttering the one prayer Foote refuses to answer" (Freedman 61).

Because change is unavoidable, flexibility becomes crucial: "In Horton Foote's world, compromise and change—being able to accept life on its own terms and to move forward—are the essential terms" (Barr 1). Those who are willing to accept the presence of loss and change survive; those who refuse are, more often than not, broken by them.

The Spiritual

Impressionistic art frequently implies and refers to a reality outside the material world; it is, in Pierre Courthion's words, a "spiritualized realism" (17) which studies the "incorporeal" (Wölfflin 27). Impressionism often generates moments of heightened awareness connected with a mysterious reality outside ourselves. Minor epiphanies, catching the outer edge of our attention, redirect our thinking, leaving us with new ways of seeing and relating to the world. Whatever we call them,

> these privileged moments, epiphanies, visionary instants, timeless moments, impressions, *instantanés*, or *moments bienheureux* do form a crucial basis for the impressionistic vision. These moments are not always transcendent, as they must be for the romantics. They are, however, the product of a change in perceptual perspective and occur at moments of heightened perceptual awareness. They may not "mean" anything beyond what they are, but they do result in a new grouping of fragmented experience. This often leads to a new way of seeing, a change in direction for the character, or an expanded consciousness. (Stowell 36–37)

Although these flashes of "expanded consciousness" do not necessarily have religious implications, the emotional content, the sense of something beyond the isolated self, is similar. As Paul Schrader notes, transcendence "in art is often equated with transcendence in religion because they both draw from a common ground of transcendental experience" (7). The obscure nature of this phenomenon makes it essentially mysterious:

> ...the criticism of transcendental art is a self-destructive process. It continually deals in contradictions—verbalizations of the ineffable. The concept of transcendental expression in religion or in art necessarily implies a contradiction.... Like the artist, the critic knows that his task

> is futile, and that his most eloquent statements can only
> lead to silence. (Schrader 8)

Inspired by Oriental, especially Japanese art (Roudebush 56), impressionism explores the "numinous," often expressed in "silence" and "emptiness" (Otto 69).

Despite its understated surfaces, Horton Foote's work is filled with fleeting moments of transcendence, suggesting spiritual realities. Without dogma or proselytizing, this "reference to the spiritual" becomes "one of the unique contributions Foote's plays have made in American theatre" (Briley 247). Christianity is, of course, inherent in the social climate of his fictional Harrison, Texas (based on his real-life hometown of Wharton, Texas); it is part of the everyday life in the history Foote describes. However, in some works—*The Trip to Bountiful* and *Tender Mercies*, for example—Christian faith is integral to the characters' lives. While Foote's stories are not evangelistic and they don't communicate a single moral message, religion is indigenous and powerful. As David Neff notes, "Foote's God remains hidden. But he is there" (31).

This sense of the divine is revealed most tangibly in the "pure sounds" and even "silence" of music, which is never "manipulative" (Davis 298). An "organic" and thus unobtrusive presence in the plays, the music, as Samuel Freedman notes, is both natural and "suggestive":

> Music plays an organic and highly suggestive role in Foote's
> work, from the hymns in "The Trip to Bountiful" to the
> norteño waltzes in "The Road to the Graveyard." These
> songs, rather than comprising a calculated sound-track,
> are the pastels on Foote's palette. (62)

By integrating Christian hymns, which "permeated the air when [he] was growing up" (Davis 299), Foote creates the feel of religious experience without insisting on its validity: "I don't see how you can listen to those old hymns and not feel something...even non-believers, you know, love those hymns. I suppose they must get something from them" (qtd. in Neff 30). The hymns are especially resonant when linked to the dominant theme of the story, as with "Softly and Tenderly," which opens and closes the film *The Trip to Bountiful*[4]:

> Time is now fleeting, the moments are passing
> Passing from you and from me.

> Shadows are gathering, death's night is coming.
> Coming for you and for me.
> Come home, come home. Ye who are weary come
>   home.
> Earnestly, tenderly, Jesus is calling,
> Calling, oh, Sinner, come home.

While these opening lines describe Carrie's heartfelt longing to return home to Bountiful, they also suggest, in Rebecca Briley's words, Horton Foote's desire to connect "the physical homecoming with the spiritual" (191).

But Horton Foote's use of music is not isolated from the rest of his vision; it is one version of what Paul Schrader names a "transcendental style" (8–9). Basing his study on the films of Japan's Yasujiro Ozu, France's Robert Bresson, and Denmark's Carl Theodor Dreyer, Schrader divides this style into three major categories or stages of presentation: (1) "the everyday," which is "a meticulous representation of the commonplace"; (2) "disparity," or "an actual or potential disunity between man and his environment"; and (3) "stasis," "a frozen view of life which does not resolve the disparity but transcends it" (Schrader 39–49). Analogous to Thomas Weiskel's "sublime moments" (23–24), these dramatic events, according to David Desser, "strive for a genuine presentation of the spiritual," as in Foote's *Tender Mercies*:

> for the viewer trained in Hollywood's abundant means who needs guidance during every "significant" moment, it might perhaps be difficult to "see" Mac's love, just as it would have been difficult to see Mac's recovery from alcoholism or his religious conversion leading to his acceptance of baptism. What even a blind man could see, but which American viewers have trouble perceiving, is that Mac's presence, his words and his actions are his signs of love. His love is what he does, what he is, what Rosa Lee helped him to become. A declaration of love amounts to a declaration of faith. And faith cannot be shown, is not subject to rational discourse; it is accepted and possessed. In transcendental style, the things we do not see are equal to those we do. (26)

Thus silence, by Foote's own admission, is "very important" in his drama (Interview 9 Nov. 1995); it is part of the "shorthand" (Porter, Interview 12 Oct. 1994) of dialogue and scene that forms Horton

Foote's version of Schrader's "transcendental style."

The poetic understatement, the intense longing of the characters, and the "sparse means" (Schrader 154) of expression in Horton
Foote's work suggest a spiritual reality beyond everyday experience.

Implications for Performance

Identifying the traits of impressionism in Foote's work provides a
performance matrix as well as a critical framework for his artistry. For
the director, actor or designer, understanding his literary impressionism helps fashion the distinctive mood, rhythm, and intensity of Foote's
style. In his book *Period Style for the Theatre*, Douglas A. Russell points
out that Chekhov's plays demand a uniquely "impressionistic" design. In presenting *The Cherry Orchard*, for example, only

> by understanding how an impressionistic painter would
> have perceived light filtered through cherry blossoms, the
> sunset hours of the day, and a chandelier-illuminated party
> can the director and the actor have an appropriate feeling
> for the settings, costumes, and atmosphere in this play.
> (361–62)

Similarly, directors who have successfully produced Foote's work have
instinctively incorporated these principles of impressionism into their
design. In *Tender Mercies*, for example, the sets help generate the quint-
essential mood and character of Foote's writing. The chipped and
faded paint on the Mariposa Motel suggests the passing of time and
an absence of concern about appearances; the newly-plowed fields
surrounding the motel suggest the emptiness—and yet fertile possibility—in Mac's life; and the earth tones inside Rosa Lee's home reflect
her warm and nurturing character.

The impressionistic quality of Foote's work is especially dependent on the skill of his actors. The unique rhythms and suggestive
nuances of his dialogue, for example, are often contingent on the
subtle pauses, inflections, and various intonations that the actors bring
to their performances. Successful actors in Foote's work must incor-
porate a keen awareness of the near-excessive need for subtlety in
their expressions and understanding of the subtext. In performing
Foote's plays, actors must understand that their dialogue is often more
dependent on what their characters *don't* say than on the actual words
being spoken. The occasional pauses that Foote drafts into the text of

his scripts are of vital importance in communicating the intention and intensity of his work.

ᕤᕥ

Notes

1. Although the structural configuration of impressionism differs from traditional designs, I disagree with Russell in his labeling of impressionistic composition as "weak" or "vague." The arrangement of specific elements must frequently be quite intricate and precise in order to create the overall effect of the work.

2. It should be mentioned that the concept of impressionism, as it will be used in this essay, is unrelated to the avant-garde "cinematic impressionism" practiced among a small group of French filmmakers in the 1930s. This "impressionist" school of filmmaking was led by Louis Delluc (1890–1924) "who founded the journal *Cinéma* and became, long before Eisenstein, the first aesthetic theorist of the film" (Cook 322). The unconventional filmic style developed by Delluc and his followers attempted to emulate the abstract visual experience of French impressionistic painting. Although Delluc's "cinematic impressionism" was based primarily on film's visual properties, most theatrical films are constructed with traditional dramatic elements in mind, taking into considerations the conventional elements of plot, dialogue, character development, and so on.

3. Foote has repeatedly been compared to Chekhov. Some have even hailed Foote as the "American Chekhov" (Berson F1).

4. The song used in the film version of *The Trip to Bountiful*, "Softly and Tenderly," was changed from "There's Not a Friend Like the Lowly Jesus," which was used in the stage version (Briley 180).

Works Cited

Anderson, George. "Ambitious 'Dragons' Opens PPT Season." *Pittsburgh Post-Gazette* (PA) 29 Sept. 1988: 26. The Horton Foote Papers. Southern Methodist University.

Atkinson, Brooks. Rev. of *Texas Town* in *New York Times*. Horton Foote Papers. Southern Methodist University.

Barr, George Terry. *The Ordinary World of Horton Foote*. Diss. U of Tennessee, Knoxville, 1986.

Berson, Misha. "The Foote Factor: Oscar-Winning Dramatist Visits for Special Weekend at Belltown Theatre Center." *Seattle Times* 23 Aug. 1993, final ed.: F1.

Briley, Rebecca Luttrell. *You Can Go Home Again: The Focus on Family in the Works of Horton Foote*. Diss. U of Kentucky, 1990.

Broude, Norma, ed. *World Impressionism: The International Movement, 1860–1920*. New York: Abrams, 1990.

Brown, Tony. "Horton Foote Catches Us 'Dividing the Estate.'" Rev. of *Dividing the Estate* by Horton Foote. *The Charlotte Observer* 31 Dec. 1991: A-1. Horton Foote Papers. Southern Methodist University.

Cook, David. *A History of Narrative Film*. New York: Norton, 1981.

Courthion, Pierre. *Impressionism*. Trans. by John Shepley. New York: Abrams, 1972.

Davis, Ronald L. "Roots in Parched Ground: An Interview with Horton Foote." *Southwest Review* (Summer 1988): 298–318.

de Vries-Evans, Susanna. *Impressionist Masters: Paintings from Private Collections*. New York: Crescent, 1995.

Desser, David. "Transcendental Style in *Tender Mercies*." *Religious Communication Today* Sept. 1985: 21–27.

"Dialogue on Film: Horton Foote." *American Film* 12 Oct. 1986: 13–14, 16.

Edgerton, Gary. "A Visit to the Imaginary Landscape of Harrison, Texas: Sketching the Film Career of Horton Foote." *Literature/Film Quarterly* 17.1 (1989): 2–12.

Foote, Horton. *Roots in a Parched Ground, Convicts, Lily Dale, The Widow Claire: The First Four Plays in the Orphans' Home Cycle*. New York: Grove, 1988.

——. Interview. 9 Nov. 1995.

——. *To Kill a Mockingbird, Tender Mercies, and The Trip to Bountiful: Three Screenplays by Horton Foote*. New York: Grove, 1989.

Freedman, Samuel G. "From the Heart of Texas." *New York Times Magazine* 9 Feb. 1986, sec. 6: 30–31, 50, 61–63, 73.

Gerdts, William H. *American Impressionism*. New York: Abbeville, 1984.

Harms, William A. *Impressionism as a Literary Style*. Diss. Indiana University, 1971.

Hauser, Arnold. *The Social History of Art. Vol. 4: Naturalism, Impressionism, The Film Age*. New York: Vintage, 1951.

Kanfer, Stephan. Rev. of *The Roads to Home* by Horton Foote. *The New Leader* 5 Oct. 1992: 22–23.

Kelder, Diane. *The Great Book of French Impressionism*. New York: Artabras, 1980.

Kirschke, James J. *Henry James and Impressionism*. New York: Whitston, 1981.

Lawrence, Larry. "Plays Follow Replacement of Old Ways." *Abilene Reporter-News* (TX) 13 Aug. 1989. Horton Foote Papers. Southern Methodist University.

Muller, Hurbert J. "Impressionism in Fiction: Prism vs. Mirror." *American Scholar* 7 (1938). [Rpt. in *Literary Impressionism, James and Chekhov*. By Peter H. Stowell. Athens, GA: U of Georgia P, 1980]

Neff, David. "Going Home to the Hidden God." *Christianity Today* 4 Apr. 1986: 30–31.

Otto, Rudolf. *The Idea of the Holy: An Inquiry into the Non-Rational Factor in the Idea of the Divine and Its Relation to the Rational*. Trans. by John W. Harvey. London: Oxford UP, 1950.

Pacheco, Patrick. "Remember Me: In Their Searches For a Lost Time, Playwrights Neil Simon and Horton Foote Reveal Two Distinct Visions of America." *Daily News-City Lights* n.d.: 5. Horton Foote Papers. Southern Methodist University.

Porter, Laurin. Interview. 12 Oct. 1994.

Rapetti, Rodolphe. *Monet.* New York: Arch Cape, 1990.

Reinert, Al. "Tender Foote: Horton Foote Continues to Find Big Themes in Small-Town Life." *Texas Monthly* July 1991: 110, 132–37. Horton Foote Papers. Southern Methodist University.

Richards, David. "The Secret Aches of Broken Families: 'The Roads to Home' Travels into the Heart of Loneliness." Rev. of *The Roads to Home* by Horton Foote. *New York Times* 4 Oct. 1992, sec. 2: 5.

Roudebush, Jay. *Mary Cassatt.* New York: Crown, 1979.

Russell, Douglas A. *Period Style for the Theatre.* Boston: Allyn and Bacon, 1980.

——. *Stage Costume Design.* NY: Appleton-Century-Crofts, 1973.

——. *Theatrical Style: A Visual Approach to the Theatre.* Palo Alto, CA: Mayfield, 1976.

Sarris, Andrew. "Do Audiences Want Mercy?" [Rev. of *Tender Mercies*] *The Village Voice* 8 Mar. 1983: 39.

Schrader, Paul. *Transcendental Style in Film: Ozu, Bresson, Dreyer.* Berkeley: U of California P, 1972.

Shiff, Richard. *Cézanne and the End of Impressionism: A Study of the Theory, Technique, and Critical Evaluation of Modern Art.* Chicago: U of Chicago P, 1984.

Simon, John. Rev. of *Lily Dale* by Horton Foote. *New York* 8 Dec. 1986: 115.

Smith, Amanda. "Horton Foote: A Writer's Journey." *Varia* July/Aug. 1987: 18–20, 23, 26–27.

Stowell, Peter H. *Literary Impressionism, James and Chekhov.* Athens, GA: U of Georgia P, 1980.

Symons, Arthur. *Studies in the Seven Arts.* NY: Dutton, 1910.

Weiskel, Thomas. *The Romantic Sublime: Studies in the Structure and Psychology of Transcendence.* Baltimore: Johns Hopkins UP, 1976.

Wölfflin, Heinrich. *Principles of Art History: The Problem of the Development of Style in Later Art.* Trans. by M.D. Hottinger. New York: Dover, 1950.

Wood, Gerald C., ed. *Selected One-Act Plays of Horton Foote.* By Horton Foote. Dallas: Southern Methodist UP, 1989.

"To Be Quiet and Listen"
The Orphans' Home Cycle *and the Music of Charles Ives*
Crystal Brian

On March 23, 1973, Horton Foote's father, A. H., died after a long illness. Not quite a year later, on February 19, 1974, Foote's mother, Hallie, also passed away. The impact of the double loss on the playwright was great. Within a year he had lost the two strongest connections to his past—to the material which provided substance for his artistic vision. After his mother died, Foote journeyed to Wharton and spent several weeks cleaning out the frame house at 505 N. Houston Street—the house which had symbolized so much in the lives of his parents. After returning to his home, a remote farmhouse in New Hampshire to which the writer had retreated in the mid-Sixties, Foote resumed his lifelong need to puzzle out—to understand why—becoming focused on his memories of Hallie and A. H. and of the town in which they had lived their lives. Such reflections became the inspiration for arguably his definitive work: *The Orphans' Home*.

Far from his birthplace of Wharton, allowing memory and the music of Charles Ives to fill his imagination, Foote created the story of Horace Robedaux and his search for a home, thus immortalizing the memory of a father he had "never understood" (Interview, 28 Sept. 1992) and a mother whom he had adored. Writing by a wood-burning stove in winter and in a screen-house in summer, often inspired by Ives, he composed his series of plays set in and around Harrison/Wharton in the first quarter of this century. Foote has called the cycle a moral and social history of a particular place and time (Interview, 6 Sept. 1990), but the plays are rendered with the unflinching vision and evocative imagery of a poet. Beneath the tranquil and literal surface of Foote's work lies a darker vision of insanity, alcoholism, racial injustice, brutality, sickness, death and despair. *The Orphans' Home* is a tapestry carefully woven with the strands of family and community—of generation following generation as the inhabitants of one small town cope with economic and social change. Gradually a pattern emerges—the universal cycle of birth, death, and re-birth, of destruction and survival.

As unique as the plays are, it is difficult to analyze how Foote infuses "the quotidian" with such "universal emotion" (Price xii). Foote's ability to use the most specific particularities of time, place, and character in achieving the archetypal is as mysterious in its origin as the courage a Foote character manages in the face of adversity. The word "grace," with its connotations of the spiritual and of the ineffable, best characterizes both the playwright's style and his creations. Foote is a playwright whose medium is not primarily text but a unique integration of words and movement more typical of musical composition.

There is an enormous influence of music on Foote's writing, beginning during the Forties when he worked with many modern dancers and composers. However, with the plays of *The Orphans' Home*, Foote finally achieved a seamless synthesis of music, dance, and text. This melodic and organic structure, in the words of Reynolds Price, makes Horton Foote "the supreme musician among our great American playwrights":

> More even than with Tennessee Williams, Foote's method (and his dilemma) is that of the composer. His words are black notes on a white page—all but abstract signals to the minds of actor and audience, signs from which all participants in the effort (again all those at work on both sides of the stage or camera, including the audience) must make their own musical entity. (Price xi–xii)

The structure of Foote's work, especially *The Orphans' Home*, is hard to describe because the whole composition relies on the creation of a "musical entity" which is itself a collaboration between writer, text, actors, designers, director, and audience.

The musical inspiration for the cycle was a composer for whose work the Texas playwright feels a profound affinity:

> Often when I was resting from working on the nine plays in *The Orphans' Home* cycle, I would listen over and over to the music of Charles Ives. I got to know the symphonies, the songs, the sonatas, the concertos, the piano pieces—all of it intimately. Not just passively listening, but questioning: why this choice, why this quote from a

> hymn, from a march, why this structure. (Foote, Spalding
> Lecture, n.p.)

In Foote's time of grief and creativity, Ives offered the writer a long-sought comfort and the energy of a "kindred spirit":

> I was always searching around for a kind of comfort....
> And I guess I'd always been looking for a kind of kindred
> spirit. And I stumbled on Ives; and, the minute I heard
> him, I knew this was my boy. (Interview, 15 March 1993)

Foote is conscious that for him, as for Ives, music is "one way of defining a sense of place":

> I remember, as a boy, sitting on my porch at night, or on
> the gallery, and down in the flats I could hear black mu-
> sic, or once in a while in the distance you could hear a
> little Mexican band, or I could hear a child practicing, or
> Sunday nights you could hear a choir in the distance. So
> it was part of it, part of life. All you know now is that
> inevitable radio or television; but it's not only the music,
> it's also the sounds. And, particularly in small towns, I
> think you're very conscious of it. (Interview, 6 Sept. 1990)

Similarly, in film Foote experimented with natural sounds, even si-lence:

> I'm really just beginning in film, but I know one thing I
> don't like: I hate manipulative music. And I feel that in so
> many of our films, producers don't trust the film; they
> don't trust the actors, and they want to tell us how to feel.
> They turn up Dolby sound, and I find it very distracting
> ...the pure sounds interest me. (Davis 298)

Once again, Foote says he follows the lead of Charles Ives: "Of course so many of his themes were folk themes. And I began to try as much as I could to use that approach in my films, so they kind of created their own music" (Davis 298). From Ives the playwright learned, he says, to integrate found and folk themes into his dramatic method.

It was from his father, the composer and conductor George Ives, that Charles Ives inherited the legacy of a transforming and unique compositional technique—a musical aesthetic free of preconception about what constitutes beauty in the musical form.

> Once a nice young man (his musical sense having been
> limited by three years' intensive study at the Boston Con-
> servatory) said to Father, "How can you stand it to hear
> old John Bell (the best stone-mason in town) sing?" (as
> he used to at Camp Meetings) Father said, "He is a su-
> preme musician." The young man (nice and educated)
> was horrified—"Why, he sings off the key, the wrong notes
> and everything—and that horrible, raucous voice—and
> he bellows out and hits notes no one else does—it's aw-
> ful!" Father said, "Watch him closely and reverently, look
> into his face and hear the music of the ages. Don't pay too
> much attention to the sounds—for if you do, you may
> miss the music. You won't get a wild, heroic ride to heaven
> on pretty little sounds." (Ives, *Memos* 132)

Like his father, Ives appropriates familiar material, such as hymns,
popular songs of an earlier era and ragtime melodies, and then uses
this material in a completely unconventional—and decidedly unsentimental—manner. The composer uses the old melodies allusively,
never quoting them as a means of invoking nostalgia but rather filtering
them through his own polytonal and dissonant aesthetic, forcing the
listener to hear in a new way what seems familiar.

At the outdoor religious services of Ives' childhood, farmers, families, and field hands would congregate to worship and sing old hymns
such as "Nearer My God to Thee," "In the Sweet By and By" and
"Beulah Land" (material which later found its way into many of Ives'
compositions). The singing at those meetings bore no relationship to
what a refined music critic might have called art, but Ives perceived
the music of the "let out soul" in those rough voices.

> Father, who led the singing…would always encourage the
> people to sing their own way. Most of them knew the
> words and music (theirs) by heart, and sang it that way. If
> they threw the poet or the composer around a bit, so much
> the better for the poetry and the music. There was power
> and exaltation in these great conclaves of sound from
> humanity. I've heard the same hymns played by nice cel-
> ebrated organists and sung by highly-known singers in
> beautifully orchestrated churches, and in the process ev-
> erything in the music was emasculated—precise (usually
> too fast) even time—"ta ta" down-left-right-up—pretty

> voices, etc. They take a mountain and make a sponge
> cake [out] of it. (Ives, *Memos* 133)

The "authenticity" of the music Ives heard at the camp meetings of
his youth was a powerful formative influence in his later aesthetic—
an aesthetic of "perception" as much as presentation.

Early musical impressions imprinted themselves on Horton Foote's
psyche in a remarkably similar way:

> There was music, too, of a kind—certainly hymns aplenty.
> My mother was pianist and later organist for the Meth-
> odist church, and at an early age I was taken to Sunday
> School where I learned to sing many of the hymns. Be-
> sides the hymns, the music I remember most were senti-
> mental popular songs that she would play some evenings
> while my father sang. He had collected sheet music for
> popular songs since he was a young man and brought
> them all with him when he married my mother. She would
> play, and he would sing "Good Night Mr. Elephant," "My
> Sweetheart's the Man in the Moon," "After the Ball," and
> "Hello Central, Give Me Heaven." (Foote, *Seeing and
> Imagining* 6)

Although the playwright's medium is traditionally the written word,
Foote's transformation of reality mirrors that of Ives' impressionistic
transcription. As a child Foote listened, and what he heard eventually
assumed—in the realm of his memory and imagination—a musical
structure and dimension. He remembered the storytellers he listened
to as a child, "but each teller, I soon observed, had his own embellish-
ments. It was like a theme with variations in music" (Foote, "Seeing
and Imagining" 6). Foote used many of these stories in his plays "like
recurring themes, sometimes only alluded to, sometimes the central
action" (Foote, Spalding Lecture n.p.). He, like Ives, recalls impressions from his childhood, always modified and transformed as material for his plays.

In selecting the found material with which to layer his plays, Foote
also is guided by an aesthetic defined by Charles Ives—in his "Epi-
logue" to *Essays Before a Sonata*. Truth would be achieved through the
rejection of conventional ideas of beauty and art and the strict adher-
ence to the artist's perception of the world as he saw it, the composer
says, in lines which anticipate the Modernist Movement:

> If the Yankee can reflect the fervency with which "his
> gospels" were sung—the fervency of "Aunt Sarah," who
> scrubbed her life away for her brother's ten orphans, the
> fervency with which this woman, after a fourteen-hour
> work day on the farm, would hitch up and drive five miles
> through the mud and rain to "prayer meetin'," her one
> articulate outlet for the fullness of her unselfish soul—if
> he can reflect the fervency of such a spirit, he may find
> there a local color that will do all the world good. If his
> music can but catch that spirit by being a part with itself,
> it will come somewhere near his ideal—and it will be
> American, too…. In other words, if local color, national
> color, any color, is a true pigment of the universal color, it
> is a divine quality, it is a part of substance in art—not of
> manner. (Ives, *Essays* 80–81)

In Ives' mind, "color" would be a natural by-product of a truthful
depiction of the local. Any strained attempt on the part of a composer (or any artist) to inject arbitrary "color" would result in an affected
or "quaint" depiction of the source material and the loss of any
universal relevance. And the beautiful can come from the disturbing
or dissonant, as Ives writes in an essay accompanying his *Concord
Sonata*:

> Beauty in music is too often confused with something
> that lets the ears lie back in an easy chair. Many sounds
> that we are used to do not bother us, and for that reason
> we are inclined to call them beautiful. Frequently…when
> a new or unfamiliar work is accepted as beautiful on its
> first hearing, its fundamental quality is one that tends to
> put the mind to sleep. (Ives, *Essays* 97–98)

This sense of a new order which includes both "found things and
dissonance" is what Foote himself describes as central to Ives' music.
The playwright says the composer has

> his own order. In other words, it uses found things and
> dissonance in order to create order. I'm no great music
> theoretician, but I know that the earlier conventions of
> music were to find principles of harmony. And Ives was
> out to break all that up. And to create a new kind of syn-
> thesis…. I think to teach people to look at things in a
> different way—that's more his synthesis, his principle. And

> to listen. And to find beauty in what many people would
> think was not beautiful. (Interview, 15 March 1993)

The art of Ives and Foote is the antithesis of escapist—it encourages
the listener, the viewer, to look at the world around him in a new
way—to hear the music which is present in everyday life.

In exploring the genesis of the last movement of his *Second
Orchestral Set*, Ives has provided a vivid illustration of the way in which
everyday experience inspires creation for those with the ability to "be
quiet and listen" (Foote, Interview 28 Sept. 1992). The composer
describes the experience of returning home from his downtown office
on the day after the *Lusitania* had been sunk. The news in the morning papers had terrified many, who assumed the act of aggression
would inevitably lead to war. As Ives crossed the train platform, he
found a crowd of people waiting for the train, which had been de-
layed. While he waited with the crowd, he noticed the sound of a
hand organ playing in the street below; soon, some workmen sitting
beside the train tracks began first to whistle, then to hum the tune,
singing the refrain.

> A workman with a shovel over his shoulder came on the
> platform and joined in the chorus, and the next man, a
> Wall Street banker with white spats and a cane, joined in
> it, and finally it seemed to me that everybody was singing
> this tune, and they didn't seem to be singing in fun, but
> as a natural outlet for what their feelings had been going
> through all day long. There was a feeling of dignity all
> through this. The hand-organ man seemed to sense this
> and wheeled the organ nearer the platform and kept it up
> fortissimo (and the chorus sounded out as though every
> man in New York must be joining in it). Then the first
> train came in and everybody crowded in, and the song
> gradually died out, but the effect on the crowd still showed.
> Almost nobody talked—the people acted as though they
> might be coming out of a church service. In going up-
> town, occasionally little groups would start singing or
> humming the tune.
>   Now what was the tune? It wasn't a Broadway hit, it
> wasn't a musical comedy air, it wasn't a waltz tune or a
> dance tune or an opera tune or a classical tune, or a tune
> that all of them probably knew. It was (only) the refrain
> of an old Gospel Hymn that had stirred many people of

> past generations. It was nothing but—"In the Sweet By
> and By." It wasn't a tune written to be sold, or written by
> a professor of music—but by a man who was but giving
> out an experience. (Ives, *Memos* 92–93)

Had Charles Ives not happened to be standing on that platform at
that particular moment, this peculiar conjunction of events might
have passed unnoticed as countless similar moments do every day.
Ives' unique perspective captured and transformed a seemingly hap-
hazard series of events into a haunting, even disturbing evocation of
human tragedy and transcendence.

Horton Foote's description of *The Orphans' Home* as a moral and
social history reveals that the playwright's creative process also begins
with actual events; as he says, "the literal" is "what really gets me
going." (Interview, 28 Sept. 1992):

> The time of the plays is a harsh time. They begin in 1902,
> a time of far-reaching social and economic change in Texas.
> The aftermath of Reconstruction and its passions had
> brought about a white man's union to prevent blacks from
> voting in local and state elections. But in spite of political
> and social acts to hold onto the past, a way of life was
> over, and the practical, the pragmatic were scrambling to
> form a new economic order. Black men and women were
> alive who knew the agony of slavery, and white men and
> women were alive who had owned them. (Foote, Intro-
> duction to *Four Plays* xii–xiii)

But, like Ives and the *Lusitania*, Foote personalizes history, looking
deeper than the literal surface of events and finding a resonance missing in the abstract:

> I remember the first time slavery had a concrete face for
> me. I was on a fourteen-mile hike to complete some phase
> of becoming a Boy Scout. I stopped in a country store for
> a bottle of soda water and on the gallery of the store was
> an elderly black man. As I drank my soda water we got to
> talking and he asked me my name, and when I told him
> he said he had been a slave on my great-great-grandfather's
> plantation. I have never forgotten the impact that made
> on me. Slavery up until then was merely an abstract sta-
> tistic that I'd heard older people talking about. "Our family
> had one-hundred-sixty slaves, one-hundred-twenty" or

> whatever, but as I looked into that man's tired, sorrowing
> face, I was shocked to realize that this abstraction spoken
> of so lightly ("we were good to them," "we never mis-
> treated them") was a living, suffering human being. The
> tales of the past had a new reality for me after that.[2] (Foote,
> Introduction to *Four Plays* xii–xiii)

As Foote explains, what he creates is "like a collage. A piece here and
a piece there…. But I do work directly from my own experience—
from what I have observed or heard, or from people I know. I do try
to create something new out of all that. I don't literally report" ("Conversation with Horton Foote" 24)

But the most striking similarity which links Horton Foote and
Charles Ives is not their use of "found material"; it is their conviction
that authenticity in the depiction of everyday reality will inevitably
lead to transcendent creation, a belief explained by the tenets of their
underlying philosophical and spiritual beliefs. Ives was a great
admirer of the New England Transcendentalists—Emerson and
Thoreau, in particular. Ives' *Concord Sonata* (and its accompanying
essays) reveals the enormous philosophical and spiritual influence
which Transcendentalist belief had on him. For most of his life, Horton
Foote has been a student of Christian Science, a system of philosophical and spiritual beliefs with many metaphysical tenets which
may be traced back to the Transcendentalists.

A major concept shared by the two philosophies is the perception of spiritual belief "in terms of the immediate possibilities of experience rather than with reference to a future realm of experience"
(Gottschalk 277). This shared belief regards human experience as a
whole rather than being composed of two opposing (secular and sacred) components. In this way of thinking, dualities perceived by many
conventional religious systems—dualities of earthly and heavenly or
natural and supernatural—are dispensed with. The ultimate, or spiritual, is understood "in terms of that which is immediate—
experienceable in man's present life-situation" (Gottschalk 277). Such
a belief makes it clear why Ives would be so drawn to the use of found
material in art as a means of achieving spiritual enlightenment.

The Transcendentalists' identification of religious experience with
"the illumined perception of nature" (Gottschalk 278) is very close to
Christian Science's belief that man can discover spiritual truth via the
contemplation and study of material reality (Gottschalk 282). This

process of discernment is somewhat akin to scientific exploration, in which experiments with elemental materials are conducted in order to gather data in a search for truth. Such a description is strikingly apt for the creative techniques of Horton Foote. Given the similar bases of their philosophical and spiritual beliefs, it is not surprising that both Ives and Foote should have evolved parallel aesthetics within their separate media.

Thus the insistence of both artists on truth connotes something much more than the literal. It is an attempt to distill life to its most essential elements, presented without manipulation or distortion. In keeping with this conviction, any specific system of belief—whether labelled "religious," "philosophical," "ethical" or "political"—would never be directly conveyed through their work for fear of "proselytizing" or "teaching" in a manipulative way. In his *Essays*, Ives characterizes truth as "substance," whereas dishonesty to the source and a strained striving for effect constitute "manner."

> Substance can be expressed in music, and...it is the only valuable thing in it.... In two separate pieces of music in which the notes are almost identical, one can be of substance with little manner, and the other can be of manner with little substance. Substance has something to do with character. Manner has nothing to do with it. The substance of a tune comes from somewhere near the soul, and the manner comes from—God knows where. (Ives, *Essays* 77)

The power of Horton Foote's work is at least partially linked to his use of found material in the most literal sense—utilizing music, events, and characters from his own past. However, if the playwright had not gone beyond the literal, he would have achieved only what Ives has called "manner," the strained striving for effect which characterizes many writers described as "regionalists." Early in his career as a playwright, Foote had recognized the limitations of such writing. He dedicated himself, in both artistic and spiritual realms, to cultivating the sensitivity and perception which enables the artist to recognize a moment—as Ives experienced standing on that platform waiting for the train—as comprising a revelation of the essential nature of the human condition. Foote is a writer of "substance," creating truths both specific and universal. This quality of perception is not a mechanical technique which can be learned but rather a reservoir "somewhere near the soul" from which Horton Foote draws his power and profundity as a writer.

The mysterious process by which the spiritual is revealed in the material is best described in Foote's work, as it was in Ives, by using the metaphor of music. Reynolds Price, for example, compares Foote's sparse, poetic dialogue to musical notes which require a sensitive actor/reader/musician to interpret and bring to life, "signs from which all participants in the effort...must make their own musical entity" (Price xi). Thus Price explains Foote's film adaptation of *1918*, the seventh play of *The Orphans' Home Cycle*, as a collaborative song of praise in the face of suffering:

> From the bare lines of Horton Foote's original text—and from nowhere else, really, except the voluble faces of the actors—there pours finally a joyful and unanswerably powerful psalm of praise: Suffering (to the point of devastation) is the central human condition and our most unavoidable mystery. Yet we can survive it and sing in its face. The only tonal parallels that come easily to mind—for similar findings, wisdom, and credibility—are the conclusion of *A Long Day's Journey into Night* or the rapturous final claim of Chekhov's *Uncle Vanya*. Yet even they, for all their grandeur of human love and pardon, are not bolstered by such a glacial weight of evidence as Foote provides in the prior and succeeding plays of his cycle, rich as it is in all the emotions from farce to tragedy to transcendence. (Price xii)

Richard Gilman, in his study of Chekhov (*An Opening into Eternity*), discusses a similar musical quality in the Russian dramatist's writing. Quoting a passage from an 1887 short story entitled "The Enemies," Gilman notes Chekhov's recognition of "the subtle elusive beauty of human grief, a beauty which would not be understood or properly described for a long time to come, and which, it seems, only music can render...Kirilov and his wife were silent, they were not crying; it was as if they were conscious of the lyricism, as well as the burden of their loss" (Gilman 108). Chekhov's plays, Gilman says, "aren't 'musical' because of any large function granted to the formal art or through any direct imitation of it, but because Chekhov has found music's verbal and gestural equivalents, its dramaturgical counterpart" (Gilman 109). Chekhov's prose itself replicates the techniques of musical composition.

> The music...is a matter of the relationships among all their [the plays] parts, the subtleties of connectedness, the alternations of rhythms and cadences, the way words and physical movements, language and gesture, build up in reciprocity states of the soul, its existence as form and its inhabitation by form. It's also very much a matter of spaces, rests, things left unsaid or undone but implicit, tacit, like hovering notes unsounded, and of climaxes deferred or never, though they constantly beckon, taking place. (Gilman 109)

When Gilman defines Chekhov's lyricism as "a musical exhalation, as it were, an essentiality of perception," he could easily be describing *The Orphans' Home Cycle*. Foote uses "found" material throughout the cycle of the plays. Characters sing hymns and popular songs, the strains of dance music drift through open windows, characters sit and listen to the church soloist next door practicing; yet the literal use of music—which lends to the "authenticity" so vital in the work of Foote and Ives—is only the most obvious way in which Foote has drawn upon music as inspiration. The themes with which Foote concerns himself, the circumstances of the plays and the ways in which characters react to those circumstances are the foundation for the lyricism of the playwright's art. In Foote's dramaturgy themes and variations surface and resurface, altered by the sometimes comedic, sometimes tragic tonal contexts of the nine plays.

The Orphans' Home Cycle is structured as a musical composition, each play with its distinctive style and tone becoming a movement in a symphony. For example, the central event of the first and last plays is the death of a father, the first play, *Roots in a Parched Ground*, dramatizing the death of Horace Robedaux's father and the last play, *The Death of Papa*, the death of Elizabeth's father. As if in response to these deaths, *Convicts* and *Cousins*, the second and eighth plays of the cycle, explore relatedness. In *Convicts*, set on a Texas prison farm in 1902, the playwright dramatizes the final hours of a lonely old alcoholic's disconnection from the convicts he mistreats on his plantation. *Cousins*, on the other hand, takes the complex interrelationships of two families to ludicrous lengths, leading us to conclude that we are all related; only false beliefs lead the human race into the atrocities relatives commit on, or on behalf of, one another.

Such atrocities lead to physical symptoms in *Lily Dale*, the third play of the cycle, where Horace's reaction to rejection for the second time by his mother and sister manifests itself as a flu-like delirium which almost kills the young man. In *1918*, the seventh play of the cycle, a variation on the motif appears when Horace—now a young man married to Elizabeth—succumbs to a real influenza and almost dies. Because Horace has no understanding with which to combat the false realities of sickness and death, even his marriage to Elizabeth cannot protect him, although their love is a healing and regenerative force throughout the cycle.

Opposing such sickness and death is Horace's search for someone to love and belong to in *The Widow Claire* and *Valentine's Day*, the fourth and sixth plays of the cycle. In *The Widow Claire*, Horace comes very close to marrying a young widow with two children, a woman he is drawn to in large part because her plight echoes the tragedy which befell his own family. Ultimately, Claire chooses to marry for security, and Horace is once again rejected. In *Valentine's Day*, he marries Elizabeth and begins his own family. At the end of the play, he and Elizabeth are reconciled with Elizabeth's parents, Mr. and Mrs. Vaughn (who had disapproved of Horace and Elizabeth's elopement) through the impending birth of a child, and Horace finally becomes part of a family.

Courtship is the fifth and central play of the cycle, wherein Horace first meets and courts Elizabeth. Foote places the marriage of his father and mother at the center of his cycle because his conviction is that love can conquer many ills and heal the deepest and most hopeless of psychic wounds. This personal conviction is reflected in the primacy marriage is given in his cycle, functioning as metaphor and recurring motif on both a personal and religious/philosophical level. In the cycle, if there is any hope for redemption in the material realm, it is through the regenerative power of love. Marriage, in its ideal form, is seen as a reflection of the love God holds for mankind—a sacred bond.

Within this symphonic structure, Foote also uses found music to define place, period and mood. On a deeper, metaphoric level, however, a particular character's reaction to music reveals something fundamental about that person's response to life itself. Again, in a way clearly reminiscent of Ives, Foote uses the specific—the authentic—

to evoke deeper truths. In the first play of *The Orphans' Home*, for example, Foote says,

> I tried to differentiate the two families in *Roots in a Parched Ground* through the use of music. In the Thornton house, music in some form is almost constantly being played or sung, while in the Robedaux house there is the silence of death. (Foote, Texas A&M University Lecture n.p.)

Similarly at the end of the play, George Tyler closes his door, and the faint music from the Thornton house fills the silence as young Horace walks alone across the stage, his solitary figure symbolizing the beginning of the journey which is to come. The closing image shows Horace between two worlds—music and silence, life and the unknown—the moment revealed and intensified through what one can say without words.

In other plays music similarly restates and emphasizes the dominant motifs. In *Convicts*, probably the most poetic of Foote's cycle plays, music is linked with images of mankind in chains and various symbols of death. As Foote explains,

> In *Convicts*, I use the songs, "Ain't No More Cane on the Brazos," "Rock Island Line" and "Golden Slippers." The first two are heard offstage, sung by the convicts as they work. "Golden Slippers" is sung by a convict, who can't really sing, at the burial of Soll, the owner of the plantation having forbidden any hymns to be sung at his funeral. The great folk singer, Leadbelly, told me many years ago that he sang "Rock Island Line" while he was working on a Texas prison farm. (Foote, Texas A&M University Lecture n.p.)

In *Lily Dale*, which portrays Horace Robedaux's thwarted attempt to reconnect with the family which has rejected him, the song "Lily Dale" becomes a metaphor for a past, which Horace desperately needs to remember but which his mother and sister are determined to forget. When Horace sings the song and tells Lily Dale that she will have to learn it so she can sing it for her own children, she answers that she wishes to forget about the past and any memory of the father she and Horace shared. Foote closes the play with a scene emotionally heightened and given texture through the counterpoint of music. Horace is on his way back to Harrison. He meets a woman on the train and implores her to pray for him and his family; simultaneously, Lily Dale—on another side of the stage—plays and sings the song "Lily Dale" with her mother, Corella. The song not only functions as evocative underscoring for Horace's desperate plea; it also makes the audience profoundly aware of the chaotic and ironic nature of human existence—that the healing which the song might have provided had it been played earlier is now impossible.

Horton Foote uses music and dance more overtly in *The Widow Claire*—and in the play which follows (*Courtship*)—than he does in any of the other cycle plays. Claire has a Victrola which she plays constantly when entertaining gentleman callers. Since Horace is a very good dancer—having been taught by his Thornton aunts—Claire and Horace dance around the living room during much of their time together. In a sense, *The Widow Claire* and *Courtship* are companion plays, for they dramatize Horace's first attempt to build his own family (an attempt that ends in failure) and his second attempt, which, due to the strength and faith of Elizabeth Vaughn, results in a marriage which completely transforms and regenerates him. The motif is introduced in the first play within the tonal context of regret and lost hope; when it reappears in the second play, it has been altered, the tone now one of love and possible fulfillment. For Foote, dance functions as a metaphor for the willingness of man to trust in the deepest intuitions and intimations of the heart and soul. If words cannot adequately express Horace's profound quest for regeneration through love, then dance and music must convey that for which there are no words.

Valentine's Day—with *Courtship* and *1918*, the plays immediately preceding and following—is the most musically structured of the cycle plays. The motif of regeneration through love, introduced in *The Widow Claire* and modified in *Courtship*, reappears in yet another variation in *Valentine's Day*. In a manner reminiscent of the polytonal and multi-themed compositions of Charles Ives and the plays of Chekhov, *Valentine's Day* concludes with the various storylines finding no neat resolutions; the characters whose stories have been introduced sit in Horace and Elizabeth's room, each occupied with his or her own concerns, thoughts and feelings woven together in a rich, musical tapestry of poetic image and song.

As Mr. Bobby recounts the horrific story of Mr. Billy Lee's effeminate son, Mr. Vaughn imagines the wedding which he opposed so strongly but now draws strength from, Miss Ruth struggles with a broken heart, and Elizabeth makes plans for the future. Four separate stories—all interrelated but each very different in tone—are being told. Mr. Bobby provides a poignant counterpoint to Mr. Vaughn's concern for Brother, who is rapidly developing his own problem with alcohol. Miss Ruth sings a hymn she has been practicing for Sunday church service, and Elizabeth joins in—both singing the same song, yet in diametrically opposed emotional contexts. Details of Elizabeth and Horace's wedding—the kind of flowers she carried, the dress she wore—are contrasted with news brought by Bessie (a mysterious little girl who appears to live in a different reality) that Mr. George Tyler has stabbed himself to death in the middle of Harrison's main street (Foote, *Valentine's Day* 84–107). These contrasting stories—the groundwork for which has been painstakingly laid out not only in the previous scenes of *Valentine's Day* but in the first five plays of the cycle—build to a climax understated in its dramatic action but over-whelming in its emotional impact. In scenes such as this, Foote's musicality is most clear, for he weaves themes, images, and emotional states into a concurrently dissonant and harmonious whole.

In *1918*, Horton Foote creates a portrait of the tragedy and hope which result from a society's confrontation with death. In the final scene, Foote again weaves themes and textures of defeat and triumph, life and death, in a conscious imitation of Charles Ives.

> In *1918*, I tried to bring off an Ivesian experiment. I wanted several times during the play to have a collection of sounds—music in the room where a scene was being played and, simultaneously, music from the house next door and music down the street. When I was directing the play at H.B. [Herbert Berghoff Studio], I tried very hard to achieve this effectively—as is done in so many of Ives' scores—but it never quite worked, and I had to modify it. Again, in the film, *1918*, I tried it, and it worked somewhat better—but never really as I wanted it to. (Foote, Texas A&M University Lecture n.p.)

The final scene of the play may not—in the playwright's perspec-tive—be the perfect Ivesian experiment; however, Foote's use of Ives' techniques lends this scene a uniquely musical tone. Brother has just called, asking to come back home, and Mrs. Vaughn has insisted he get back on the train to Galveston and not return until he has completed his job on a cotton boat. The town is celebrating the Armistice, and Miss Ruth, having rented a house for herself close to the Robedauxs', practices her church solo. Mr. and Mrs. Vaughn and Horace gather near Elizabeth and the new baby, as the strains of Miss Ruth singing "Peace Be to This Congregation" fill the room. As Ruth sings, Elizabeth asks Horace what kind of flowers have been placed on their dead baby's grave. As Horace and Elizabeth speak, Mr. Vaughn tells his wife that a character who had earlier lost her son is adopting a boy. The motifs of children lost and of rebirth form a moving counterpoint to the singing of the unhappy and unfulfilled Miss Ruth. Elizabeth begins to sing in the final moments of the play, and the playwright uses the counterpoint of thematic motif and music in an almost subliminal, yet devastating, communication of the inevitable duality of human experience in which hope and despair, life and death mix in seemingly chaotic fashion.

Playwright, novelist, and critic, Reynolds Price, has suggested:

> It's a famous and lamentable limitation of modern aesthetic criticism—whether of the graphic and plastic arts, literature, music, or performance—that it has proved generally helpless in the presence of apparent "simplicity," the illusory purity of means and ends toward universally comprehensible results.... Any sympathetic viewer of the recent films and plays of Horton Foote is likely to share the critic's dilemma. Were you as deeply moved as I was by his *Tender Mercies* (1983)? Then can you tell me why? Explain to me how actors—even as perfect as those he found, even so resourceful a director—could employ so few and such rhetorically uncomplicated speeches toward the flawless achievement of such a calmly profound and memorable face-to-face contemplation of human degradation and regeneration. I confidently suggest that even St. Augustine in his *Confessions* went no farther toward the heart of that dark mystery than Horton Foote. And I—novelist, poet, playwright, and critic—cannot hope to begin to tell you how he has made that longest and hardest of journeys. (Price ix–xi)

In his introduction to a collection of Foote's plays, director Robert Ellermann echoes Price's perception of Foote, calling the playwright "our 'mystic in the theatre'."

> Horton Foote is an artist of spiritual transcendence. His characters are the conflicts of the soul struggling for inner peace. At the center of his plays is loneliness, loss, grief, fear, courage and love; the existential state of our common humanity.... The conflicts between characters in a Foote play are rarely motivated by the egotism we label "success" and "failure." His creations are on a path of action which inspires all of the world's great religions. These men and women are seeking the experience we call God. To be enlightened, they are willing to face the divine nothingness of reality and the "infinite within" of the human spirit. (Ellermann vii)

In order to achieve his sense of the mysterious and spiritual, Horton Foote avoids "theatricality" in the conventional sense (dramatic reversals, suspense, etc.) He constructs a fictional world which gives the illusion of being very close to life; however, Foote's dramaturgy has a preoccupation which goes beyond the aesthetic. In refusing to focus on "action" and "theatrics," Foote achieves—intentionally—an almost meditative quality. He wants to make people look at theater—and by extension, life—in a way different from that to which they are accustomed. In much the same way that Charles Ives felt ears had to be retrained in order to understand his music, Foote feels people need a different way of looking and listening to understand his plays (Interview, 28 September 1992). His unique style feels out of sync with the fast-paced, outwardly oriented perceptions of Western Civilization because Foote's vision can be seen clearly only when perception moves beyond the intellectual and analytical. To understand Foote's work, artist and audience alike must trust the intuition of the soul, for it is that to which Horton Foote speaks most profoundly.

ೞ

Note

1.   Foote has often referred to Katherine Anne Porter's description of her own creative process, a process closely akin to the playwright's own.

> By the time the writer has reached the end of a story, he has lived it at least three times—first, in a series of actual events that, directly or indirectly, have continued to set up the condition in his mind and senses that causes him to write the story;

second, in memory; and third, on re-creation of this chaotic
stuff. (Porter 467)

When Foote refers to the childhood experience of meeting an ex-slave,
he is again evoking the sort of moment Katherine Anne Porter has
described as "what happens to a child when the bodily senses and the
moral sense and the sense of charity are unfolding, and are touched
once for all in that first time when the soul is prepared for them."
(Porter 482)

Works Cited

Davis, Ronald L. "Roots in a Parched Ground: An Interview with
Horton Foote." *Southwest Review* 73 (Summer 1988): 298–
318.

Ellermann, Robert. "Introduction." *Horton Foote: Collected Plays. Vol.
II.* Lyme, NH: Smith and Kraus, 1996. vi–viii.

Foote, Horton. *Courtship, Valentine's Day, 1918: Three Plays from the
Orphans' Home Cycle.* New York: Grove, 1987.

——. *Cousins, The Death of Papa: Two Plays from the Orphans' Home
Cycle.* New York: Grove, 1989.

——. "Fairleigh-Dickinson College Lecture." Horton Foote Papers.
Southern Methodist University.

——. *Roots in a Parched Ground, Convicts, Lily Dale, The Widow Claire:
Four Plays from the Orphans' Home Cycle.* New York: Grove,
1988.

——. Introduction. *Four Plays.* By Horton Foote. New York: Grove,
1988. xi–xv.

——. "Conversation with Horton Foote." *The Dramatists Guild Quarterly* 29:1 (Winter 1993): 24.

——. "Seeing and Imagining." Louisiana State University. 19 April
1989. Horton Foote Papers. Southern Methodist University.

——. Interview. 6 Sept. 1990.

——. Interview. 28 Sept. 1992.

———. Interview. 15 March 1993.

———. Interview. 8 April 1995.

———. "Spalding University Lecture." Horton Foote Papers. Southern Methodist University.

———. "Texas A&M University Lecture." Horton Foote Papers. Southern Methodist University.

Gilman, Richard. *An Opening into Eternity.* New Haven: Yale UP, 1995.

Gottschalk, Stephen. *The Emergence of Christian Science in American Religious Life.* Berkeley: U of California, 1973.

Ives, Charles. *Essays Before a Sonata, the Majority and Other Writings.* Ed. Howard Boatwright. New York: Norton, 1962.

———. *Memos.* Ed. John Kirkpatrick. New York: Norton, 1972.

Porter, Katherine Anne. *The Collected Essays and Occasional Writings of Katherine Anne Porter.* Boston: Houghton Mifflin/Seymour Lawrence, 1970.

Price, Reynolds. Introduction. *Three Plays.* By Horton Foote. New York: Grove, 1987. ix–xiii.

Subtext as Text
Language and Culture in Horton Foote's Texas Cycle
Laurin Porter

It is an irony worthy of one of his plays that until he received the 1995 Pulitzer Prize for *The Young Man from Atlanta*, Horton Foote, prolific dramatist, screenwriter, producer, and director for nearly fifty years, was relatively unknown in academic circles. The first reference to Foote's work doesn't appear in *The MLA Bibliography* until 1981, almost fifty years after he wrote his first play; his *Orphans' Home Cycle*, a nine-play series written in the 1970s, wasn't published in book form until Grove Press brought it out in three volumes in 1988 and 1989. Perhaps this neglect is due to the fact that he is primarily known for his screenplays, such as the Oscar winners *To Kill a Mockingbird* (1962) and *Tender Mercies* (1983) and Oscar nominee *A Trip to Bountiful* (1985). Perhaps it is because at first glance Foote's plays appear rather conventional, dealing with seemingly sentimental themes such as the need for family and tradition and the redeeming power of love.

A closer look, however, reveals that while his dramas may deal with fairly standard themes, in their understatement and self-imposed restraint they recast conventional dramatic structures and modes of expression. Consider, for example, the fact that his plays use almost no stage directions. We are given no physical descriptions of the personae, no indications of their emotional responses—only dialogue. The dialogue is likewise peculiarly restrained in both its lexicon and its emotional overtones. In *The Orphans' Home Cycle*, the subject of this essay, Foote limits himself to the ordinary language of average people living in a small Texas town at the turn of the century. Their diction is flat, sparse, and unadorned. There are very few long speeches, with many one or two-word responses: "Yes, Ma'am," "No, Ma'am." The following conversation between *Roots in a Parched Ground*'s protagonist, twelve-year-old Horace Robedaux, and Mr. Ritter, a drunken friend of his father, is typical:

> MR. RITTER: Were you with your father when he died, Son?
>
> HORACE: No Sir.
>
> MR. RITTER: Was anybody with him?
>
> HORACE: My grandmother.
>
> MR. RITTER: Not your mother?
>
> HORACE: No Sir.
>
> MR. RITTER: That's right—they were separated.
>
> HORACE: Yes Sir.
>
> MR. RITTER: Any hope for a reconciliation?
>
> HORACE: No Sir.
>
> MR. RITTER: Why not? There's always hope, I think.
>
> HORACE: He's dead.
>
> MR. RITTER: Oh, of course. (*Four Plays* 52)

Likewise, in *Courtship*, the fifth play of the cycle, the first kiss of Horace and Elizabeth Vaughn, a passionate declaration of their budding romance, passes unremarked by either of them. In the midst of a conversation on Elizabeth's front porch, the stage directions merely state, "They kiss" (*Three Plays* 26). Though this will mark the turning point in both their lives, Elizabeth matter-of-factly resumes their conversation. In Foote's plays, what is unsaid is often more important than what is said.

The plots, likewise, seem flat. The action is relatively uneventful, with highly dramatic events—births, deaths, a wedding—taking place either offstage or between the plays. There are no villains, and overt conflict is limited. It is no accident that the playwright with whom Foote is most often compared is Chekhov,[1] another master of the seemingly shapeless plot. The cycle plays are also remarkably brief, most fewer than eighty pages. Four have two acts; five have only one. One has only to glance at them to observe how radically they depart from the more traditionally constructed plays of O'Neill, Miller, Williams or their more contemporary counterparts. These plays' rhetorical restraint and seeming simplicity, however, can be misleading, for the power of both their staged and filmed versions is immense.

It is undoubtedly their very atypicality that makes Foote's dramas difficult to discuss theoretically and perhaps helps account for their mild critical reception. Because they lie outside our usual categories and strategies, they elude the various critical nets that we cast. In his introduction to volume two of the *Cycle*, Reynolds Price addresses this issue. Pointing to the elegance of Greek temples and Oriental scroll-painting, a William Blake lyric or an Appalachian ballad, he comments,

> It's a famous and lamentable limitation of modern aes-
> thetic criticism…that it has proved generally helpless in
> the presence of apparent "simplicity," the illusory purity
> of means and ends toward universally comprehensible
> results. Where is there a genuinely illuminating discus-
> sion of Blake's "Tyger," Gluck's "Dance of the Blessed
> Spirits," or Joan Baez's traversals of the Child ballads?
> (Introduction, *Three Plays* ix–x)

Placing Foote's art in this same category, he writes of *Tender Mercies*,

> Explain to me how actors—even as perfect as those he
> found, even so resourceful a director—could employ so
> few and such rhetorically uncomplicated speeches toward
> the flawless achievement of such a calmly profound and
> memorable face-to-face contemplation of human degra-
> dation and regeneration. I confidently suggest that even
> St. Augustine in his *Confessions* went no farther toward
> the heart of that luminous dark mystery than Horton Foote.
> And I—a novelist, poet, playwright, and critic—cannot
> hope to begin to tell you how he has made that longest
> and hardest of journeys. (Introduction, *Three Plays* xi)

It is my contention that the apparent simplicity and ease of these plays masks a complexity of construction that accounts for the strange power to which Price refers. To understand this paradox, one must carefully consider language and its relationship to culture in these nine plays.

In an interview with John L. DiGaetani which appears in *A Search for a Postmodern Theater*, Foote points out that in poems and plays he's especially fond of, the effects are often achieved by "suggestion rather than statement" (68). When DiGaetani says, "You feel that understated language is important in the theater," Foote responds, "I think language in general is of enormous importance—language is everything to me" (68). Later in the same interview he says, "Writing has been one of the great joys of my life. I love reading, I love being read to, I love words, I love writing—the whole process" (71).

Given his love for words, it is perhaps surprising that his language doesn't call attention to itself. If anything, it disappears. All of his *Cycle* characters, for example, use more or less the same vocabulary. With occasional exceptions, language is not used to indicate social class. Instead, it becomes a kind of leveler, a font into which all dip with much the same results. This homogeneity of lexicon and syntax reflects a culture which, though not without its problems, is coherent, whole, of a piece. Unlike the characters in a Mamet play— *Glengarry Glen Ross* for example, of whom this same statement could be made—the linguistic sameness of Foote's characters does not indicate a cultural and spiritual poverty. Indeed, its power derives precisely from the characters' shared values and attitudes, social conventions, and individual and collective pasts. Even when individual characters rebel against them, societal norms and expectations, though never overtly articulated, are known to all. Thus to decode the meanings residing in the dialogue, one must make explicit the cultural realities of this particular time and place. As we do so, it will become clear that undergirding the cultural matrix of these nine plays are the central issues: (1) How does the individual fit within the larger context: family, town, world? and (2) How does what is said, the bits and pieces of conversation, fit into a larger whole?

This Emersonian matter, the relationship of the one and the many, the part and the whole, is uniquely reflected in the structure of the cycle itself. Each drama in *The Orphans' Home Cycle* is self-contained, yet part of a larger saga; together they trace the life of Horace Robedaux, a young lad of twelve who has just lost his father and in the following eight plays creates a family of his own. The narrative, based loosely on Foote's family history and set in Harrison, Texas, the fictional counterpart of Wharton, Foote's hometown, covers a period of twenty-six years, from 1902–1928. It is a moving story, one which gathers momentum and complexity as it goes. By the final pages, the reader has encountered three generations and three families (those of Horace's mother, his father, and his wife) and learned a good deal about the other residents of Harrison, whose stories weave in and out of Horace's, with the town becoming a kind of extended family. As in Faulkner's Yoknapatawpha saga, Foote's cycle extends beyond the story of the

Robedauxs and Harrison, Texas, to the entire South, tapping finally the depths of human experience. The action takes place against the backdrop of historical, social, and economic developments: World War I, the flu epidemic of 1918, and the economic upheavals of the cotton-dependent small town after the Civil War and on into the twentieth century.

Roots in a Parched Ground, the opening play, tells the story that announces the themes of the entire cycle. The title is taken from William Carlos Williams' poem "Raleigh Was Right": "Love itself a flower/ with roots in a parched ground." The poem is an affirmation of Raleigh's parody of Marlowe's famous "Come Live with Me and Be My Love," a bucolic pastoral extolling the joys of peasant life. Williams, like Raleigh before him, takes an unsentimental look at love, knowing that though it blooms in unlikely and inhospitable soil, it often does not have the roots to sustain it. In this play Horace loses his father, who dies while still a young man of alcoholism and broken dreams. Paul Horace, the father, has been estranged from his wife Corella for several years due to conflicts between their two families, and Horace is caught in the middle of these warring camps. By the time the play is over, Horace is for all practical purposes an orphan. His father is dead, his mother has remarried and moved to Houston with his sister Lily Dale, and his paternal grandmother and her family have moved. In the final scene Horace looks for empty whiskey bottles to sell, vowing to save enough money to buy a tombstone for his father's grave. All the adults in his life, including two friends of his father who promised to take care of the boy, have failed him. Seeing himself alone in the world, Horace sets about finding a home, a quest that will be pursued through the next eight plays.

The play begins in obvious disorder. Horace is caught between two warring families: the vibrant, music-loving, warm and unpretentious Thorntons on his mother's side and the highly refined and educated, somewhat cold and distant Robedauxs on his father's. The physical division of stage space reinforces this split, with stage right designated as the Thorntons' and stage left, the Robedauxs'. Horace moves uneasily between these two camps, literally and figuratively. His parents' separation several years earlier has solidified the tensions and misunderstandings between the two families of which Horace is a part, and the suffering which ensues as he tries to find his place in the world is painful to watch. His father lies dying in the Robedaux family home, while just a few doors away the Thorntons are celebrating a reunion with singing and dancing. His mother Corella, back from Houston where she's been working making shirts, refuses to speak to her estranged husband and later won't even go to his funeral, so bitter is she about the circumstances that ended their marriage, yet neither her feelings nor their origin is verbalized.

Horace's last visit with his dying father is a particularly poignant scene, though understated in typical Foote fashion. The entire interaction is controlled by Horace's unfeeling, domineering grandmother, who summons Horace in, directs what he is to say, then dismisses him. His only words are, "Hello, Papa," and "Goodbye, Papa." Yet in the sequel play, Horace, in naming those who care for him, can only think of his father. "My daddy cared about me, but he's dead," he says matter-of-factly (*Four Plays* 97).

By *Roots'* end, Horace has come to the understanding that he's on his own. The adults who should look after him have either died, moved away, or failed him, and at twelve he is alone in the world. It may not seem the stuff of great tragedy, but as a statement of the existential condition it wields great power in its simplicity. Horace's life is as drained of possibility as the empty whiskey bottles he seeks, and the last action—his father's friend Mr. Ritter giving him a dime—is painfully ironic.

In this play, as in all nine, what is left unsaid is often more important than what is said—a hallmark of Foote's style and the first rhetorical trait I would like to examine. In a scene early in Act I, for example, when Horace talks to his dying father, it is clear both that his father loves him and that he has been fairly uninvolved in his son's life, though nothing is said directly about either fact. Paul Horace asks Horace if he's going to school and is concerned to learn he's not because his teacher (whose name Horace Sr. doesn't know) thinks he's "dumb." He asks his son to bring his books the next day so he can help him, corrects his grammar (no one else bothers to do so), and answers all of his many questions. Young Horace asks his father if he's a lawyer, for instance, and if Mr. John Howard is his partner, then inquires about a tragedy in John Howard's life in which his two children were killed. His father is the one person both wise and caring enough to guide Horace through the vicissitudes of childhood to a productive adult life, but he is dying.

Thus it's doubly tragic that on his deathbed, as Horace is called in to say goodbye, the boy is not free to speak his heart to his father, primarily because his Grandmother Robedaux is present and controlling what can and can't be said. We have observed in previous scenes that she is both negative and manipulative, repeatedly complaining, for example, in her son's name of the music coming from the Thorntons' home, though he himself says he enjoys it. In conversations about the disintegration of Paul Horace's marriage, it is implied that perhaps the key factor was his mother, two brothers, a sister, and her daughter Minnie moving in with the young struggling couple. The burden of assuming their financial support drove Horace Sr. to drink and ultimately broke his spirit. Thus we know both first and second-hand that this woman, who sees herself as innocent, a long-suffering martyr, manipulates reality to suit her own vision.

When Horace, who has been summoned by his grandmother, enters the sickroom with his younger sister Lily Dale, the scene is orchestrated by Mrs. Robedaux, who draws the children to her and says, "Dear Lord, why have you brought this suffering on this precious child of mine? Spare him, I pray you, for the sake of these two innocent children who so need a father's love and guidance" (*Four Plays* 35). When her son moves his lips, she says, "Speak to him, children" (36). "What shall I say?" Horace asks, and she tells him to say hello. Those will be the only words he is allowed: "Hello, Papa," and when he is told to leave, "Goodbye, Papa" (37).

We know Horace suffers deeply the loss of his father. When he learns of his father's death and observes his mother's bitter response to this news, he doesn't comment, exiting quickly, ostensibly to check on his fishing lines. Lily Dale then says that he goes to the river to smoke, and his Grandfather Thornton grabs him and shakes him. The fact that he has just lost his father is evidently not as important as the possibility that he smokes or that he calls his sister a liar when she accuses him. Later, with his friends, when asked about his parents' separation, he remains silent; when his friend Thurman says, "I bet you feel sad about your papa dying" (*Four Plays* 45), he simply leaves. Deep emotions are not articulated or publicly displayed; for the most part, Foote doesn't even allow them to be seen on stage.

Similarly, when Corella is told by her brother Albert that her husband is near death, she merely says, "Oh?" and continues her sewing. We are given no stage directions to indicate her emotional response or Horace's as he sits there and watches; we're only told that after a moment he gets up and leaves (*Four Plays* 7). When Paul Horace actually dies, we get a bit more information, which helps us understand Corella's unemotional response. Her mother wonders whether they should pay their respects or send food, and Corella says, again, in front of Horace, "I'm not going near them. I'll not put my foot in that house" (42). Though she thinks the children should go to the cemetery, she refuses to:

> I couldn't stand being near them and if I went and stayed apart from them…(*Pause.*) Well, you know. Oh, don't look at me that way, Sis. I am very bitter still and I can't help it. (*Four Plays* 42)

According to Corella, proper forms must be observed; even if she cannot bring herself to attend the funeral, the children should pay their respects. It's unacceptable even for Corella's own sister to pry into the reasons for this decision. Corella simply states her position, and no one gainsays her. To do so would violate an unspoken but ironclad code of behavior.

In terms of dramatic exposition, we note that Foote withholds both Corella's emotional response to Paul Horace's death and the reason for her bitterness towards his family. We have to piece together for ourselves from second-hand information the reasons for their failed marriage and Corella's subsequent rancor. In this, as in other matters, Foote's use of language forces us to do what the townspeople have already done: sift through the two families' versions of the story and come to our own conclusions (hence the effectiveness of dividing the stage space and action between the two opposing families). Cousin Minnie's reaction is perhaps the strongest—ironically, since she's of another generation and seemingly the least affected by her aunt and uncle's separation. Yet she refuses to call Corella by name, referring to her by pronouns only. When Lily Dale comes to see her dying father, Minnie says to her, "I'm his favorite. I guess you know that" (*Four Plays* 33). We gather that her identification with her uncle is strong, especially since she and her mother were abandoned by her own father. She blames Corella for the failure of the marriage, accepting at face value the version she has probably heard from her Grandmother Robedaux. "Your mama is to blame for it, you know," she says to Lily Dale. "She deserted him when he needed her. All she was ever interested in was money. When he got sick and couldn't work, she left him" (38).

Lily Dale, on the other hand, is told a different version by her elders. Trying to sort it out, she tells Horace, "Aunt Virgie says it isn't true. She says Papa is being killed by whiskey and cigarettes and worry. Worry because he has to feed and clothe his relatives. She says his family are all shiftless and lazy" (*Four Plays* 38). Then Lily Dale gives us the one account we have of the final, irrevocable split:

> I won't ever forget it. Walking down the street at two in
> the morning in our nightgowns with the neighbors all
> watching from their windows, Minnie screaming at
> Mama, Grandma Robedaux crying, Mama crying...Uncle
> Terrence calling to everybody to be calm. (38)

As readers, then, we must sift through various versions of the story, testing one against the other, judging the degree to which a given character is prone to exaggerate, embellish, distort. Foote will neither give us a single, direct account of what happened nor allow the characters who are most involved to reveal their feelings. We, like the children, in this case, can only observe the adults and come to our own conclusions.

As we watch Horace trying to decide on a course in life, we see a final example of Foote's indirection. Horace has noted his father's concern that he continue his education and become a lawyer, and when he learns that his mother and her new husband are coming to visit, he takes the notion that he'll move to Houston with them and study law. Even though he hasn't attended school for some time, he starts going regularly, coming to check his fishing lines at daybreak so he can make it to school on time. He also quits chewing tobacco when he learns that his stepfather doesn't chew. He tells his friend Larry, "He doesn't chew, he doesn't drink, he doesn't smoke. As a matter of fact, he doesn't have any bad habits at all" (*Four Plays* 74). He's obviously eager to please his new father and awaits the visit with great anticipation. Thus when he's rejected by Mr. Davenport, who dotes on Lily Dale but feels boys should work for a living as he himself once did, Horace's hopes are dashed. "Lawyers are a dime a dozen," Pete says; "I wouldn't let a son of mine study for the law" (82). Corella, sadly, is no help. When Horace works up his courage to ask if he can come live with them in Houston, she tells him they have no room, at which point Lily Dale insists on performing a piece on the piano and the subject is dropped.

Foote doesn't dwell on this scene. The lights fade quickly and come up again on Horace, down by the river smoking his pipe and saying to his friend that it's "too noisy" at his house; he prefers the quiet (*Four Plays* 83). He also states flatly that he's decided not to go to Houston (he "doesn't care" for cities) or to school, since "lawyers are a dime a dozen" (85). When his friend asks him what he calls his stepfather (titles are important in this community), Horace simply says, "Mr. Davenport" (83). In masterful understatement, to the question "Do you think you'll ever call him anything else?" Horace replies, "Nope." This is not to be his father. His life has changed forever in a few short moments. He's decided he'll go to the Gautier plantation and work with his Uncle Albert for "my grub, all the tobacco I want, and four bits a week," adding, "I'm on my own" (84). The turning point of his life, the end of his childhood, is contained in these four words.

What do these examples tell us about the cultural milieu which informs this play and the eight that follow? What Southern mores and linguistic conventions do they reveal, and how does Foote's language both shape and reflect these realities?

One of the most obvious axioms of behavior that we observe is that children must not question, challenge, or even take the initiative with their elders. Horace cannot challenge his grandmother's authority, for instance, even though his father is dying and he knows he may never see him again. Although he is a bit more free to take the initiative with his father when Mrs. Robedaux is not present, even then there are certain topics he does not bring up, things we assume he would like to know, like why his father and mother are separated (or even what "separation" means, since he clearly doesn't know), how his father feels about dying, what impact this will have on his own future. Horace must guess, surmise, and piece together from whatever information he can gather the facts of his past and his prospects for the future.

The cultural value informing this rule of behavior is that children should respect their elders. A closely related value which extends this conversational restraint to adults is that of privacy. Corella's sister Mary assumes it would be a violation of her privacy if she presumed to ask Corella her reasons for not attending her husband's funeral. While it may have some advantages, the dictate "Thou shalt not interfere" can also have negative consequences. One poignant example of this occurs at the end of *Valentine's Day*, the sixth play of the cycle, which tells the story of Horace's marriage to Elizabeth Vaughn. A seemingly desultory conversation occurs in the final moments of the play between Horace, Elizabeth, her father, and two residents of the boarding house where Horace and Elizabeth live. In typical style, this seemingly aimless discussion touches upon matters that range from joy to heartbreak: Horace and Elizabeth's wedding day; her parents' disapproval of the match; the death of Elizabeth's two infant sisters over twenty years earlier; the suicide of Mr. George Tyler that very day; and the building of Horace and Elizabeth's first home, a gift from her now-reconciled parents. In the midst of all this, Mr. Bobby, a boarder whose own life is in disarray, mentions the time Mr. Billy Lee whipped his "sissy" son Edgar. In one of the few references to homosexuality in the cycle, we see quickly sketched this tragic story:

> BOBBY: Edgar, Edgar Lee. Now what made me think of him? Oh, yes. We were talking about Mr. Billy Lee. (*There is silence.*) Mama saw Mr. Billy Lee whip Edgar once. She was over at Mrs. Lee's visiting one day and Mr. Billy came home and she said she heard him say, "Take that dress off," and then Edgar run across the yard in his sister's dress and Mr. Billy run after him and he grabbed him halfway across the yard and had his buggy whip and she said he beat him until she thought he would kill him. She said Mrs. Lee kept right on talking as if nothing had happened. (*Three Plays* 106)

Not only does Bobby's mother not interfere at the time, though we infer she was upset or at least dismayed at what she saw, no one at the boarding house comments on the episode, whatever their feelings may be. The next line is Mr. Vaughn's to Elizabeth: "What kind of flowers did you say the Norton girl carried at your wedding?" Billy Lee is at the mercy of his father. No one, not even his own mother, interferes in what each presumably believes is a father's right to "discipline" his child.

A third cultural commandment interdicts any display of deep emotion, except in the most private of situations. When after almost a year of refusing to speak to Elizabeth, who eloped with Horace on Valentine's Day, Mrs. Vaughn calls to ask if they can bring over some Christmas presents, not a word is said by either about their estrangement. Elizabeth tells Horace about their phone conversation:

> It was Mama! She said, "Do you know who this is, Eliza-
> beth?" and of course I did and I said, "Mama." And she
> said, "Yes," and then she said, "Merry Christmas," and I
> began to cry. And she began to cry and then she said,
> "May we come over in a few minutes? We have a few
> little presents for you." And I said, "Yes," and that was it.
> (*Three Plays* 64)

When her parents and brother arrive shortly thereafter, it is as if nothing
has happened, and nowhere else in the cycle do they ever discuss it.
The Vaughns simply accept Elizabeth back into the fold, along with
Horace, as if no explanation of their harsh, even cruel behavior is
necessary. If either Elizabeth or Horace is bitter, we are never to know;
their respect for their elders and their sense of propriety forbid their
talking about it, perhaps even to each other.

Similar examples abound. The first kiss Horace and Elizabeth
exchange, mentioned earlier in this essay, passes unremarked by either, although its significance is clear. At the end of *Courtship*, though
nothing seems to have happened except Horace's paying Elizabeth a
call, she says quietly to her sister Laura, "I'm marrying Horace
Robedaux."

LAURA: If he asks you.
ELIZABETH: If he asks me. (*Three Plays* 49)

Though she has made a decision which will change her life, the audience must infer the deep emotions never revealed in the seemingly
desultory conversations.

In all these matters, social conventions and a degree of formality
foreign to a contemporary audience provide a way of managing feelings which might otherwise overflow and destroy the apparent tran-
quility of the community. Certain prescribed rituals characteristic of
this time and place function as rituals do everywhere: as containers
for emotion. Standard forms of address, for instance, are insisted upon.
Children respond to their parents, as to all elders, with "Ma'am" and
"Sir." First and last names are generally used in speaking of one another—Mr. John Howard, Mr. George Tyler—though if the relationship is fairly close, they address one another with the title and first
name only: Mr. Bobby, Miss Ruth. These forms of address sometimes

indicate class distinctions. Horace calls the black gravedigger "Sam" in *1918*, while Sam responds with "Mr. Horace" (*Three Plays* 111, 170). If Sam weren't so comfortable with him, it would be "Mr. Robedaux." Even married couples observe these formalities. Mrs. Vaughn addresses her husband as "Mr. Vaughn" and wouldn't dream of using a pet name in public. We observe the changes that come with time in Horace and Elizabeth, who call each other by first name only; Horace even kisses Elizabeth hello in front of Bobby Lee and Miss Ruth.

It is also standard to inquire after someone's family when speaking as a matter of course; it is assumed, given the great value placed on family in the Southern culture, that this is a question of paramount importance. Answers to questions are kept brief and to the point and must always be polite. It goes without saying that swearing and the use of obscenities are never permitted in the presence of a lady, and sexual matters are not considered appropriate topics of conversation. Though in the course of the cycle we learn of infidelities, broken marriages, abortions, and babies born out of wedlock, these things are generally inferred or whispered rather than openly discussed. In this world, behavior as well as speech is strictly governed by rules of decorum.

Once again, these customs and the values they reflect cut both ways. When tragedy strikes, everyone responds in predictable and supportive ways: food is brought to families who have experienced a death or a loss; one goes to pay one's respects. Thus grief does not have to be endured in isolation. The community at its best functions as an extended family. Since everyone knows the rules, there is a degree of comfort and ease, of knowing where one fits in the network of relationships, knowing what is expected. Unlike today's world, which for the most part values spontaneity, individuality, and freedom from restrictive codes of behavior yet experiences the social isolation that can accompany these values, the citizens of Foote's Harrison know who they are. "Identity crisis" is not a term that they would understand.

Yet they, too, must all find their way in the world, and while their strict and often restrictive mores provide a clear starting point, they can also get in the way. The taboo against talking about sexual matters, for instance, particularly evident in *Courtship*, can have devastating results.

The action of this play is deceptively simple. The title suggests that it will portray a couple engaged in some form of courting ritual which will eventually lead to a marriage, a standard plot structure of romantic comedy. Yet the only overt action that could be categorized as such occurs when Horace leaves the dance which Elizabeth and her younger sister Laura are forbidden to attend and comes to call. His brief conversation with Elizabeth on her front porch, along with an even briefer one later in the evening, are the only times Elizabeth and Horace are together that evening. Both episodes combined amount to no more than ten minutes of stage time. Indeed, the play is more about the difficulties of marrying happily than it is about romance; on one level "Non-Courtship" might be a more accurate title. To underscore this point, Foote has young couples, ostensibly at the town dance, waltz across the stage from time to time, "unseen" by the actors but reminding the audience of what Laura and Elizabeth are missing. Yet in spite of the brevity of their actual encounters that evening, by the play's end, Elizabeth has decided that she will marry Horace if he asks her. As with all the cycle plays, the information which shapes this decision is conveyed between the lines, by inference and indirection; the essential action is interior. A close inspection of the dialogue reveals how Foote accomplishes this.

The central issue of *Courtship* involves the way in which one chooses a life mate, a critical decision for both men and women. The life of Mr. Vaughn's brother Billy, we are told, was ruined by his choice of wives—first the "vain, extravagant, foolish" Stella (*Three Plays* 29) and then the dissipated Asa, who led him to drink and debauchery. His sister Lucy married a man twenty years her senior who left her a widow at thirty-two with four children to feed. Other examples of failed or unhappy marriages abound. At different points in the evening, both Elizabeth and Laura pose the critical question, "How can you ever be sure?" (22). An important question for anyone contemplating marriage, this issue was especially critical to young women of this era, since they were totally dependent on their husbands financially, and divorce was not an option if the marriage didn't work out. In this community, the selection of a husband was without doubt the most important decision of these young women's lives.

This issue is uppermost in Laura and Elizabeth's mind, especially since their father has forbidden them to go to the dance and discourages their beaux, including Horace, from coming to call. We learn in the course of the evening that both Elizabeth and Laura, when spending the night with girlfriends, had sneaked out with boyfriends: Elizabeth and her friend for a buggy ride; Laura and Annie Gayle and their callers for a walk around the block—hardly shocking fare for a contemporary audience.

The dangers of this kind of behavior, however, of deceiving one's parents and acting on one's own impulses, are illustrated by two tragic events that function as a shadow plot to Elizabeth's story: the deaths of her friend Sybil Thomas and a former beau, Syd Joplin. Foote weaves these stories, like those of the other townspeople, into seemingly disconnected conversations, though these two receive special emphasis, functioning as comments upon Elizabeth's pending decision. We first learn of Syd Joplin's recent death in a conversation between Laura and Elizabeth early in the evening. Laura asks Elizabeth if it's true that at one time she had planned to elope with Syd since their parents forbade her to see him, and Elizabeth admits that it is:

LAURA: Are you still in love with him?

ELIZABETH: No.

LAURA: Were you ever really in love with him?

ELIZABETH: I thought so.

LAURA: Do you think if you had married him you would have still loved him?

ELIZABETH: No.

LAURA: Wouldn't it be terrible to think you were in love with someone, marry them, and then find out you weren't?

ELIZABETH: Yes. (*Three Plays* 7)

Beneath Elizabeth's one- or two-word responses is the drama of a young woman finding the courage to decide for herself and act courageously.

The desire for certainty in the face of love's mystery is a theme which recurs throughout the play. It surfaces again at the second mention of Syd Joplin, this time in Elizabeth's conversation with Horace. Horace asks Elizabeth if she had been in love with Syd, and she replies that she thought so and almost eloped with him but didn't because she was afraid her parents would never speak to her again if she did:

HORACE: Did you think they meant it?

ELIZABETH:	Yes, I did.
HORACE:	Is that why you didn't marry him?
ELIZABETH:	I guess so. I guess I also wasn't sure myself.
HORACE:	If you had been sure...would you have eloped?
ELIZABETH:	I guess so. If I were sure. How can you ever be sure? (*Three Plays* 22)

This conversation, which makes explicit the parallel between the two relationships, is typical of the pattern of communication throughout the cycle. Both Horace and Elizabeth are aware that what they're really talking about is not Syd Joplin but their own relationship and whether Elizabeth would be willing to elope with Horace.

None of this can be said directly, however, nor can they speak of their feelings. Instead, they seek confirmation indirectly. Horace wants to know if she'll write when he is away on a business trip; she wants to know if he dates while he's on the road. They talk about how old their parents were when they got married, about his sister's marriage, and Sybil Thomas's hasty marriage that afternoon. Horace speaks of his goal to own a dry goods store; Elizabeth says she's wearing the ring he gave her; and in the midst of all this, they kiss, then go on with their conversation as if nothing had happened.

Syd comes up one more time at the end of the play during a climactic confrontation between Elizabeth and her father. Mr. Vaughn, discouraging Elizabeth from seeing Horace, points out that he'd been right in breaking off her relationship to Syd in spite of her protests, and even Elizabeth admits that in the end she was glad she didn't marry him. Yet she is about to make the same decision regarding Horace, who, like Syd, is considered "wild."

Their conversation is interrupted with the news that Sybil Thomas has just died. Elizabeth's friend Sybil, we learn, six months pregnant, had corseted herself tightly to hide her disgrace from her parents. When the truth came out, she and her boyfriend were hastily married; that evening, the night of the play's action, she goes into premature labor. The baby is born dead, and Sybil herself later hemorrhages and dies. The impact of this story is heightened by the way in which Foote allows the information to leak out gradually. At first we learn in a conversation between Laura and Elizabeth that Sybil is four-months pregnant, then from Horace that she and her boyfriend Leo Theil got married that afternoon. This is followed by conflicting reports that Sybil has died, the baby has died and Sybil has recovered, and then finally that Sybil was actually six-months pregnant and her labor induced fatal hemorrhaging—a sobering announcement which spreads quickly throughout the town. The dance is called off and everyone immediately walks to the Thomas home, despite the late hour, to pay their respects.

This event, juxtaposed as it is with Elizabeth's pending decision about marrying Horace, reverberates on several levels. In the first instance, it suggests that acting on passion as Sybil did, defying societal mores and deceiving one's parents, can lead to disaster. The parallel clearly isn't lost on Elizabeth. Mrs. Vaughn, who has just learned about Laura and Elizabeth's illicit escapades, makes this connection explicit when she confronts her daughters late that evening. "Think about poor Sybil Thomas the next time you start slipping around with boys in a buggy in the middle of the night," she says (*Three Plays* 35).

At the same time one could argue that it is the very repressiveness of this society that killed Sybil in the first place, the tight corset functioning as a symbol of a rigid, restrictive society that refuses to accept or even acknowledge sexuality. Nowhere is Sybil's character impugned; Elizabeth describes her as "always jolly...[with] a very sweet disposition" (*Three Plays* 37). The reluctance of the adults of this generation to discuss sexual matters is illustrated by Laura's naive questions about abortion. When she asks Elizabeth how women "get rid of" unwanted babies and Elizabeth doesn't know either, Laura says,

> I guess we'll never know. I don't trust Anna Landry and I don't know who else to ask. Can you imagine the expression on Mama's face, or Aunt Lucy's or Mrs. Cookenboo's if I asked them something like that? (*Three Plays* 42)

This same phenomenon is dramatized before our eyes when Mrs. Vaughn, sent by her husband, comes to have a talk with Laura and Elizabeth near the play's end. The news about Sybil is known, and Elizabeth has confronted her father about her feelings for Horace and her anger at Mr. Vaughn's restrictive behavior, during which her ring from Horace falls off its chain inside her dress and clatters to the floor. The parallels between Sybil, Syd, and Elizabeth are in the open, and the Vaughns are fearful that Elizabeth is about to make a terrible

mistake. In this frame of mind, Mrs. Vaughn asks her daughters if
they have any questions. Immediately, Laura says,

LAURA:	How did you know you were in love with Papa?
MRS. VAUGHN:	I just did.
LAURA:	How could you be sure?
MRS. VAUGHN:	I just was. (*Pause.*) Elizabeth, do you have any questions?
ELIZABETH:	No, Ma'am.
LAURA:	Elizabeth thought at one time she was in love with Syd Joplin. How come she wasn't?
MRS. VAUGHN:	She was wrong.
LAURA:	Why was she wrong?
MRS. VAUGHN:	She just was. (*Three Plays* 47)

At this point, Mr. Vaughn joins them and his wife reports, "The girls
and I have had a nice talk" (48). In her mind they have, yet Laura's
question, arguably the key issue of the play, goes unanswered. It isn't
that Mrs. Vaughn is willfully withholding information from her daughters; she doesn't know any more than they do. There are some things,
she insists, "you just know." She sidesteps the question of *how* one
knows or tests this knowledge, nor does she romanticize by saying
"follow your heart" or "trust your intuition." She hasn't given this
matter much thought, we gather. She fell in love and got married and
her history has taken on the aura of inevitability.

It should be noted that sexual questions are not even posed.
Though clearly there is much that Laura and Elizabeth would like to
know, they realize that their mother's invitation to ask questions doesn't
include this topic. Once again, what is not said is more telling than
what is.

The play ends with Elizabeth saying aloud to herself, "I'm marrying Horace Robedaux...if he asks me" (*Three Plays* 49). She has
weighed carefully all that she has seen and heard this evening—the
table talk of her aunts Lucy and Sarah, a widow and "old maid,"
respectively; the news about Syd's and Sybil's deaths; her conversations with Laura, who is equally terrified of being unmarried and
marrying the wrong man. Thus if we read carefully, even though noth-

ing has been said overtly, we are prepared for the fact that these seemingly unrelated snippets of casual after-dinner conversation are actually key factors in Elizabeth's decision. The subtext is more important than the text. The true action of this play, as in all the *Cycle* plays, is interior.

It is important to understand that Foote's restrained, indirect use of language reflects the mode of communication common to the period and milieu he is depicting. The dialogue rings true precisely because it emerges from a specific cultural context. The values that it reflects are those of that time and place: proper forms of address (Ma'am and Sir, Mr. and Mrs.), emotional restraint, family, privacy, decorum. Subjects like sex, abortions, homosexuality, and illegitimate births are not discussed in polite company or if so, only in hushed voices when no children are present. All of these topics occur in Foote's cycle; critics who dismiss him as sentimental are mistaking the era's rhetorical restraint for his own. His is a clear-eyed, unsentimental picture of the world he knew as a boy.

Language has great power in Foote's world but a power of a different sort from that of other American playwrights. His characters are all storytellers of one kind or another; they delight in anecdotes, family legends, local gossip. It is one of his most Southern characteristics. In a lecture Foote once gave entitled "The Artist as Myth Maker," he told of his childhood, growing up listening to the talk on his front porch summer evenings like today's children watch television:

> Although I've always liked to read, I grew up in a place and time when there was no radio, no television, no VCRs, and no movies on Sundays, and strictly rationed during the weekdays, so people often entertained themselves by talking. In my family the talk was often about the past as in Miss [Katherine Anne] Porter's *Old Mortality*—my mother had been to Kid Key College and was certainly bright enough, read occasionally, but mostly she loved to talk, and my father loved to talk, and my grandmother, and my great aunts and uncles—all loved to talk. And I often found their talk more interesting than the books I was reading. (4)

These stories became a sort of oral history. "They told their stories endlessly," he said: "Their families had all come to Texas early, none later than 1836, and they seemed to me to remember everything that had ever happened to them" ("Myth Maker" 4)

He quickly learned, however, as he went on to explain, that the versions of these stories changed slightly with each teller. Referring to Porter's work again, Foote said in his lecture:

> Miss Porter has written: No legend is ever true, but I believe all of them are founded on some sense of truth. And even these truths appear in different lights to every mind they are presented to, and the legend is that work of art which goes on in the human mind, adding to and arranging, harmonizing and rounding out, making larger or smaller than life, and holding the entire finished product in a good light and asking you to believe it. (6)

He went on to add, "It is true, no memory is really faithful, it has too far to go, too many changing landscapes of the human mind and heart, to bear any sort of really trustworthy witness, except in part" (6).[2]

In Foote's plays, information is not conveyed in a direct, linear, cause-and-effect fashion. Bits and pieces of family conversations, stories that are told and retold by various characters must be added to whatever action is dramatized on stage in order to get some sense of the whole. Moreover, one must be careful to weigh the veracity of the storyteller, to take into account his or her stake in the story, proximity to its occurrence, and so forth in order to determine to what extent it is or isn't true.

In *The Orphans' Home Cycle*, Horton Foote crafts the authentic language of his coastal Southeast Texas into a delicate but unbreakable web, weaving individual lives into a larger whole. A bit like Emerson's sentences, each of which seems to stand alone but in some mysterious fashion coheres to form a whole paragraph and essay, Foote's characters, through his dialogue, create a world both familiar and strange. As readers and audience, we, like the characters in these plays, must sift through their stories, consider the sources, make judgments and connections, and draw our own conclusions. It is like piecing together a puzzle, except that the pieces are presented so quietly and unobtrusively we're not aware of doing so. While he recognizes and embraces the subjectivity and complexity of all experience, his language is designed to help us find new ways to discover ancient truths.

⁊

Notes

1. Al Reinert, for example, in an article in *Texas Monthly* (July 1991: 137), refers to Foote as a "Gulf Coast Chekhov."

2. Katherine Anne Porter, another Texas writer, has had a profound influence on Foote's work, perhaps even more than other playwrights. When one recalls her themes—memory and the past, families and the ways in which they both liberate and imprison, the importance of place in shaping life experience—it is not hard to understand why.

Works Cited

DiGaetani, John L. *A Search for a Postmodern Theater: Interviews with Contemporary Playwrights.* Westport, CT: Greenwood, 1991.

Foote, Horton. "The Artist as Myth-Maker." Katherine Anne Porter Memorial Lecture. U of Texas at Arlington. Arlington, TX, 16 Nov. 1988. Horton Foote Papers. Southern Methodist University.

———. *Courtship, Valentine's Day, 1918: Three Plays from the Orphans' Home Cycle.* New York: Grove, 1987.

———. *Roots in a Parched Ground, Convicts, Lily Dale, The Widow Claire: Four Plays from the Orphans' Home Cycle.* New York: Grove, 1988.

Price, Reynolds. Introduction. *Three Plays.* By Horton Foote. New York: Grove, 1986.

Performing *The Death of Papa*
A Review
Kimball King

From February 5, 1997, until March 2, 1997, Horton Foote's *The Death of Papa* was performed on stage for the first time by the Carolina Playmaker's Repertory Company at the Paul Green Theater in Chapel Hill, North Carolina. That the world premiere of Foote's play should take place in the Paul Green Theater was an appropriate tribute to the late playwright Green, who as a University of North Carolina alumnus and major twentieth-century playwright is a worthy precursor of Foote. A fellow Southerner, he also was concerned with racial injustice and high moral and ethical principles. Then, too, he used Southern experience as a microcosm of universal conflicts and their attempted resolutions.

The Death of Papa is the ninth and final play in Foote's *The Orphans' Home*. It brings a kind of closure to the playwright's evaluation of Horace Robedaux, Sr., the "orphan" of the series and the fictitious counterpart of Foote's own father. "Papa" in the play is Robedaux's father-in-law, Henry Vaughn, who has died immediately preceding the play's opening scene. The chief witness to the play's subsequent events is a ten-year-old boy, Horace Robedaux, Jr., a surrogate for the author himself, who attempts to forge his own emerging identity as he observes his parents', uncle's, and grandmother's reactions to the death of the family patriarch. Young Horace must confront the social and economic issues of his region as well as its complex class system and racial divisions while he attempts to understand his stoical, obstinate father and loving but oddly passive mother.

For an eighty-one-year-old playwright to represent himself in the person of a little boy suggests Foote's continuing odyssey of understanding himself and his universe. Regardless of his chronological age, Foote does not hesitate to revisit events that shaped him as an artist and a man. All of the plays in *The Orphans' Home* cycle provide both the playwright and his audiences with the opportunity to process world events and personal situations into a comprehensible, meaningful pattern. With an impressive sense of symmetry, this ninth play in the series parallels the initial play, *Roots in a Parched Ground*. While *Roots* explores the impact of Foote's paternal grandfather's death on his family and hometown of "Harrison" (Wharton), Texas, *The Death of Papa* measures the effects of Foote's maternal grandfather's demise on the same community a decade earlier. The chronology of the plays suggests that the playwright first attempted to comprehend his father's character as a means of coming to terms with his own nature, only to discover in his maturity that the story of the second grandfather, including the impact of his death, was needed as well.

Foote's attendance at the Playmaker Theater's "gala" performance on February 7 emphasized the biographical nature of his Texas plays. Furthermore, the role of Foote's mother, Elizabeth Vaughn Robedaux in *The Orphans' Home* cycle, was played by Hallie Foote, the author's daughter. The spectacle of a woman playing her own grandmother caring for a husband and son, who are in actuality the actress' grandfather and father, respectively, added not only authenticity but a powerful psychological dynamic to her performance. Since all of the "good" women in Foote's plays are versions of his mother and his late wife, Lillian, portraying this composite of one's own mother and grandmother would be an enormous challenge to the actress. But Hallie Foote convincingly and winningly mastered the role.

America's infatuation with celebrity accounted in part for the sold-out performance schedules of *The Death of Papa*. Not only Hallie Foote, but Ellen Burstyn, Matthew Broderick, and Polly Holliday were featured players in the drama. As the patriarch's widow, Ellen Burstyn expressed with great sincerity both her grief for her lost husband and her excessive tolerance for her alcoholic son. Polly Holliday as Horace Robedaux, Sr.'s mother, Corella Davenport, exploited the comic overtones of her role, especially satirizing Corella's defense of ignorance and her general distrust of intellectual pursuits and self-knowledge. Yet even the "strident" women in Foote's works are more insecure than wicked. While Corella denies she failed to nurture her only son, she makes herself available to his family at times of crisis and wishes him success and happiness. Similarly, the complaining daughter-in-law who torments her husband and his mother in Foote's earlier *A Trip to Bountiful* is generally concerned about the old lady's health and hesitates to leave her when she's having "a spell." Granted, she wants the mother-in-law's pension check, but she also feels a responsibility for her. Irksome women in Foote's plays are too preoccupied with personal disappointments and their inferior status in a patriarchal society to emerge as villains.

Ray Virta, as Horace Robedaux, Sr., was appropriately reserved and non-judgmental. His character has stoically adjusted to a harsh world, and he finds solace in stubbornness and unexpressed opinions. "Brother" Vaughn, Papa's only surviving son, is a composite of the playwright's alcoholic uncles. Matthew Broderick brought a poignancy to a basically unsympathetic character. Weak, envious, and boastful, Brother squanders his widowed mother's money and ultimately becomes involved in a drunken act of violence. Yet the almost archetypal pattern of a patriarch's son, who can never measure up to the father in either his family's or his community's opinion, makes Brother's dilemma recognizable and universal. Injured during rehearsals, Broderick walked on stage with a stiffened leg. This disability stressed his character's vulnerability. Especially when a townsperson says that Henry Vaughn was a robust man "who never was sick a day in his life," one can imagine the torment of a physically handicapped son, small in stature, whose own father was the town's *father figure.*

In all of Foote's works there is a blending of naturalistic surfaces with religious or mystical overtones. Dramatic events are created out of everyday occurrences, yet the playwright manages to reveal the uniqueness of each character and the intensity of painful or pleasurable moments in his or her life. While it is possible to enjoy *The Death of Papa* as a statement about parent-child relationships and the contributions of one individual to the community, the greatest pleasure in Foote's canon is derived from seeing or reading a number of his works and observing the interplay of related characters and events. Like Faulkner in his Yoknapatawpha series or the Englishman Trollope in his Barchester or Palliser novels, Foote presents a panoply of characters who may have minor roles in one work but become the protagonist in another. His method of presentation, though popular with novelists, is rare in the theater, although another Texan, the late Preston Jones, attempted a similar but less ambitious blending of personalities and situations in his Texas Trilogy. Like the novelist Sherwood Anderson, Foote allows his hometown of Wharton, Texas (renamed "Harrison"), to be a shaping influence of character development and group experience.

Unlike Anderson, however, Foote always provides a sense that a divine providence is guiding seemingly random secular events. While the playwright does not proselytize, he treats religious experience seriously. Whether it is the total immersion of born-again Baptists in *Tender Mercies* (Foote's 1983 screenplay), the singing of hymns in *The Trip to Bountiful,* or the emphasis on joining the church in *The Death of Papa,* Foote, a practicing Christian Scientist, stresses the importance of spiritual commitment. But he is not dogmatic. An enlightened character, such as Elizabeth Robedaux (Foote's representation of his own mother) refuses to tell her son who will go to heaven or who to hell because she lacks the hubris to prognosticate about divine will. Similarly, when Brother Vaughn questions God's wisdom in allowing his "worthy" father to die, while sparing his own tormented and ineffectual life, it becomes clear that the playwright considers such speculation improper. Whether it is the recovering alcoholic folk singer in *Tender Mercies* raging that his innocent daughter's life was taken in a car crash while his own was saved, or the protagonist in *A Trip to Bountiful* sadly recalling the death of her children, the audience/reader is encouraged to accept life's major events, rather than to rail against them.

This same stoical passivity extends to the role of parents in shaping their children's lives as well. Elizabeth Robedaux, musing on the leniency of her parents toward her decadent brother, asks why some parents get their children "out of scrapes" and those offspring ultimately turn into responsible citizens, while others are later disgraced or ruined. While Foote seems to be denying the power of sensible parenting, he is arguing for individual responsibility and personal salvation. One cannot leave *The Death of Papa* or any other Foote play without believing that an individual's worth is based ultimately on his or her ability to make informed and often painful choices. A blend of Christianity and stoicism becomes the final defense in a puzzling world. People inevitably leave home in search of an identity outside their community but generally return at some point to discover themselves within that familiar arena.

Foote is sensitive to issues of racial justice, and it is not surprising that he was chosen to write the famous screenplay for Harper Lee's novel *To Kill a Mockingbird*. In *The Death of Papa*, Elizabeth, deeply moved by the poverty of black families in her community when she attends a servant's funeral, cannot account to her young son for social injustices perpetrated in the name of race. She can only comment, "I don't know why; that's just the way it is." Not only society's flawed sociological structures but the land itself can destroy a generation of hard workers, both blacks and whites. The failure of the cotton crop is slowly bringing down Harrison, Texas, in 1923, a full year before the stock market crash added to national woes. Yet, returning to manage the land, as Horace Robedaux does when his father-in-law dies, suggests that the traces of an agrarian ideal can occasion a spiritual or emotional rebirth.

Horace, Sr., whose formative years as an orphan provide the title for Foote's nine-play cycle, at the conclusion of this play is on the verge of inheriting the home of his deceased father-in-law. Rejected earlier in the cycle as an unsuitable mate for the Vaughn's daughter, an older Horace, now a principled, caring, and dependable son-in-law, may preserve the Vaughn family's legacy. *The Death of Papa* ends with a family meal in which Mrs. Vaughn and Brother plan their departure from Harrison, and the formerly distrusted son-in-law promises to manage their interests conscientiously. The many threads of Foote's biographically-based fictional universe are tied together although God's purposes and individual decisions remain undisclosed. The value of kindness, forgiveness, and personal integrity prevails, and one leaves a quiet play with a sense of fortitude in the face of a seemingly capricious march of events.

ↀ

Horton Foote's Film Aesthetic
S. Dixon McDowell

After more than fifty years of dramatic writing, Horton Foote is once again at the top of his career. In 1993 TNT's Masterworks Series produced a made-for-TV movie of his play *Habitation of Dragons*. A year later Gary Sinise commissioned Foote's adaptation of Steinbeck's *Of Mice and Men*. And then in 1995 a season of his plays at the Signature Theatre culminated in his play *The Young Man from Atlanta*, winning the Pulitzer Prize for Drama. It is ironic that his films—sometimes disparaged by critics for being slow, talky, and anti-cinematic—have been the catalyst for this renewed interest in his dramas. The present interest in Foote as a playwright is founded, for example, on the success of two films in the early 1980s: *Tender Mercies*, for which Foote won his second Academy Award, and *The Trip to Bountiful*, which provided an Academy Award for Geraldine Page. And yet, while the Pulitzer recognizes his contribution to theater, his films are often considered marginal; even allies like Alan J. Pakula, for whom Foote wrote the film adaptation of Harper Lee's *To Kill a Mockingbird*, while praising Foote's naturalistic style and unique voice, admit "his work is not particularly of this time" (Pakula Interview).

Partly this is because, despite his two Academy Awards, Horton Foote is not a commercial Hollywood screenwriter. His work is character driven and, when he has artistic control, shot on location with low budgets. His films usually have few stars and virtually none of the cinematic flash of even a B-grade Hollywood action film. Even the classic *To Kill a Mockingbird*, which was produced on Universal Studio's lot by Alan J. Pakula and directed by Robert Mulligan, may now seem "anti-cinematic" compared with contemporary Hollywood fare. However, when Foote's body of work is viewed in the context of both international cinema and American independent filmmaking, it reveals a consistent alternative film aesthetic.

International and American independent films, while using lower budgets, typically demand more from their audiences than Hollywood.

Many of these films avoid excessive technique not just for financial reasons but cinematic ones as well. John Sayles, for example, whose work in independent cinema inspired Foote's early efforts, said of his film *Matewan*,

> Our one general decision was to stay away from self-con-
> scious, authorial kinds of camera moves. As often as pos-
> sible we wanted the characters and the action to lead the
> eye, rather than have the camera drag it around. Though
> bravura camera moves can add a lot to a certain kind of
> movie, establishing a grand style or an ironic distance from
> the story, we wanted the audience to be inside the story
> and to forget about the movie-makers as much as pos-
> sible. (88)

International filmmakers from Bergman to Wim Wenders have at times opted for a less overt cinematic style of presentation as well. Instead of acrobatic camera work, complex editing, and costly special effects, many international and independent films combine a more complex narrative style, outstanding performances (often by other than box office stars), and a rich and authentic *mise-en-scène* which creates a literary texture. These are also the three key values of Horton Foote's film aesthetic.

Foote's films clearly place the writer and his literary voice in a higher position than they have in Hollywood. Typically in Holly-wood the writer is commissioned to complete a script based on some-one else's idea. That script is then rewritten numerous times under the direction of the producer, a major box-office star, and/or the di-rector. Often a series of writers are hired, the final script becoming a "collaborative effort" with a shared writing credit. But a film con-trolled by Horton Foote and his collaborators is true to a single script and screenwriter.

Foote writes primarily out of a personal literary compulsion not driven by commercial concerns. A script by Horton Foote has but one author and one voice. When examined as a body of work, Foote's films show the kind of thematic and stylistic unity that is expected in a writer of literature. Such integrity may actually hinder the career of a Hollywood screenwriter, who is expected to bend his or her talent to a plethora of competing visions and commercial pressures. Outside of a few writer/directors (Woody Allen is perhaps the most notable), no other screenwriter can demonstrate the remarkable consistency of voice evident in Foote's films.

This elevation of the writer and the written word has only been possible in Foote's films by going outside Hollywood. As Arthur Penn clarifies,

> Hollywood is in quest again and again and again of that two-hundred-million dollar grossing film. That two-hundred-million dollar grossing film, as we've seen from the precedent films, is by nature usually a one-person movie. It's either "Rocky" or it's Schwarzenegger or, you know, "Batman" or one of those absurdities. There couldn't be anything more anti–Horton Foote than that.... He writes about the unit, the human unit, whether it be a family unit or a town unit. But certainly the small human unit, is his canvas.
>
> So, well, the obvious thing is, you don't go to Hollywood. You try to do some other kind of films. And he's done that...more-or-less successfully, not without a great deal of pain. (Interview)

Although Foote earlier in his career worked "on assignment" for Hollywood studios, he does not claim these projects as his work. In fact, Foote distances himself from the Hollywood "treatment" of both *Hurry Sundown* and *The Chase*. In the case of *Hurry Sundown*, Foote recalls that Otto Preminger wanted to make "some kind of epic out of something that was big enough already" (1988 Interview). On *The Chase* Arthur Penn recalls that Sam Spiegel had several writers working on the adaptation of Foote's book with the resulting script resembling a "dog's breakfast" (1990 Interview). The strength of Foote's stories comes from the singularity and genuineness of the writer's voice at the center; once that is lost, then the rest collapses.

Movie executives are fond of proclaiming the scarcity and indispensable value of good writing; however, attributing a film to the screenwriter unless that writer is also the director of the picture is unprecedented in Hollywood. Film is considered a "director's medium," indicated by the opening credits of most films reading "a film by" whoever directed it. It is thus significant that both *1918* and *Convicts* were released as *Horton Foote's 1918* and *Horton Foote's Convicts*. Lewis Allen, producer of *1918*, explains:

> Well Horton is kind of unique.... On all the smaller films he kind of directed the actors and it was kind of his total vision of the thing.... The direction was simply trying to...to realize his vision totally. I would always say they are Horton Foote films myself...Ken Harrison that was the director of "1918".... He had done a couple of short films but never done feature.... So he deferred to Horton pretty much shooting what Horton had there. Horton had really cast it all himself too.... So they really were his films. (Interview)

This is not to deny the importance of the director in the filmmaking process. World-class directors have used their cinematic styles to elevate simple genre films to the level of art. However, in a Horton Foote film, it is the director's ability to understand, capture, and protect Foote's delicate writing rather than the director's cinematic virtuosity that is of primary importance. The realism of Foote's writing requires controlled and unobtrusive direction. The director in a Horton Foote film must respect the writing and voice at the center of the work. As Peter Masterson, director of *The Trip to Bountiful* and *Convicts*, has said,

> In a Hollywood production sometimes you don't know who the writer is. There may be three or four writers. There is no way to develop a writer's voice. So it becomes a director's kind of visual idea. There is no writer's voice at the center.... I think we've lost some good writers because of that. (Interview)

Robert Duvall takes an even stronger position regarding those who would direct Foote's work:

> there're certain New York directors that cannot direct Horton's stuff...some famous men. And I also feel there oughta be a line of guys at the Mason Dixon Line with shotguns clicking 'em and saying, "You New York guys can't come down here and play us 'cause you don't know what you're doin'." (Interview)

Even when directors as talented as Arthur Penn and Otto Preminger have tried to open up a Horton Foote story, they have diminished the material. Alan Pakula points out the rewards and pitfalls of directing a Horton Foote script:

> [Horton] does deal with the landscape of the soul. These
> people take...journeys through life as well as going from
> Tyler to so forth and all the lovely names of those places.
> It is a metaphor. You don't play the metaphor. You never
> comment on Horton's work. It's there for you.... It's like
> the poetry in Chekhov and it demands the most
> controlled work from film directors, with theatrical
> directors, and from actors because it's exhausting. And
> finally, if you violate the truth for theatrical effect, it's all
> gonna fall apart in your hands. If you push it and try to
> make it into something more souped up and...more sen-
> sational or more obviously theatrical, it will crumble. It
> will, it will show you up for the cheap, theatrical charla-
> tan you are because it has such an integrity of its own.
> (Interview)

In Horton Foote's movies, the director must stay with the metaphoric
and poetic; the "sensational" and "theatrical" will destroy the material
and betray the director.

On the other hand, Horton Foote is interested in more than the
words on the page; he respects directors and freely admits that he has
learned to appreciate the economy of the visual in cinema. He appre-
ciates, for example, the narrative economy of a simple scene in his
film *Tomorrow* in which Jackson Fentry stops to milk a goat for the
child he has determined to raise. There is no dialogue, just the simple
visuals of milking the goat along a road. Foote also points to the closing moments of *1918* in which

> Elizabeth has the baby, and the flowers have been put on
> little Jenny's grave, which she's been so reluctant to give
> up and to surrender to death, that, as she's taking this
> new life to her, the helplessness of,...the inevitability of
> the releasing of Jenny when the flowers are blown over,
> and nobody's there to pick them up or to put them back
> on the grave, and they're just scattered, and Jenny's alone
> in wherever she's gone to, wherever she is. I know that it's
> [*1918*] been considered, in a sense, a non-movie which is
> puzzling to me because I guess all the movies I like, then,
> are non-movies...I guess my instinct is towards this kind
> of film because true action, to me, is internal.
> (Interview 1988)

These images may not be the dynamic tricks Hollywood would have chosen, but they are extraordinary moments of genuine dramatic action.

The success of Foote's collaboration with Bruce Beresford on *Tender Mercies* came from their development of a shared vision. As Foote recalls,

> So finally EMI had gotten involved, and they suggested this Australian director, Bruce Beresford. Well, I went running down to see *Breaker Morant* because I'd never seen his work and I was very taken with it, but I thought, "My Heavens. This is the most insane idea in the world. I don't think he's gonna respond to it to begin with. And secondly, what in the world does he know about it?" But they sent it to him. And he responded right away and said, "If I can get along with the writer, I'll do it." So he flew in, and we did get along very well. I'm devoted to him. And I took him down to Texas to look at the terrain. And he looked around, and he said, "This is just like Australia." And felt immediate kinship with it. (Interview 1988)

An Australian, Bruce Beresford nevertheless sensed the need for rapport with the writer and a sense of place that he could use in the film. The careful selection of a director who will protect and realize the vision in Foote's writing has been the major reason Foote has worked primarily as an independent. Unlike Hollywood writers, who rarely have any power over the selection of director, Foote carefully guards his work by taking an active role throughout the process.

Likewise the casting of a Horton Foote film is not about packaging, bankability, or star power; actors are chosen for the ability to sustain a genuine and controlled performance. Foote gives the actor realistic and resonant lines which demand disciplined and subtle articulation. And because Foote is both sympathetic and unsentimental about his characters, the actors must respond without sentiment or condescension. Robert Duvall puts it this way:

> His literary voice is very special, very unique, one of the best in America, I think. I always said when I was younger, I said it was like sandpiper prints on a beach, very simple, very deep, like rural Chekhov. You know it's something that you can't push, you can't goose. You can't mess with

> it. You gotta let it happen. You gotta meet it halfway and
> let it bring you along because if you start to force it, then
> you're in trouble. It's true with any material, but espe-
> cially his. It's very delicate. (Interview)

Foote's aesthetic involves hiring actors who, like Robert Duvall, meet
the script "halfway and let it bring you along."

The dialogue Horton Foote gives these actors is meticulously
authentic, accurately depicting the play's region, but the words also
transcend mere dialect, often becoming poetic and revelatory. Foote's
characters are not uncomplicated people although they may speak in
rhythms and idioms that seem quaint and unsophisticated. In the
language one might hear at a farmers market can be profound issues,
often unrecognized by the characters themselves. When Mac Sledge
is coming out of the feed store in *Tender Mercies*, a woman asks, "Were
you really Mac Sledge?" Mac replies, "Yes, ma'am. I guess I was."
Although couched in the unself-conscious cadence and dialect of rural Texas, the theme of the movie is highlighted in this simple exchange: Mac's quest for identity and peace. Likewise when Carrie
Watts finally boards the bus to Bountiful, she says, "The Lord is just
with me today" and then wonders why the Lord isn't with her every
day. A rambling widow who talks mostly out of habit and nervous-
ness, Carrie, like the most sophisticated intellectual, still needs meaning and purpose in her life.

Performance is central to Horton Foote's film aesthetic. He trained
as an actor and began to write only as part of improvisational acting
exercises. As actor Matthew Broderick explains, Foote has a deep respect for the creativity an actor brings to his material:

> His writing is just from an actor's point of view, and pretty
> much any actor who's worked on his stuff, I think, feels
> it's beautifully written for acting. It's not just something
> that's nice to read, or "Look at that beautiful speech," or
> something. It all works beautifully between two people.
> You never have all that strange exposition that you some-
> times have with other stuff I do.... And it's lovely to do.
> It's elusive in a way. It's a subtle kind of work, but it's, uh,
> totally thrilling when it goes well, as an actor. (Interview)

Foote's writing gives the actor specific action and precise dialogue
while leaving room to invent. Gifted actors respond by playing up to
the level of the writing.

Foote was taught as an actor not to play emotion but to play a specific event or action and let it create the emotion. His writing and his films work the same way. Foote emphasizes the details of a character's idiosyncratic speech and behavior, leaving much of the thematic content in the subtext. The result is not an obvious, externalized drama; it challenges the audience to attend to his meticulously drawn re-creation of specific people in a particular place and time. The reward for patient attention to Foote's subtle language and resonant action is the creation of genuine emotion in the audience.

While there is no evidence that Foote consciously imitates the principles of neo-realist film, his aesthetic places his work much closer to the films of post-war Italy than mainstream Hollywood. Most obviously, like the neo-realists, the writer uses an ordinary person's struggle to reveal social problems. Foote's characters, while not the poorest of the poor, are ordinary people facing everyday conflicts that at first seem of little consequence to the greater world. The larger issues are implied in the details of everyday life, not an artificially exaggerated plot. In both neo-realism and Horton Foote's films, the seemingly normal relationships within a family or small town create a wider world in miniature. Implied in the very personal and particular conflicts are universal human emotions.

Also like the neo-realist films, Foote's work has little external dramatic action—apparently nothing happens. Mrs. Watts goes to Bountiful only to be found and brought back to that wretched apartment in Houston. Young Horace Robedaux does not get paid for the six months of labor he has done for Mr. Soll, nor does he get the tombstone for his father's grave. Mac Sledge does not regain his lost prominence in the country music world. However, the internal changes of each of these characters are monumental. Mrs. Watts fulfills her dream of going home, reconnects with her son, buries her dead past, and finds strength to go on. Horace learns to cope with the death of his father by experiencing the deaths of two convicts and Mr. Soll. Mac overcomes despair and learns to accept the graceful love of a wife and adopted son. These profound actions are all internal. The Italian neo-realists sought to heighten authenticity in their films by rejecting the artifice of studio production. Among the earliest filmmakers to value shooting on location, they also used non-professional actors to deepen the sense of reality. All of Foote's independent films have been shot on location in Texas, Louisiana, or Mississippi. Even *Baby, the Rain*

Must Fall with Steve McQueen was shot on location in his home town of Wharton, Texas. In *Tomorrow* Robert Duvall and Olga Bellin were supported by non-actors in the roles of the preacher, shopkeeper and jury members. Even in *Tender Mercies* Foote, Beresford, and Duvall chose Tess Harper, who had never acted in a feature film, to play Rosa Lee.

Location shooting and casting against star-typing are essential to realizing the third element in Horton Foote's film aesthetic—his relentless pursuit of authenticity. Like the neo-realists, Foote instinctively presents an image of the real place, time, and people he writes about. Although fictional, they are most often versions of actual events he knew or heard about as a boy growing up in Wharton, Texas. In the most literal sense, his writing preserves these events in a more organized and formal medium.

> I'm trying…to enforce on a body of material order, which, given its raw self would seem like chaos. And I think, mainly, that from the time I was that high I was surrounded by really first-rate storytellers. And they made myths and legends out of the history of my little town and my family and people who I'd never known. And so I was surfeited with those stories, and then of course my own observation began to take place and my own sense of what was happening.… I…never really know what is going to surface, but when I've found it, I know that instinctively my thrust is to bring a sense of form, a sense of order to that material. (Foote, Interview 1988)

While seeking the order of "myths and legends," Foote's stories record as faithfully as possible the details of actual events.

Horton Foote insures this authenticity throughout casting, rehearsing the performances, and establishing the *mise en scène*. On the set he oversees the process, though he seems oblivious to all the activity around him, often reading or writing until a rehearsal or take. Then he moves closer or listens in a headset to the dialogue. As soon as the director calls "Cut!" he usually goes back to his reading or writing, but if he perceives a violation of the authenticity of the work, he is quick to express concern. His relaxed vigilance does not intrude on the director or the actors, but it is a safeguard for his work. As Foote himself expressed on the set of *Convicts*,

> I just kind of keep an eye on things, you know. And so far
> I'm very approving of everything. Pete [Masterson] and I
> work the same way with actors.... Some writers don't want
> to be on the set. But when it is personal material as this is,
> I think it is essential for the writer to be there.[1] (Inter-
> view 1989)

The writer typically monitors but doesn't intrude on the set.

The fact that Foote, even while living in the East, has written almost exclusively about his hometown and its surroundings indicates the primacy of setting in his work. The landscape and culture of rural southeast Texas are not just the backdrops for his stories; in a way, they *are* his stories. His stories and themes grow out of the particular people and settings of his childhood:

> I have a suspicion that it's true, that without knowing it,
> your themes are established by the time you're eight or
> nine years old. And the rest of your life you are dealing
> with those themes...I go back South often, but I've not
> consistently lived there...since I was seventeen or eigh-
> teen, and yet I don't even question the fact that when I
> take up a piece of paper and a pen or pencil I know that I
> have begun to think about the South. Um, it isn't that
> I'm not fully aware of all the rich wonderful life around
> me here in the East or all over America. I just don't think
> in those terms. I don't hear those voices. (Foote, Inter-
> view 1988)

It is as impossible to imagine setting a Horton Foote story in a urban locale as it is to place *Mean Streets* or *Taxi Driver* in Dallas. And yet in Foote's hands these small places become microcosms of universal human concerns.

In order to maintain an authentic look for his fictional world, Horton Foote employs a relative stasis that gives his films a look strikingly different from that used in mainstream Hollywood productions. The cinematic art is more obvious when fluid camera movement and dynamic editing energize the visuals. But Foote's films, even in the hands of Joseph Anthony, Robert Mulligan, and Bruce Beresford, are presented in long, often static shots that let the action play out before the audience without making the camera an active participant. Since this inactivity was present in earliest motion pictures and is similar to the presentation of a play on a proscenium stage, critics often consider Foote's films as lacking cinematic sophistication. The fact that all his recent personal film work, except for *Tender Mercies*, was first a stage play may seem to support this argument.

But the relative stasis in Horton Footes's films is a specific cinematic choice designed to preserve the authentic look, in performance and texture, of Foote's literary writing. Andre Bazin in his influential essay on the virtues and limitations of montage indicated that a subtle sense of falseness is created by the use of cinematic technique rather than longer unedited takes. He found that master shots in *The Red Balloon* made the fantasy—that a boy is being followed by a red balloon—more believable whereas editing, as in *White Mane*, punctured the illusion (Bazin 43–49). Once the audience subconsciously realizes that the sequence of a boy being dragged by the horse in *White Mane* is an editing technique, not an actuality, they may experience less genuine emotion when the film cuts to a close-up. Worse yet, a cut or camera move may push powerful writing and the performance over the top. They could become distractions in a scene like Mac Sledge's "I don't trust happiness" speech which requires a delicate sense of the real and immediate.

Horton Foote's literary writing also requires a distinctive style of editing and visual presentation. Just as an action-adventure film calls for fast editing, camera gymnastics, and a high-energy score, a Horton Foote script needs time to do its delicate work. The richness of the dialogue and the subtlety of the narrative require more careful attention from the audience than is true of most Hollywood films. Picking up the pace in a Horton Foote film would not allow the audience the time to experience the emotional content. Similarly, the emphasis on performance is supported by master shots, with little camera movement. The stage-like construction allows the actors to play off one another as they would in theater. The width of the master also allows for gesturing with their whole bodies, not just their faces, as in a close-up. Through subdued editing and restricted camera movement, the image becomes transparent, drawing the audience into a life-like image.

Two excellent examples of the intentional choice of the unconventional wide shot occur in *Tender Mercies*. The first is when Mac Sledge, who has just denied remembering singing a hymn to his estranged daughter, turns his back to the camera and in long shot sings the song. Most filmmakers would certainly not have played the scene away from the camera and probably would have gone to close-up. But, if a more traditional presentation were chosen, the subtle rocking of Duvall's body to the beat of the song would be lost. The other scene is perhaps the most famous in the film: Mac is tilling a small plot of ground in the back of the house after his daughter's funeral. He leans on his shovel and says, "I don't trust happiness...I never have and I never will." By avoiding the obvious choice of a close up, the filmmakers ask the audience to focus on the words and the emotion of the whole scene, including Rosa Lee's powerful silence.

This focus on visual contexts requires an equally authentic presentation of locations. The familiarity of Foote's rural settings may at first seem passive, especially if compared to modern urban landscapes or futuristic visions in budget-driven Hollywood films. But, when given the proper visual treatment, the rural towns, flat sprawling fields, and open horizons lend themselves to a composition in depth which resists dynamic montage. Without the elegant *mise-en-scène* of a film like *Remains of the Day*, the depth of the shots may seem exaggerated, with little to draw one's eye toward the frame. But Foote's stories grow out of this landscape and the camera must keep them rooted there. In order to express Mac Sledge's impulse to grow and change, Bruce Beresford and Russell Boyd allowed the camera to dwell on the recently tilled farm field that lay behind the house in *Tender Mercies*. Depth made the field Mac's own. As this brief scene indicates, cinema is well suited to events which can be externalized. Often a wide variety of camera shots are edited together into a dynamic visual presentation of a scene. The action of the camera and editing reinforces the action in the scene. However, narrative fiction is finally not external; it is about the significant internal action of a person struggling with something and making a decision. Horton Foote's experience in theater as both an actor and a writer gives him the confidence to portray these internals through dialogue and specific, subtle external images and movements. In his cinematic style, opening up is not only unnecessary, it is distracting.

The fact that Foote's writing is so realistic and specific makes it less dependent on technical manipulation for its impact. Indeed, the cinematic artifice that would be perfectly valid in another context may well drive Foote's naturalistic writing over the top by exaggerating and sentimentalizing it. The internal dramatic action of Foote's films must be allowed time to do its quiet but persistent work on the audience. Thus the stasis and slow pacing of Foote's films is not merely the result of cinematic primitivism, theatrical origins, or tight budgets. It is rather an appropriate choice to preserve the films' literary voice, afford the actors the room to create, and enhance the feeling of authenticity of the films.

ⵦ

Note

1. Foote recalls an incident during the production of *The Chase* that serves as counterpoint to his pleasant experience with Peter Masterson on *Convicts*. Lillian Hellman, who was paid to write the screenplay, had left the project and Foote was asked to return to "do a little work":

    > the first day of shooting I went down on the set to check everything. He [the producer, Sam Spiegel] asked me to go and check it for authenticity, and there was an Indian squaw sitting in the drugstore. And I went running back, and I said, "Sam, my God! What's an Indian squaw doing in my town? I never saw an Indian!" He said, "What?" He got so excited, and he went running for the phone. He called.... So Sam tried to stop it, but he said, "Horton, it would cost me fifty thousand dollars to redo that scene." So I said, "Well, let her stay." So you now see that scene. There sits the Indian squaw with a papoose! (Foote, Interview 1988)

    While the audience may never be aware of the inconsistency of a Native American woman appearing in the scene, for Foote it is a violation of his basic aesthetic. Unlike "regional" filmmaking which provides only "local color," Foote's stories try to authentically re-create the region around his Wharton, Texas, home. He is true to that place.

Works Cited

Allen, Lewis. Interview. 17 February 1993.

Bazin, Andre. "The Virtues and Limitations of Montage." *What Is Cinema?: Essays Selected and Translated by Hugh Gray.* Berkeley: U of California P, 1971. 43–49.

Broderick, Matthew. Interview. 19 February 1993.

Duvall, Robert. Interview. 24 September 1992.

Foote, Horton. Interview. 9 August 1988.

———. Interview. 21 October 1989.

———, screenwriter. *Baby, the Rain Must Fall.* Dir. Robert Mulligan, Prod. Alan J. Pakula. With Steve McQueen and Lee Remick. Columbia Pictures, 1965.

———, screenwriter. *Convicts.* Dir. Peter Masterson. With Robert Duvall and James Earl Jones. MCEG-Sterling, 1990.

———, screenwriter. *1918.* Dir. Ken Harrison. Prod. Lewis Allen, Peter Newman, and Lillian Foote. With Matthew Broderick, William Converse-Roberts, and Hallie Foote. Guadalupe Entertainment and Cinecom, 1985.

———, screenwriter. *Tender Mercies.* Dir. Bruce Beresford. With Robert Duvall, Tess Harper, Betty Buckley, Ellen Barkin, Wilford Brimley. Antron Media/EMI Films, 1982.

———, screenwriter. *Tomorrow.* Dir. Joseph Anthony. Prod. Paul Roebling and Gilbert Pearlman. With Robert Duvall and Olga Bellin. Filmgroup Productions, 1972.

———, screenwriter. *The Trip to Bountiful.* Dir. Peter Masterson. Prod. Sterling VanWagenen. With Geraldine Page, John Heard, Carlin Glynn, Richard Bradford, and Rebecca DeMornay. Island Pictures, 1985.

Masterson, Peter. Interview. 20 October 1989.

Pakula, Alan J. Interview. 6 October 1990.

Penn, Arthur. Interview. 7 October 1990.

Sayles, John. *Thinking in Pictures: The Making of the Movie* Matewan. Boston: Houghton Mifflin, 1987.

Singing in the Face of Devastation
Texture in Horton Foote's Talking Pictures
Susan Underwood

During the final moments of an interview with Gerald Wood on March 18, 1990, later printed in *Post Script*, Horton Foote explained his particular treatment of realism, using an example from his screenplay for *The Trip to Bountiful*. When asked to clarify comments made in earlier interviews, in which he described his work as "textured," Foote responded:

> Well, I think texture is revealed in the specifics. For instance, in *Bountiful*—not the play but in the screenplay—when they're waiting on the bus to Corpus Christi and someone says, "Do you know what that means in Spanish? The body of Christ." Well, they'd never heard of that. And suddenly Mrs. Watts is intrigued with that, and she asks the Black woman if she knew that, and the Black woman says no, she did not know that. They ask a Spanish man, who can't even understand English, so he doesn't even know what the question is. I mean, that, to me is texture. It has nothing to do with the forward action of the thing, but it has to do with what enriches it. (12)

Echoing this explanation, in his article about Foote's film career, critic Gary Edgerton notes that Foote's "technique is important because it forgoes plot cliches for deeper resonances. Primary attention is forcefully shifted away from the more immediate, melodramatic potential...to scenes of reflection and understatement which suggest meanings well beyond the simple actions and words" (11).

Such attention to detail breathes the very life not only into Horton Foote's screenplays but his plays as well. Within the vibrant texture in this brief scene from *The Trip to Bountiful*, Horton Foote has instilled a crucial irony that is predominant in much of his work—that the most ordinary or familiar aspects of life, even those most portentous moments, may remain as elusive as a foreign tongue to the hard of hearing. Although the characters may not readily see what is plain yet sublime in their lives, Foote's exacting attention to texture conveys to his audience the clarity of meaning beneath the predominant dramatic action.

A similarly disguised but momentous drama enriches *Talking Pictures*, the first of the Horton Foote plays in the Signature Theatre Company series, produced in 1994. In this play, Foote's vision of the human experience, although expansive, is expressed with great subtlety; it is "understated" (Wood, Introduction xv). Foote himself has remarked that in his favorite poems and plays, "the effects are often arrived at through suggestion rather than statement" (DiGaetani 68). He marks his characters' dilemmas and joys with simple language, in an unassuming dialogue that reveals the oblique complexities of their inner lives.

In order to understand Foote's method, the viewer must look closely at repeated words and images and even whole songs and hymns, all of which coalesce and reverberate like a musical passage. The texture in *Talking Pictures* is literally composed. Foote has said that "music is a part of the texture of life, a part of the texture of the life I that I know anything about" (DiGaetani 68). Indeed, Reynolds Price has called Horton Foote "the supreme musician among our great American playwrights" (xi). Such resonance is revealed most often in the characters' most myopic observations, in moments during which the plot is stopped and attention is placed upon seemingly inconsequential dialogue. It is this attention to dialogue that grounds Horton Foote's central concern: the common man and woman facing with grace and resilience the vast unknown.

The physical drama of *Talking Pictures*, then, is not of principal importance; it is only a vehicle for the minutiae, the elements of the common life which convey Foote's ultimate purpose. The essentially unspoken drama of the play is found in such specific moments which reveal the characters' most crucial motivations, fears, and reactions. Nevertheless, these characters are usually unchanged by any revelation. Because it is through such intimate details that the audience glimpses the characters' simple curiosity, their yearnings, and their crises, with little transformation in their actual lives, *Talking Pictures* relies upon dramatic irony for expression of what Foote calls the "texture" of the play. No one seems moved much from his or her own small life. However, the tone at the close of the play is incredibly hopeful, for Foote presents his characters in the play's final moments balanced at the edge of discovery. They are set in a course that will go on, outward, continuing, despite the hazards and vagaries of life. Edgerton says of this aspect of Foote's "texture," "There is a psychic turbulence seething beneath the calm and restraint of Horton Foote's fictional world; his characters...must all face the pain of tragedy and disappointment by learning to accept life on its own terms, and move forward" (11–12). At the play's end the characters are set to move in a particular direction, toward the foundation of community, human compassion, and, principally, toward assurance in the need and ability of humanity to go on despite the chaos of the world; this is the only real hope in Horton Foote's vision.

The result is a delicate balance between comedy and tragedy. Tragic circumstances in *Talking Pictures* are often conveyed in humorous terms, and the final scene, freighted with loss and the prevailing unknown, offers both serenity and hope. Although the comic elements of the play should not distract from the sobering realities of the characters' lives, it would be easy for a director to view Horton Foote's *Talking Pictures* through the distorted lens of high comedy, to interpret the play as farce or social satire. It would be tempting to portray in easy patronizing humor the simple notions and complicated lives of the characters to exploit the tension between their morality, their religious beliefs and the encroaching secular world.

However, Carol Goodheart's fall 1994 production of *Talking Pictures* finely balanced the serious implications of even the most humorous moments. Played with pathos, the script maintains the integrity of its dramatic undertones and the serious universal themes. Thus, Foote's comic moment is made poignant by the force of its own sobering resonance, and the "texture" of the play is strengthened by the blending of the dark moment with the light. Standing seemingly quite apart from the structure, plot, and significant serious themes, the comic moment actually suggests the most serious motivations of the play, probing the deeper lives of the characters and suggesting their capacity for discovering stability by creating human connections. This production of *Talking Pictures* not only revealed but reveled in Horton Foote's talent for dwelling upon the textures of life, the nuances, the shades, the little things which time and modernity have let escape us. Foote conveys the visceral moment, felt as well as seen, with a language simple and precise and evocative. This experience may be deceptively humorous, yet within it lies the consequence and power, however still and quiet, of Horton Foote's larger thematic concerns: family, endurance of the human spirit, romantic love, the tragic past, and faith and resilience, despite the inexorably tragic future.

The issue of faith, the predominance of affirmation, is certainly one consequence of the sanguine tone of the play's texture. The old saying "God is in the details" is made incarnate in Horton Foote's *Talking Pictures*. The characters' daily experiences are imbued with a sense of the religious; their conversations often resound with unself-conscious spiritual questioning, which is inextricable from their private turmoil. However, Foote's use of religious matter is neither simplistic nor didactic. He merely shows that spirituality is one of many common, everyday elements in the characters' lives, and thus it becomes a matter of texture, of detail. As Fred Chappell asserts, the characters' need for human connection is distilled in their religious querying:

> There is no defense but there are some momentary stays against confusion. While the community exists, it is possible and comforting to take a place in it. Religion offers no final answers for Foote's stricken searchers, no final security, but it does give a steady solace, some of which is social in nature. The best attitude to take seems that of Mac Sledge in *Tender Mercies*, whose quizzical Christian stoicism puts more than a measure of faith in human relationships and none at all in worldly circumstance. (36)

Chappell's example from Foote's screenplay is certainly reminiscent of the textural implications present in *Talking Pictures*. The characters' conceptions of faith—their active yet actively questioned beliefs—reveal their search for stability and sustenance, their need for strength beyond themselves, their desire for a centered life within family and community.

Within this tension between the search for solace and the chaos of the world lies the central drama of the play. For all its seeming narrowness and simplicity, the world of *Talking Pictures* is a place of upheaval, personal turmoil, and doubt. It is a chaotic world on the brink of becoming, like the lost town in *The Trip to Bountiful*, a world of the past, a world flung apart by the forces of modern society. However, even the precariousness is not pure. Although his characters suffer and face the unknown, they are also resilient, unwittingly steadfast; a transcendent atmosphere veils all their sorrows. This is the crucial paradox noted by Gary Edgerton: "Foote's impassioned desire to affirm and celebrate life is ever-present, even as the characters of Harrison struggle and generally fail to understand why misfortune and calamities happen" (12).

The setting of the play is that of many of Foote's screenplays and stage productions, the small Texas town of Harrison, whose sole movie theater, the Queen, is one of the last holdouts in the state against the technological advance of the talking picture. Only by moving from town to town has Myra Tolliver, one of the play's central characters, been able to continue supporting herself and her fourteen-year-old son, Pete, by playing the piano at the silent movies. Although she has been able to find enough work to provide basic needs, she is burdened by the knowledge that "they may stop making silent pictures altogether" (181). However, the encroaching modern world has already impacted Myra's life. At a time and place where a woman's personal needs are subordinate to those of the family, Myra is divorced although her husband was neither abusive, nor unfaithful, nor a drunkard. She tells Willis, her suitor, who is similarly situated, having separated from his wife due to her infidelity, that they "just outgrew each other" (190), certainly a very modern notion. It is perhaps most telling of their precarious position that Myra and Pete have no home of their own; they are boarders in a single room in the Jackson household. The mother and son relationship is also being challenged because of this lack of a stable home. Pete wishes to go and live with his father, who has a new wife and sons and a swimming pool in Houston.

In an echo of such flux and instability, Mr. Jackson has his own working worries. A railroad engineer, he is about to be "bumped," a term used to describe his replacement on the train from Harrison by someone with greater seniority from another city. The Jackson family realizes that this problem signals yet another in a long line of moves as Mr. Jackson, in turn, bumps someone in the nearby town of Cuero. The uncertainty of this single situation is overshadowed by several conversations concerning the serious possibility that buses will soon take the place of trains altogether. Mrs. Jackson asks, "What'll happen to the trains if everybody starts riding the bus?...one day we could wake up and find there are no trains at all" (198). Her question foreshadows circumstances beyond the setting of the play, texturizing the immediate drama with the audience's sense of the fragility of these seemingly simple times.

This difference in historical perspective between characters and observers is the basis of the dramatic irony which resonates throughout *Talking Pictures*. The audience, which knows the certain extinction of silent films, the near-obsolescence of passenger trains, the desolation of small towns, is aware of the immediate significance of the play's time frame. The characters who are immersed in the summer heat and chaos and all those insecurities of family, home, and job are also ironically caught up in a time much more carefree and easy than the time to come. These are the final innocent moments before economic darkness, cultural collapse, and extreme personal hardship. It is the summer of 1929. The characters are on the verge of the Great Depression.

To strive for equilibrium in such a world, the characters maintain an individual spirituality, a resilience based sometimes in orthodox religion but grounded more specifically and vitally in the communion of family, in the knowledge of the past, in the power of human resilience in the face of mutability. Although the apparent embodiment of strength, Myra Tolliver is searching for relief from her exile and solitude; she needs stability and peace. Her faith is necessarily practical. While like the Jackson family she is a Methodist, she tells Willis, himself a Baptist and worried about their differences, that she doesn't "care about that at all" (193). She does not openly discuss her beliefs, but it is obvious that she has gone through great spiritual suffering, in large part due to the repercussions from her divorce, including rejection by her father. She tells Willis: "My daddy said if I left [my husband] he'd never speak to me again and he didn't until the day he died and then he just barely nodded to me when I went into his room" (190). This brief detail, though concerning neither plot nor theme, is crucial to our understanding of Myra's motivations, her loss and her search, a part of the texture of her character.

So too are her revelations to Willis concerning her mother. Remembering her mother's dream to travel, she wistfully tells Willis that "she never got out of Nacogdoches." Soon after he asks her mother's name; she responds that it was Corinne, she tells Willis, adding, "like Corinne Griffith, the movie star. My mama died when I was sixteen" (211). Such an abrupt juxtaposition of painful truth with movie trivia is typical in Myra's conversations. As in many other instances, Myra's constant indulgence in the imaginary world of the picture show slips into her discussions of real life. She unburdens the hard realities of her world with talk of not only movie plots but also the troubled lives of movie stars. She finds within the darkened theater a sorrow deeper than her own and, too, a commiseration, an assurance that she is not alone.

However, in reality, Myra is an orphan, without a husband, tremulous about her future. The words "lonely" and "lonesome" become emblems of Myra's character as she sings songs from the movies about loneliness. One song she has learned is from the soundtrack to the movie *The Singing Fool.* The character of the grieving father sings after his little boy's death:

> Friends may forsake us/Let them all forsake us/I still have you, Sonny Boy./You came from heaven/and I know your worth,/You made a heaven for me right here on earth./ But the angels they got lonely/And they took you because they were lonely/Now I'm lonely too, Sonny Boy. (182)

Her sweet rendition of this song from the Al Jolson film is made more poignant by the fact that Pete has become frustrated and scared about the precarious lifestyle they lead. He wishes to go and live with his father in Houston. Though he does eventually decide to remain with her, Myra struggles for a time with the dilemma of her own impending aloneness. She admits to Willis that her primary reason for leaving her husband Gerard was that she was "lonesome." Moved by her confession, Willis in turn admits his own loneliness.

In the play's most romantic scenes, it is obvious these two characters, though not in love, need companionship; they crave human understanding and hope to discover it within each other. When they continually discuss the heat in their rooms at night, the erotic implications are overshadowed by the realities of their lives. Layers of dialogue emphasize their connection, and the texture of details expands the sense of close yearning. Willis tentatively confesses his concern for Myra, hinting that he likes her son, that he doesn't drink, and that his job is secure, at present. He tells her, in the play's most moving moment, that he has told his boss he is making "personal plans," and he continues, "I don't know what you think about me exactly, but I think you're a mighty fine person" (192). In the subtle current

between them, these two search for a shimmering hope against loneliness.

Katie Bell Jackson, the sixteen-year-old Jackson daughter, is herself searching for her place in the world as she outgrows her family,
the rote rules of religion, and the confines of small town life. She is
the central character in Foote's subtext, guiding the other characters
and the audience to question the here-and-now, to consider "what if"
and "why." While comic to the audience, her naive questions are un-
nerving to the other characters. Myra in particular is a great curiosity
to Katie Bell, whose preacher, Brother Meyers, has warned against
the sin of frequenting the movie theater. Katie Bell quizzes Willis:
"Do you think people that attend picture shows are going to Hell?...
Brother Meyers says if they go on weekdays they are liable to go and
if they go on Sundays they are bound to. I certainly don't think Myra
is going to Hell, do you?" (186). It is apparent that Katie Bell's questions are quite rhetorical and reveal that she is beginning to trust her
own heart above the narrow interpretations of organized religion. On
a deeper level, her speculations explore her need to have reinforced
her nascent compassions, which do not square with conservative apho-
risms. Even her mother cautions her, concerning their pastor, Brother
Meyers, "He's a good man, but extreme in his views" (187). Katie Bell
continues to be intrigued by the didacticisms of a higher authority,
but she is drawn by the example of her family to trust an inner voice
that tells her to look further, ask, search.

This is evidenced in other conversations in the play but nowhere
more tellingly than in the subtle strains of a discussion between Myra
and Katie Bell and her older sister, Vesta, about *The Singing Fool.*
With Myra's help, Katie Bell retells the plot:

> I remember there was this man and he was a famous singer
> and he was married. Right?... And they had a little boy
> and he loved his little boy very much, but then he and his
> wife were separated and one night when he was to sing
> his little boy got sick and died. But he had to go on stage
> and sing anyway, even though his heart was breaking....
> Miss Myra said everybody in the picture show was cry-
> ing. (181–82)

Immediately after Katie Bell reels off her story, Vesta is reminded of a
story she has heard in church. The pointed juxtaposition of these two

stories, one from a secular and the other from a religious source, reveals yet another layer of detail to enrich the whole. Vesta attempts to retell the story of a "poor widow who had no money and no job...she had starving children and everything" (182–83). Here Vesta interrupts herself to reiterate to Katie that the woman has no husband. She defines her world, as does Katie Bell, in tactless yet innocent terms. She explains in front of Myra: "If you're a widow, your husband is dead. And if you're a grass widow your husband is alive and you're divorced. Myra is a grass widow" (182). This immediate comparison heightens the sense of Myra's situation as a single mother in precarious circumstances. It also reveals that although captivated by and insightful of the many fictions around them, the two girls do not understand fully the drama happening under their own roof.

Vesta continues, but once more Katie Bell interrupts. She leaps ahead to what becomes for the audience the punchline; however, in the comic moment, a hard truth is revealed. She says: "I know what happened. She prayed to God and he saved them" (183). Vesta asks, "How did you know that?" To which Katie Bell responds innocently: "Because that's what always happens when Brother Meyers tells a story" (183). Surprisingly, Vesta makes no defense of Brother Meyers but immediately turns to Myra and asks once more about the *Singing Fool.* Obviously Katie Bell and Vesta are both more moved by the humanity of this story, can comprehend more readily the universal implications of the perseverance of the human spirit, which attempts to lift itself alone out of darkness and sorrow. Their curiosity and sympathy are piqued by such resilience and by the haunting image of human suffering. While the two girls reveal their capacity for empathy and mistrust of an easy answer or the idea of an absolutely benevolent god, the irony remains that they seem unable to practice such compassion within their real lives.

Still, the Jackson family members, in particular the mother, are quite sensitive to much of Myra's dilemma, though they do not communicate this concern to her. Katie Bell is especially inquisitive about the lives of others; she is the one who introduces them to a Mexican boy she has met in town, much to the dismay of Vesta. This young boy, Estaquio, acts as perhaps the greatest catalyst in the play. He has travelled with his father to establish a Mexican Baptist church, and he arrives at the Jackson household reveling in his zealous faith. He appears at first overbearing, spouting prayers and reciting Bible verses, singing hymns—all in Spanish—to the cautious delight of Mrs. Jackson. When he asks Katie Bell to visit him in Mexico, she says that it is too far and that she doesn't comprehend the language. However, in reality, Mexico does not lie so far from Harrison, only across the Texas border, and as Katie Bell soon sees, the language is a crucible, holding what is already familiar. Estaquio's world brought close, his uniquely familiar rhetoric delivered in a foreign tongue, provides a foil for the lives of the other characters, who reel in the face of even the simplest new experience.

Estaquio's zeal is understandable given the specifics of his own tumultuous life. He tells Katie Bell:

> The devil got hold of my Mama, you know.... My Papa prayed and prayed but he won out. She ran off and left Papa and me. She hated Church. Hated the Bible. Hated hymns. Hated Jesus.... We saw her on the street one day in Mexico City, but when we went up to her she said she didn't even know who we were. (196)

Estaquio's faith is ironic; what drove his mother away is what stays him from despair, his own defense against personal loss. His faith has been bought at the greatest sacrifice, the rhetoric he uses to sustain his strength being particularly telling. He recites, "Jehova es mi salvador, nada me faltara.... The Lord is my Shepherd. I shall not want." He sings, "Roca de la eternidad...Rock of Ages" (197). Both the verse from Psalms and the Christian hymn "Rock of Ages" are standard fare at times of grief or mourning. Repeating them reminds Estaquio to look beyond the moment of anguish. He seeks reaffirmation and comfort; despite his ecstatic devotion, he yearns toward hope against uncertainty. Estaquio's sincerity and his hard-won belief intrigue Mrs. Jackson and Katie Bell, both sheltered from what is even remotely different from themselves. Estaquio brings Mrs. Jackson a Spanish-language Bible, which amazes her. If she has any prejudice similar to her husband's, it is overwhelmed by her curiosity at hearing familiar Christian doctrines repeated in a foreign tongue. She asks Estaquio to sing more in Spanish and to read from the Bible. He reads the "first few verses of Genesis":

> In the beginning God created the heaven and the earth.
> En el principio creo Dios los cielos y la tierra.
> And the earth was without form and void.

> Y la tierra estaba desordenada y vacia.
> And darkness was upon the face of the deep.
> Y las tinieblas estaban sobre la faz del abismo.
> And the spirit of God moved upon the face of the waters.
> Y [el] Espiritu de Dios se movia sobre la faz de las aguas.
> (205)

Mrs. Jackson repeats, in the form of a question, "Spirit of God?" as if she had never before attended to the verse. Immediately she asks Estaquio to sing "Blessed Assurance," the full implication of the title resounding from the middle of the play to the end. Assurance in a world of dynamic transitions and uncertainty is perhaps the most precious commodity. It is certainly at the heart of the characters' search and the most important unnamed element in the play's design.

Songs and verses create much of the meaning within the texture of *Talking Pictures* as they appear variously in the play, from beginning to end. In the final scene, for example, when Estaquio's father must abandon his mission to establish a Mexican Baptist church, the song "Rock of Ages" suggests the need for order in the face of change. Katie Bell and her family are set to move to Cuero. However, all is calm in the moment, as she sits with Myra and Willis on the front porch. They are "lost in their own thoughts" (224), having decided to marry. Katie Bell announces her dream, "I bet I get to Mexico one day" (224). When Katie Bell practices singing "Rock of Ages" in Spanish at the conclusion of the play, some in the audience will view her as a "singing fool." But she is not merely seeking faith in the unspeakable divine; she is pressing toward assurance against uncertainty, toward support, which she finds in the complex architecture of the human community, human ritual, and human love.

Reynolds Price writes of Horton Foote's film *1918* that the "players…achieve a final effect of genuinely transcendent volume" (xii) in the resonant rhythms. The same could be said of the characters in *Talking Pictures*. The texture resonates through their common and intimate conversation like a single sustained musical note. Between turbulence and chaos, and through dramatic irony, Foote creates a subtle, muted tone, conveyed in profoundly shaded voices, which serves as a mainstay against the prescience of calamity. But that prescience manifests itself in a naive and noble stoicism. Of suffering and resilience in life and of his opportunity to speak to humanity, Horton Foote says, "I think…that there's dignity in everyone. Certainly everybody is striving.... And if they're defeated, as many people are, that's moving, too" (Broughton 5). The power of music within the texture reveals a movement toward humanity and compassion which Foote asks the audience to share. Reynolds Price's comments on *1918* also explain the power of Katie Bell's singing to reveal our vulnerability and our potential. He writes of Foote's "bare lines":

> [T]here pours finally a joyful and unanswerably powerful psalm of praise: Suffering (to the point of devastation) is the central human condition and our most unavoidable mystery. Yet we can survive it and sing in its face. (xii)

☙

Works Cited

Broughton, Irv. "Horton Foote." *The Writer's Mind: Interviews*. Ed. Irv Broughton. Vol. 2. Fayetteville: U of Arkansas P, 1990. 5–23.

Chappell, Fred. "Understand Me Completely." *Chronicles* 13.11 (November 1989): 35–37.

DiGaetani, John L. "Horton Foote." *A Search for a Postmodern Theater: Interviews with Contemporary Playwrights*. Westport, CT: Greenwood Press, 1991. 65–71.

Edgerton, Gary. "A Visit to the Imaginary Landscape of Harrison, Texas: Sketching the Film Career of Horton Foote." *Literature/Film Quarterly* 17.1 (1989): 2–12.

Foote, Horton. *Talking Pictures. Horton Foote: Four New Plays*. Intro. Jerry Tallmer. Newbury, VT: Smith and Kraus, 1993. 175–224.

Price, Reynolds. Introduction. *Courtship, Valentine's Day, 1918: Three Plays for The Orphans' Home Cycle*. New York: Grove, 1987. ix–xiii.

Wood, Gerald C. "Horton Foote: An Interview." *Post Script* 10.3 (Summer 1991): 3–12.

———. Introduction. *Selected One-Act Plays of Horton Foote*. Ed. Gerald C. Wood. Dallas: Southern Methodist UP, 1989. xiii–xxii.

Boundaries, the Female Will, and Individuation in *Night Seasons*
Gerald C. Wood

Horton Foote has always had high regard for women. He was raised by a loving and attentive mother. And as a boy he was the center of attention in an extended family which included grandmothers and aunts who loved to tell him stories. Later, in his late twenties, he met Lillian Vallish at a bookstore in New York City and within a few months they were married. Just as the writer's father believed marriage brought peace to his life, Horton centered his adult emotions on Lillian and their family. His long, happy, and successful marriage, which produced four children, has been a delight for the writer. Throughout his life, women—from his mother to his two daughters—have brought him joy, intimacy, and direction; as he once told me, "I give enormous credit to women for everything" (Interview).

Such sympathy and adoration would be of little interest to interpreters of Horton Foote's work if women didn't play important roles in his work for theater, television, and film. But they do. Foote creates a variety of female characters—lost and focused, sad and happy, weak and strong—the most interesting of whom express significant life issues for twentieth-century females. Without a conscious political agenda, Horton Foote is careful to point out that women pay a price for traditional roles in the patriarchy. He studies the social and psychological barriers keeping women from courage and freedom, his central human values.

These are the issues in, for example, *The Tears of My Sister*, first aired on television for Gulf Playhouse, August 14, 1953. The play was the second of two experiments with point of view (the first was *The Death of the Old Man*, telecast on July 17 of the same year), or camera eye, that Horton Foote wrote for producer Fred Coe; like *Old Man*, *Tears* was directed by Arthur Penn. Throughout *The Tears of My Sister* the camera assumes the position of Cecilia Monroe, who is anticipating the marriage of her older sister, Bessie. Although Cecilia

fights the loss of her innocence, during the play she is slowly introduced to the reasons for Bessie's repeated tearful episodes. After the
death of their father, the older sibling feels the pressure to marry a
wealthy man, not the man she loves. She slides toward this conclusion, the play explains, because of the emotional and financial poverty that accompanies the loss of Mr. Monroe. The women—the two
girls and their mother—have become dependent on men, feeling
powerless to make choices and change their lives. Worse than this
impotence is the inauthenticity they feel as the objects of male fantasies. As Cecilia explains,

> Mama says men understand not a thing about the sor-
> rows of women. She says it just scares them. She says all
> men want women to be regular doll babies all the time.
> Happy and good-natured and with no troubles. (*Selected
> One-Acts* 161)

Unable to share these dark feelings of confusion and powerlessness
with men, the women are condemned to an artificial, child-like state.
In Horton Foote's theater, such inauthenticity is horrific.

   The Tears of My Sister is remarkable because, written in 1953, it
examines marriage as a dehumanizing business transaction. It demonstrates that since women are not trained either psychologically or
professionally to assume powerful roles in the public world, they are
rudderless when the protection of men is withdrawn, as the Monroes
are when the father dies. Worse yet, they collaborate in an auction of
their affections and allegiances to men of means. Left to their own
financial and emotional resources, the women are forced to betray
their own wills. And from Horton Foote's point of view, they are left
without the freedom to choose and act freely, to become themselves.
Though they blind themselves to the real causes, the Monroes cry
because they can never become individuals; they are always the objects of the men who can offer them a shallow form of safety.

   Just as debilitating are the social expectations which make identity so difficult for women. In *Blind Date*, another one-act play (produced at The Loft Studio in Los Angeles in 1982), the main character
is Sarah Nancy, a young woman who rebels against the traditional
expectations for women. As she prepares for a date, her aunt Dolores
reminds her that girls need to be "peppy" and "gracious" at all times
(*Selected One-Acts* 369). But Sarah Nancy ignores the advice and the

mystique of Dolores, deciding instead to use her sarcasm on her blind date, Felix Robertson. When he tries to sing, Sarah declares, "If you can sing, a screech owl can sing...I'd rather listen to a jackass bray than you sing. You look like a warthog and you bray like a jackass" (*Selected One-Acts* 386). Significantly, Felix accepts this honesty, the subsequent leveling between the two young people becoming the basis of their growing friendship. Only in genuine emotion, even if that includes destroying old roles for women, can females find themselves. Without these changes, little identity—and no intimacy—can be realized, according to Foote's play.[1]

There is an alternative, and hope, in Horton Foote's imaginative world. His norm is found in the story, based on his mother, of Elizabeth Vaughn in *Courtship*, the fifth play of the nine-play cycle *The Orphans' Home*. Her father, Henry Vaughn, carries the weight of the patriarchy; he is the wealthiest man in town, all the women in the family look to him for guidance, and he believes his girls can find all necessary security from him. And Elizabeth's last infatuation was not a wise one; she was saved from unhappiness, as her father well knows, by Henry's intervention. Despite the burdens of her father and history, Elizabeth has fallen in love with Horace Robedaux, an orphan who has a reputation for wildness. While death and sexual intrigue fill the streets of Harrison, Elizabeth finally decides to marry Horace, if he asks her, even if the lovers have to elope.

In the context of the times, this a most courageous act for a young woman. The implied sexuality is dangerous, previous affections have been betrayed and lost, her father and mother have previously given correct advice, and her sister fills the night air with fear verging on hysteria. Especially in the conversations with Laura, the sister, all the risks are outlined; pregnancy, insanity, suicide, alienation, death are all most real possibilities. And yet Elizabeth decides to trust her feelings and judgment in order to marry Horace. Although *The Orphans' Home Cycle* focuses on the power of the marriage of Elizabeth and Horace, *Courtship* is about a single woman's courage and power to choose. It is not a sentimental, or even romantic, tale in the traditional sense; it celebrates marriage less as an institution than an act of self-definition and assertion. By marrying Horace, Elizabeth risks everything for a life decision; she becomes a person.

Between the two poles of female identity—*The Tears of My Sister* and *Courtship*—lies *Night Seasons*, the second in the Signature Season of Horton Foote plays. Employing a sweep of time and history unusual in a Foote play, *Night Seasons* is an impressionistic play covering 1917–1963 in the lives of the Weems family in Harrison, Texas. It has a complicated plot involving alcoholism, unhappy marriage, suicide, and lost loves. While it moves back and forth in time and among many characters, it focuses on Laura Lee Weems, the daughter, who during the play entertains both a beau, Mr. Barsoty, and a fiancé, Mr. Chestnut, but she never marries. Laura Lee's explanation is that her mother controlled her life; as Josie, the mother, describes it, "Laura Lee always accused me of interfering in her life" (*Four New Plays* 68). And Josie does interfere. Throughout the play the Weemses live in rented rooms because Josie decided to leave their home and refuses to return (72–73). When the mother feels that Chestnut, a baker, is beneath her daughter, Josie asks the father and brother to offer Mr. Chestnut a position at the bank (71–72).

But the focus of the play is not parental abuse; it is how Josie, Laura Lee, and the other Weemses conspire to sabotage the daughter's commitment to men outside the family. As Laura Lee explains to her father, Josie approved of Mr. Barsoty "because she knew I didn't want to marry him" (74). But even when Laura Lee feels genuine desire, as with Chestnut, she is poisoned by the fear she will end in a loveless marriage like her brother Thurman. Laura Lee is one of the casualties implied when Skeeter, Laura Lee's young brother, tells Dolly, a cousin, that Thurman and his wife Delia won't kill each other: "They'll kill everybody else first" (80). Even her father, who saves money for Laura Lee's independence, undercuts her resolve by worrying Chestnut is a "fortune hunter" (74).

Finally, in *Night Seasons,* as in all Horton Foote's plays, each person is responsible for his or her own life; Laura Lee is not an innocent victim. Though she knows her parents didn't have her "best interest at heart" (85), she is the one unable to act. When Chestnut asks her to join him in Houston, where he is to acquire the training demanded by her brothers and father, Laura's real self is revealed: "I have to think...You go on to Houston. I need time to think" (83). She can only steal time, not redeem it. The result is a paralysis of will suggested in the many references to Laura's dying intestate; she has "no will" (78), "didn't have a will" (80), "didn't leave a will" (99–100). Stuck to her mother by perverse anger and confusion, Laura Lee can neither decide nor act.[2]

The symbols for Laura Lee's inability to be herself in *Night Seasons* are the houses she desires but never gains. One is the Reeves house, possibly a reference to the one owned by parents of Bubber Reeves in Foote's much-earlier story *The Chase*. But brother Thurman sabotages that deal by purchasing the house for one of his customers, explaining that it is too run down and expensive for Laura Lee. After the death of Mr. Weems, Josie uses grief as an excuse for not discussing houses. When Laura Lee protests, Thurman frightens her with the story of "Miss Nanie Stanfield," who "tried to live by herself and then a man started peeking in her window and she had to give up and go live at the hotel" (107). One more time, after Laura Lee agrees to live with her mother, Thurman again delays, this time taking a year for a title search, until the war intervenes. Finally, when Josie is 83 and Laura Lee 60, Josie says there is no reason for two old ladies to own a house.

As these references to houses accumulate in *Night Seasons*, it becomes clear that the pattern is not literal. Laura Lee's desire for "my own house" (98) is an expression of her need for boundaries between herself and others. Unable to establish a sense of her own identity, Laura slides into the lives of those around her. Better at taking care of others than herself, she tells her cousin Dolly, "I want to help [Lawrence] in anyway I can," though he commits suicide anyway (89). Near the end of the play, she offers Barsoty money to start a trucking business, but when he announces his engagement, she once again retreats into the family, saying "I'm sorry. Forgive me. I just thought of father...if anything should happen to him. I don't know what I'd do. I'd be very lost without father" (104–5). When asked about her ex-beau, she devalues any connection outside the family, claiming "I don't think he [Barsoty] came here to see me in the first place. I think he came here hoping to borrow money" (106). Having no house—no autonomous identity—Laura Lee becomes fused with her family and part of everything around her.

Because of her inability to act and thus define her own destiny, Laura becomes, unwittingly, a diversion for the bored gossips of Harrison. Like a chorus, they return time and again to "pretty and popular" Laura Lee and her "many beaux" (81). As caring and nurturant as she is, Laura becomes a performer in the continuing drama acted out for the citizens of the town. At the heart of her story, the citizens of Harrison believe, is her comic and sometimes frustrating inability to decide. Delia tells the story well known in town:

> Merchants hate to see her come into the store. She drives them crazy. She wants to see everything in the store, before she makes up her mind what to buy and then when she finally decides on something and brings it home, she always brings it back the next day to exchange it for something else. (108)

Laura Lee, the woman without a house or a will of her own, drifts from one conflict to another, hoping someone's need will temporarily rescue her from her paralysis.

While Foote writes of such issues instinctively, never resorting to psychological theory, in *Night Seasons* he dramatizes realities described most provocatively in recent feminist developmental psychology.[3] Nancy Chodorow, for example, challenges the Freudian assumptions concerning the ways children begin to establish their sexual identity. She assumes, as does Sigmund Freud, the existence of paradigms by which males and females in middle-class Western culture tend to experience the world. Chodorow agrees with Freud's description of the Oedipal situation initiated when young boys perceive they are different from their primary caretakers, their mothers. Although this break often is felt as troubling, even precipitous, the masculine child typically shifts his identification—and his primary emotional dependence—from his mother to his father. Once he completes the Oedipal phase, the boy can look back on his mother with a new, and empowering, sense of distance and identity. He is driven toward autonomy. Sigmund Freud and Nancy Chodorow agree that this Oedipal pattern explains the male drive for independence and anxiety over intimacy.

But Chodorow then argues that Freud failed to understand the essential developmental difference between male and female children. Believing the male experience the normative one, Freud imagined girls are condemned to feel loss and emptiness because they have no penis and are not allowed to have their father's child. Actually, as Chodorow explains, the female child—in typical middle-class culture—is strengthened by her primitive pre-Oedipal attachment to her mother, experienced as a version of the child's self. In a healthy case, rather than feeling a biological and psychological inferiority, the young female imagines a prolonged and secure fusion with the breast and maternal figure. And this connection, unlike the boy's, requires no radical separation. If she grows emotionally, the girl will later shift her affections first to the father and then to other men. But her female experience doesn't require the severing and replacing that characterizes the growth of males. As Nancy Chodorow and others theorize, this prolonged attachment to the mother leads women toward more relational, less isolated lives.

The consequences of these different paradigms are most predictive and instructive for gender identity and relations. Males are motivated from an early age to actively pursue separation, especially from patterns which are reminiscent of the mother and the feminine. But until maturity they tend to deny dependence, carry hostility toward the mother (often imagined as rejecting or abandoning), and have little interest in intimacy and nurturing—characteristics associated with the lost mother. Females, on the other hand, quickly learn intimacy skills and empathetic responses. Unlike the males, their task in maturity focuses on clarifying a sense of self, especially in relation to love objects:

> Girls who grow up in family setting which include neither other women besides their mother nor an actively present father tend to have problems establishing a sufficiently individuated and autonomous sense of self. (Chodorow, *Reproduction* 212)

Carol Gilligan takes Chodorow's work to its logical conclusion by describing the residual tasks facing the sexes in achieving an integrated and mature sensibility. Men most obviously need to return to the symbolic mother, recognizing in the process their connections and dependency. They need to work more creatively with others, become more nurturant, and finally sacrifice themselves to the natural processes. But women share a dark side which, though different, is as powerful as men's. Since adult women don't—and shouldn't—sever the identification with the primary caregiver, they tend to have problems associated with their more flexible ego boundaries. Gilligan warns that

> development for girls in adolescence hinges not only on their willingness to risk disagreement with others but also on the courage to challenge two equations: the equation of human with male and the equation of care with self-

> sacrifice. Together these equations create a self-perpetu-
> ating system that sustains a limited conception of human
> development and a problematic representation of human
> relationships. (Gilligan, "Exit-Voice Dilemmas" 155)

The stumbling block for women is caretaking which sacrifices the
self, usually driven by the need to sidestep conflict and choices which
hurt others. When these object-relation problems become extreme,
pathologies—especially in the form of masochism and lack of identity—develop.

While most helpful to understanding Laura Lee in *Night Seasons*,
these feminist paradigms need to be qualified in one way: Horton
Foote's vision is derived from, but doesn't stop with, human relations.
A Christian Scientist, the writer subtly informs his stories with a religious sensitivity which is a step beyond clinical description. In addition to being a keen observer of human behavior, Foote imagines a
radically loving God—both masculine and feminine, as best man can
understand—who should be credited for all good things. According
to Mary Baker Eddy, the founder of Christian Science, artists, for
example, should have no ego about creativity, which is a gift from
and an expression of God (*Science and Health* 263). And yet all
people—women equal to men—are also asked by God to endlessly
pursue their own sense of self. The Divine Spirit in the universe wants,
Eddy says, full personhood for all people; the creation of individuation is a primary goal of God-inspired living:

> The one Ego, the one Mind or Spirit called God, is infinite
> individuality, which supplies all form and comeliness and
> which reflects reality and divinity in individual spiritual
> man and things…. The divine Ego, or individuality, is
> reflected in all spiritual individuality from the infinitesimal
> to the infinite. (*Science and Health* 281, 336)

In Christian Science all goodness comes from God; nevertheless,
"genuine selfhood," "identity and individuality" are the rewards of
pursuing "the Christ ideal" (Gottschalk 59; "Who Is God?" 68).

Thus Horton Foote's examination in *Night Seasons* of psychological issues like female will and identity needs to be placed in the
context of his implicit religious call for loving attachments. His imaginative landscape is peopled with men and women who fail to connect
with others. And, Foote argues, it is only through identification with

loved ones, a place, or a religious tradition, for example, that peace and a sense of self are knowable. His women are especially loving because they are not obsessed with a rigid individualism which continually distances his men from the living world around them. In most of his writing, Foote is calling for more empathy, compassion, and selfless understanding—defined as female and spiritual values. But he is a dialectical writer, always studying both sides of the issues he raises. And so in *Night Seasons* he focuses on failed intention and autonomy in women, a dark variation on his study of intimacy as the basis of courage.

In Foote's imaginative world the pilgrimage to personhood begins when one confronts his or her personal and psychological past. This burdensome path, characterized by painful conflict and risky freedom, is made easier by loving connections to various cultures. Sometimes it is religion, sometimes the land, a specific community, or even work. But most often deep connection to parents, children, or a partner is the source of courageous autonomy. The healthiest power in his fictional universe is some version of a loving parent, who asks the other to be neither independent nor isolated. Paradoxically, as *Night Seasons* makes clear, such closeness relies on clear boundaries between the self and the other.

Without these boundaries, as in the case of Laura Lee, adventurous intimacy can never be established because closeness is experienced as fusion and loss of the self. This lack of personhood is initially created by parents who preach independence but secretly maintain control over their children, imagining only failure and abandonment outside the family. This is particularly problematic for female children, Foote discovers, whose attachment to the mother asks for more flexible and finally grayer distinctions between daughter and caregiver. Paralyzed by such fusion with the mother, women like Laura Lee can never move into the mature world of conflict, choice, and freedom, which they imagine as a black hole for the weak and unstable self. Although she only feels anger and helplessness, she actually chooses to follow her mother's return to an endless repetition of their past.

In *Night Seasons* this choice, which denies Laura's sense of self, is equivalent to siding with death over life. Normative is the rhythm of life itself, imagined in the metaphor of nature, which Foote used similarly in earlier plays, for example, *The Trip to Bountiful, The Oil Well, The Shape of the River,* and *Spring Dance.* According to the writer, every child is naturally drawn toward a profound sense of intimate attachment, which then encourages him or her to move beyond that bond toward other loving connections. Such benign intimacy, also recognized in a wholly loving father/mother God, nurtures individuation, which is the goal of all Foote's characters. *Night Seasons* is a dark play because Laura Lee, unable to find the boundaries between herself and others, primarily her mother, cannot find within herself the power to choose her own life. Unable to follow the archetypal movement from roots to wings and back again, Laura lives without the light of freedom or the transcendent movement of the seasons. She is lost in unredeemed time.

An advocate of family as a source of the love and generation so dear to his characters, Foote nevertheless implicates the Weemses in Laura's paralysis. Inspiring and nurturing intimacy, Foote's best families are regenerative, sacrificing their own history for individual growth. Minnie in *Cousins*, from *The Orphans' Home Cycle*, expresses the ideal pattern when she explains to Horace: "A family is a remarkable thing, isn't it? You belong. And then you don't. It passes you by. Unless you start a family of your own" (*Two Plays* 92). And yet, as the title suggests, *Night Seasons* is about the inversion of this order; it describes the dark place where the natural rhythms of nature and divinity have disappeared. While many other Foote plays offer families as a source of healing, Laura's people frustrate the individuality and courage upon which free and creative life is established. Unwilling to let Laura Lee pass by, to allow her a family of her own, the family turns tragically inward. It forms a nearly invisible—because shared—narcissism in which its members are indispensable and irreplaceable. Change and risk, cardinal virtues in other Horton Foote plays, are the mortal enemies of the Weems family.

Thus, as *Night Seasons* demonstrates, Horton Foote's imaginative world is essentially relational. His characters who find, maintain, and nurture loving attachments discover a powerful peace and contentment. Those who don't connect lovingly with their surroundings face lives of violence and self-destruction. Because intimacy is the normative value in his work, certain Foote women, those expert at loving connections, have a saint-like presence in stories like *The Oil Well*, *Tomorrow*, and *Tender Mercies*. But Foote's dramas are dialectical. The need for connection is studied against a dark background of separation. Most obviously his men—haunted by the American male's cult of radical individualism—are chronically isolated and alienated. Longing for loving connections, they repeatedly take flight—like Henry Thomas at the end of *Baby, the Rain Must Fall*—from family and responsibility. Even many of his women follow forces which lead to alienation and death rather than love and life.

Some of these forces, as Foote describes in *The Tears of My Sister*, are social and political. Women traditionally have been dependent on men economically and even emotionally. In the modern industrial and urban society, when husbands and fathers are either too close or too distant, their wives or daughters become passive smiling objects of male will and control. Like Mrs. Monroe, Bessie, and Cecilia, they become paralyzed and depressed. Feeling like victims of this patriarchal world, these women cling to its history and assumptions; unprepared for a world of change and choice, they feel their choices are not real. But Horton Foote's theater is finally more mental than sociopolitical, and so *Night Seasons* is a more complete and mature work and an even darker Foote story.

In *Night Seasons* Laura Lee is well connected—to her brothers, her father, and her mother. And, typical of a Horton Foote story, she is not asked to sever her attachments in any definitive way. All her decisions are made within loving connections; she is interdependent and should remain so. And yet, unlike Elizabeth in *Courtship*, Laura Lee cannot establish boundaries between herself and her family which stimulate conflict and lead to freedom. Without usable boundaries, she cannot choose a life beyond her biological family; lacking the will to act, Laura Lee loses both her physical body and her emotional self. Without individuation, Foote discovers in *Night Seasons*, the female mind becomes profoundly ambivalent, marked by senseless fusion and cold, reactive isolation. In such a paralytic existence, courageous action, regenerative families, and new life become impossible. Laura Lee embodies the death-in-life on the dark side of Horton Foote's relational theology.

ↄ

Notes

1.   From these many causes, Horton Foote's women exhibit every weakness of his men. Mamie Borden, in *Only the Heart* (1943), is one of his most controlling characters, male or female. Her interest in oil

wells alienates her daughter and eventually drives both the child and Mamie's son-in-law from her doorstep. Unable to learn the lessons of Foote's theater of intimacy, Mamie replaces the messiness of deep attachment with the false god of material security. At the other extreme, Georgette Thomas, in *The Traveling Lady* (1954), lives a fantasy marriage. So desperate for even the semblance of a happy home, Georgette believes Henry's lies and ignores each of his many betrayals. She loves with a remarkable intensity, but her illusions make her inflexible. Without genuine attachments, only fantasies, she drifts from one town to another. Most discontented is Annie Gayle Long, of *Spring Dance* (1982), who cannot cope with the violence in her past and subsequently slips into an imaginary world and finally an Austin sanatorium.

2.   Horton Foote's understanding of will, especially female will, doesn't imply aggression or alienating self-assertion. Foote considers such behavior destructive to the loving relationships which are normative in his dramas. In his work will is the ability to speak one's distinctive voice and mind and then act with intention and risk in both private and public situations. The goal is not separation for a cold autonomy; it is an active personhood that will accept choice and the conflict it engenders. Foote's heroic women don't retreat from freedom even as they nurture power through connection and interdependence.

3.   I want to thank Sandra Ballard, Associate Professor of English at Carson-Newman College, for introducing me to these writings in feminist developmental psychology, especially to the studies which deal with women's search for identity. From a purely developmental point of view, the most comprehensive is Louise Kaplan's *Oneness and Separateness* (New York: Simon & Schuster, 1978). The developmental style of women, especially as different from that of men, is examined in a number of texts, among them: Jean Baker Miller, *Toward a New Psychology of Women* (Boston: Beacon, 1976); Jane Flax, "The Conflict Between Nurturance and Autonomy in Mother-Daughter Relationships and Within Feminism," *Feminist Studies*, 4.2 (June 1978): 171–89; Nancy J. Chodorow, *The Reproduction of Mothering* (Berkeley: U of California P, 1978), "Feminism, Femininity, and Freud," *Advances in Psychoanalytic Sociology*, ed. Jerome Rabow, et al. (Malabar, Florida; Robert E. Krieger, 1987) 105–19, *Feminism and Psychoanalytic Theory* (New Haven: Yale UP, 1989), and *Femininities, Masculinities, Sexualities* (Lexington: UP of Kentucky, 1994); Carol Gilligan, *In a Different Voice* (Cambridge: Harvard, 1982) and "Exit-Voice Dilemmas in Adolescent Development," *Mapping the Moral Domain*, ed. Carol Gilligan,

et al. (Cambridge: Harvard, 1988) 141–58; ; *Women's Ways of Knowing*, ed. Mary Field Belenky, et al. (New York: Basic Books, 1986); Ruthellen Josselson, "Becoming Herself: Identity, Individuation, and Intimacy," *Finding Herself: Pathways to Identity Development in Women* (San Francisco: Jossey-Bass, 1987) 10–27; *Women's Growth in Connection*, ed. Judith V. Jordan, et al. (New York: Guilford, 1991), esp. Jean Baker Miller, "The Development of Women's Sense of Self" (11–26), Judith V. Jordan, "Empathy and Self Boundaries" (67–80), and "Beyond the Oedipus Complex: Mothers and Daughters" (97–121).

Works Cited

Belenky, Mary Field, Blythe McVicker Clinchy, Nancy Rule Goldberger, and Jill Mattuck Tarule, eds. *Women's Ways of Knowing: The Development of Self, Voice, and Mind.* New York: Basic Books, 1986.

Chodorow, Nancy. *Femininities, Masculinities, Sexualities: Freud and Beyond.* Lexington: UP of Kentucky, 1994.

——. *Feminism and Psychoanalytic Theory.* New Haven: Yale UP, 1989.

——. "Feminism, Femininity, and Freud." *Advances in Psychoanalytic Sociology.* Ed. Jerome Rabow, Gerald M. Platt, and Marion S. Goldman. Malabar, Florida: Robert E. Krieger, 1987. 105–19.

——. *The Reproduction of Mothering: Psychoanalysis and the Sociology of Gender.* Berkeley: U of California P, 1978.

Eddy, Mary Baker. *Science and Health with Key to the Scriptures.* Boston: The First Church of Christ, Scientist, 1934.

Flax, Jane. "The Conflict Between Nurturance and Autonomy in Mother-Daughter Relationships and Within Feminism." *Feminist Studies* 4.2 (June 1978): 171–89.

Foote, Horton, screenwriter. *Baby, the Rain Must Fall.* Prod. Alan J. Pakula, dir. by Robert Mulligan. Starring Steve McQueen and Lee Remick. Columbia Pictures, 1965.

——. *Blind Date. Selected One-Act Plays of Horton Foote.* Ed. Gerald C. Wood. Dallas: Southern Methodist UP, 1989. 366–89.

——. *The Chase*. New York: Dramatists Play Service, 1952.

——. *Courtship*. *Courtship, Valentine's Day, 1918: Three Plays from the Orphans' Home Cycle*. New York: Grove, 1987. 1–49.

——. *Cousins*. *Cousins and The Death of Papa: Two Plays from the Orphans' Home Cycle*. New York: Grove, 1989. 1–99.

——. *The Death of the Old Man*. *One-Acts*. 133–48.

——. *Night Seasons*. *Four New Plays*. Intro. Jerry Tallmer. Newbury, VT: Smith and Kraus, 1993. 63–113.

——. *The Oil Well*. *One-Acts*. 91–129.

——. Interview. 24 October 1985.

——. *The Shape of the River*. Playhouse 90, CBS, May 2, 1960. Prod. Fred Coe. Starring Franchot Tone and Leif Erickson.

——. *Spring Dance*. *One-Acts*. 347–62.

——. *The Tears of My Sister*. *One-Acts*. 152–65.

——, screenwriter. *Tender Mercies*. Dir. Bruce Beresford. Starring Robert Duvall, with Tess Harper, Betty Buckley, Ellen Barkin, Wilford Brimley. Antron Media/EMI, 1982.

——, screenwriter. *Tomorrow*. Prod. Paul Roebling and Gilbert Pearlman, dir. Joseph Anthony. Starring Robert Duvall and Olga Bellin. Filmgroup, 1972.

——, screenwriter. *The Trip to Bountiful*. Prod. Sterling Van Wagenen, dir. Peter Masterson. Starring Geraldine Page, John Heard, Carlin Glynn, Richard Bradford, and Rebecca DeMornay. Island Pictures, 1985.

Gilligan, Carol. "Exit-Voice Dilemmas in Adolescent Development." *Mapping the Moral Domain: A Contribution to Women's Thinking to Psychological Theory and Education*. Ed. Carol Gilligan, Janie Victoria Ward, and Jill McLean Taylor with Betty Bardige. Cambridge: Harvard UP, 1988. 141–58.

——. *In a Different Voice: Psychological Theory and Women's Development*. Cambridge: Harvard UP, 1982.

Gottschalk, Stephen. *The Emergence of Christian Science in American Religious Life*. Berkeley: U of California P, 1973.

Jordan, Judith V. "Empathy and Self Boundaries." *Women's Growth in Connection: Writings from the Stone Center*. Ed. Judith V. Jordan, Alexandra G. Kaplan, Jean Baker Miller, Irene P. Stiver, and Janet L. Surrey. New York: Guilford, 1991. 67–80.

Josselson, Ruthellen. "Becoming Herself: Identity, Individuation, and Intimacy." *Finding Herself: Pathways to Identity Development in Women*. San Francisco: Jossey-Bass, 1987. 10–27.

Kaplan, Louise. *Oneness and Separateness: From Infant to Individual*. New York: Simon & Schuster, 1978.

Miller, Jean Baker. "The Development of Women's Sense of Self." *Women's Growth in Connection*. 11–26.

——. *Toward a New Psychology of Women*. Boston: Beacon, 1976.

Stiver, Irene P. "Beyond the Oedipus Complex: Mothers and Daughters." *Women's Growth in Connection*. 97–121.

"Who Is God?" *Christian Science: A Sourcebook of Contemporary Materials*. Boston: The Christian Science Publishing Society, 1990. 65–71.

The Nature of Mystery in
The Young Man from Atlanta
Gerald C. Wood

In an interview we did for *Post Script*, which appeared in the summer of 1991, I asked Horton Foote what he feels about "life as a mystery." He answered instinctively and emphatically:

> Well, I think, my God, how can you say it's not a mystery? You never know what the next day is going to bring and you just sit and wait and you do the best you can with what's there.... I think it is essentially naive to think that you can really control life because you can't. You may work to better certain aspects of life in a social sense...but there's certain "givens" that you just have to accept, I think. (10)

Since Horton Foote's drama is not highly rhetorical, his characters don't discuss such cerebral issues. But this belief in mystery, like many of Foote's personal views, informs the subtext of his work. Among the many struggles his characters face but rarely articulate is the struggle between control and acceptance, which for some of them is resolved by embracing life as a divine mystery.

Take the garden scene near the end of *Tender Mercies*, for example. At first viewing, it seems tragic when Mac declares to Rosa Lee that he doesn't know why he survived an automobile accident while his daughter didn't. His words only appear as the heart-felt expression of an otherwise emotionally insulated man. But Rosa Lee has a strong presence throughout the scene; she is a witness to his pain, though she offers no palliative. By giving no explanations, even her own religious ones, Rosa Lee asks Mac to confront the limits of his will in the face of the essential muddle of human experience. And Mac responds to his wife's instructive silence. Though he is becoming a good Baptist, Mac has discovered, like a good Catholic, that there is no grace in despair, no mercy for those who fail to love the mystery of human experience.

Despite his contention that God has not answered his questions, Mac has received—through Rosa Lee—a response to his prayers. By admitting his inability to see everything clearly, to know exactly, to have God fully revealed in history, Mac gains an acceptance which, though easily confused with passivity or accommodation, is a religious offering from wife to husband. This interpretation of the garden crisis also explains the apparently loose, inconclusive structure of Foote's plays and screenplays, especially the later ones. As Horton Foote develops as a writer, his characters become less assured about their own motives and goals; consequently, there are fewer passages where they explain their feelings, mistakes, and conclusions. His mature dramas have little closure; explanations, if any, are tenuous, the endings acting more as lulls than resolutions. The human drama continues, the plays imply; only time and mystery remain.

Such issues seem to have little, if any, application to the opening scenes of *The Young Man from Atlanta*. Unusual for a Horton Foote work, this play early on admits to its literary and theatrical sources. Similar to the one-act *The One-Armed Man*, which revisits Flannery O'Connor's "A Good Man Is Hard to Find," the Pulitzer-Prize play borrows from Arthur Miller and, more immediately, David Mamet; it could be a coastal southeast Texas version of *Death of a Salesman* or *Glengarry Glen Ross*. *Young Man* opens in the office of a small Houston company seized with the post–World War II spirit of retrenchment. With his usual sense of the historical moment, and like other socially-aware American playwrights, Foote initially satirizes (in the figure of Will Kidder) the need to have "the best of everything....The biggest and the best" (2–3). Will's manic optimism is satisfied only if, as he declares to co-worker Tom Jackson, "I live in the best country in the world. I live in the best city. I have the finest wife a man could have, work for the best wholesale produce company" (3). Like previous critics of American society, Horton Foote exposes Will's inflexible desire to compete, portraying him as a man without an emotional home (3).

But *The Young Man from Atlanta* is not content with imitating the satire of other playwrights. In its very first moments Foote deflects the play from social commentary by injecting a Pinteresque intruder, a mysterious outsider who insinuates himself into the vulnerable relationship between Lily Dale and Will Kidder. This unseen Atlantan and his questionable motives denaturalize the play's political content; menace creates a theatrical sense of disorder and suspense. Subsequently, like a detective/mystery story, *Young Man* asks a number of pressing questions. Did Bill Kidder commit suicide? If so, why? What was his relationship to Randy Carter? Was Bill religious? What does the young man from Atlanta want from Lily Dale and Will? Is Pete's great-nephew Carson telling the truth? Are his motives different from Randy Carter's? Why did Bill give $100,000 to his roommate?

But even as *Young Man* fitfully pursues these questions, Horton Foote betrays his dissatisfaction with the mystery story he began in the first scenes. The play has come too close to formula and metatheater, styles too dehumanized for Foote's taste. And so, within a few moments after the opening curtain, he begins his typical dedramatization of the subject, especially its political and artistic content, in search of a more personal and realistic theater. In the first scene, for example, Will sounds like the typical detective when he asks, "Why in the middle of the day in a lake in Florida out in deep, deep water if you can't swim" (6). But, before the tension can build, Will answers his own query, defusing the generic expectations: "Everyone has their theories, and I appreciate their theories, but I'm a realist. I don't need theories. I know what happened. He committed suicide" (6). Taking its cue from this deflation, the rest of the play gives no definitive explanation of "Why" (6) his son died, and the various rationalizations, even the convincing ones, contradict each other. By the last scene *The Young Man from Atlanta* has fostered more mystery than it has solved.

Foote's most obvious motive in repeatedly deviating from genre— in this case the detective/mystery—is his creative obsession with his characters' problems with intimacy. Despite the melodrama surrounding Bill's death in *The Young Man from Atlanta*, the play's focus is not suicide. It is Will's inability to connect lovingly with his son. His indifference, the father eventually confesses, was born of narcissism:

> I just think now I only wanted him to be like me, I never
> tried to understand what he was like. I never tried to find
> out what he would want to do, what he would want to
> talk about. (105)

Sadly, Will is not the only male "never close" (105) to others. Pete, ostensibly a loving husband and stepfather, apparently has been a womanizer, and Randy Carter and Carson both claim to need father-figures. Like an Ingmar Bergman story, *The Young Man from Atlanta* is haunted by the loss of benign paternity.

This search for fathers is a symptom of a general breakdown in family order in *The Young Man from Atlanta*. While Will "can't talk to my wife" about the death of their son (5), Lily Dale confides in Randy Carter, the young man from Atlanta, rather than her husband. Will shares his deepest understandings with Tom Jackson because "I feel like you're my son in many ways" (10). Similarly, Pete and Lily Dale make the visitors from Atlanta—Carson and Randy—into images of the dead son (76, 103). According to *The Young Man from Atlanta*, intimacy—when unrealized in caring families—tends to bleed beyond safe limits, bringing more emotional chaos, vulnerability, and eventually violence.

As in many of Horton Foote's other works, this confusion of primary attachments becomes the basis of humor in *The Young Man from Atlanta*. Throughout the play Lily Dale is obsessed with "the Disappointment Club," a purported program of absenteeism designed by Houston blacks during the 30s to cause stress—disappointment—in the white homes where they were employed. Even though Lily Dale never confirms the existence of such a campaign, she embellishes the story, believing Eleanor Roosevelt its instigator. When her husband quizzes her about the supposed conspiracy, Lily insists: "I know she was. Everybody in Houston knows she was. She just hated the South, you know. She took out all her personal unhappiness on the South" (24). By projecting her own unhappiness onto the wife of the Democratic President, Mrs. Kidder justifies the aggressive Republicanism she shares with her husband. Her private confusions lead Lily Dale toward comic and potentially destructive political views.

Integral to *The Young Man from Atlanta*'s study of intimacy is its focus on grief's temptations and opportunities. Early in the play Will and Lily Dale use their new possessions to insulate themselves from loss (8); Will hopes "this new house will help us get away from a lot of memories. To celebrate the new house I'm buying my wife a new car" (11). Conversely, the loss of these luxuries, following the greater loss of their son, eventually brings the couple closer. Once he has resolved his anger toward his wife, Will begins to accept his age and health problems, give up his pride and bitterness, and see himself as "a simple man at heart" in need of meaningful work (66). For her part, as Lily Dale confronts her profound loneliness and shares it with her husband, she becomes more realistic about her son and his death. Their gains are expressed in a simple exchange of shared loss near the end of the play; Will admits "I want my son back, Lily Dale" and she responds "I know. I know. So do I" (105).

Thus, *The Young Man from Atlanta*, despite its sensational subjects, is indifferent to the causes of the son's suicide, choosing instead to study the effects of grief on the marriage of Lily Dale and Will Kidder. She needs to be more realistic about dark motives, the play determines, less a girl who calls her husband "Daddy" (25). He needs to live with all the unanswered questions about his son's death, including his failure as a father. And they both need to shift from taking comfort in their possessions to finding support in shared loss. The dramatic issue in *Young Man* is not the boy's sexual orientation or the motives of the young man from Atlanta. It is whether Lily Dale and her husband can integrate mystery into their emotional lives and find peace in their marriage—in the face of death.

Thus, in *The Young Man from Atlanta* Horton Foote uses the conventions of the detective/mystery story as a backdrop for his continuing exploration of the power of intimacy, his most prevalent artistic concern. Repeatedly the play raises social, psychological, and even moral questions which are purposely never answered. Through such cultivation of mystery, Horton Foote is suggesting that art, in its truthfulness to life, best serves its readers and audiences by not giving false assurance, expressed as closure in traditional dramatic formulas. In fact, wonder is gained by admitting that the "whys" are often unknowable and not a source of peace. Resilience and courage are gained by leaving many things with God.

This understanding eludes Lily Dale throughout most of *The Young Man from Atlanta*. Her infantile, self-obsessed religion denies the dark realities of Bill's life, leaving her vulnerable to Randy Carter's machinations. Rather than deal honestly with loss, she covers herself with innocent piety: "Every time I feel blue over missing Bill, I call his friend and I ask him to tell me again about Bill and his prayers and he does so so sweetly" (30). Her innocence leaves Lily Dale speechless after Allie Clinton's baiting question "why did this good God let your son commit suicide?" (29). Feeling powerless herself, lacking the individuation so essential to Foote's characters, Lily accepts the image of God as controlling and vindictive.

But in *The Young Man from Atlanta* black women offer an alternative theodicy, a moral norm for Horton Foote's work. As in *The Orphans' Home*, where the love between Horace and Elizabeth offers a sense of order to the violent world around them, the blacks in *Young Man* embrace a radical and healing vision of God-as-Love. Clara, the present help, says Lily Dale needs "Christian faith" (50), and Etta Doris, the former cook, benignly remembers Bill as a good-looking, friendly boy who liked baseball. Her truth is simple: "Everything changes. The Lord giveth and he taketh away.... We're here today and gone tomorrow. Blessed be the name of the Lord" (84). There is nothing else to say; acceptance is the only response to such faith and assurance. In *Young Man* everything else is a mystery.

This sense of mystery is the key to the last scene of *The Young Man from Atlanta*, one of the most resonant in all of Horton Foote's work. It begins in a clutter of information, with a narrative speed almost dizzying by Foote's usual standards: the Disappointment Clubs are reprised, Will's illness continues, Pete is moving disturbingly close to his nephew, and Lily Dale has seen the young man from Atlanta once again. Lily Dale reports that Randy waits just outside the house, arguing for his innocence and Carson's jealousy. Then Will appears from the bedroom, admitting he's "lost my spirit"; "Here I am," he says, "in the finest city in the greatest country in the world and I don't know where to turn. I'm whipped" (102). Lily Dale responds by confessing a brief assignation she and cousin Mary Cunningham had with two men some 20 years earlier. Though child-like, her confession nevertheless encourages Lily Dale to acknowledge her loneliness and need for comfort.

This ambiguity deepens as the scene, and the play, comes to a close. *The Young Man from Atlanta* offers hope in the growing intimacy between Lily Dale and Will. He controls his anger and lets go of his bitterness; he will "swallow my pride" and return—out of genuine need—to his job at the bank (107). When she offers to "help us out" by teaching music, his response is empathetic: "If you like. It might give you something to think about" (107). And yet, even as they grow closer, the husband and wife conspire to avoid the whole truth. Just as Lily Dale begins to admit the implications of Randy's declaration that "he loved" Bill "and missed him," Will cuts her off, offering the unwarranted assurance that ends the play: "everything will be all right" (110). While Will holds Lily Dale with genuine affection as the curtain falls, the ending to *Young Man* is purposely inconclusive.[1]

Most arresting is the conspiracy between husband and wife to create mystery in the final moments of *The Young Man from Atlanta*. When Lily Dale asks Will if he believes Pete's been unfaithful, Will says "I don't know. Who knows about anything, Lily Dale?" (106). The husband also refuses to speak to Randy "Because there are things I'd have to ask him and I don't want to know the answers" (108–9). Finally, as Will considers the reasons why the son gave money to his roommate, he stops himself, saying "whatever the reasons, I don't want to know. There was a Bill I knew and a Bill you knew and that's the only Bill I care to know about" (109). Will Kidder, the self-described realist early in *Young Man*, in the end chooses uncertainty rather than the truth he admires. Having spent the whole play trying to introduce Lily Dale to realities about Randy Carter, the Disappointment Club, and their son, he finally embraces an unclear future peace.

When Will and Lily Dale decide to remember "the only Bill" they "care to know" (109), everything changes. Their agreement, while colored by shared fantasy, is not innocent; it is a creative act—like the play itself—which values life without reference to truthful causes or even morality. In its final moments *Young Man* imagines the human mind—even in twentieth-century material America—still participating in its own heaven or hell. By refusing to label their son with deadly reductive and judgmental names—like "suicide" and "homosexual"—the parents no longer want truth in the literal sense. Whether Randy or Carson is the liar will not be clarified. Bill's religious belief, if any, won't be established. His anger toward his father, the hollow places in his emotional life, his despair will never be explained away. By making peace with these unknowns—by embracing mystery—the parents commit a final act of love. Keeping alive the story of their son's goodness, they retreat from reality and cross the line separating truth from faith.

In these final moments of *The Young Man from Atlanta*, Horton Foote, one of the most adamant realists in the history of American theater, reveals the boundaries of his realism. As he makes explicit in his lecture "The Artist as Myth-Maker," Foote believes the writer should be "a truth searcher," always risking the "collision of myth and reality" he finds definitively expressed in Katherine Anne Porter's "Old Mortality" (4). Even when creating fiction, Foote argues, the artist should employ myths which aren't "phoney or synthetic. They must be truly rooted in a time and place to be useful...not] degenerate into a stereotype" (5). In the South this authenticity is found in "people who love to talk, who love to remember, who love to share their re-membrances"; they are "the real myth makers" (7), he says. For Horton Foote, myth must be grounded in the real language, stories, and memo-ries of living people.

And yet in *The Young Man from Atlanta* the writer qualifies his realist argument, dramatizing instead the creative tension, the unresolvable dialectic, between reality and vision, knowledge and belief. On the one hand, the ending of *The Young Man from Atlanta* reiterates the need to be cold and hard. Lily Dale gains strength from facing the dark realities, especially the role her fantasies played in Bill's death. And Will is served by continually examining his own narcissism. Nevertheless, when Lily Dale and Will decide to remem-ber a different Bill than the one represented by the bank receipts, they are not delusional. They are participating in the invention of their world. By choosing to look and talk no further, the parents embrace life's ineluctable mystery. After a long and painful pursuit of the truth, they are hungry for myth, in this case the myth of goodness.

Just as mystery returns Foote's characters to authentic myth—not the fatuous and sentimental fabrication of genres—it sensitizes them to the power of language. As Horton Foote says in an interview with John DiGaetani, "language is everything to me" (68). But he doesn't, like many of his contemporary dramatists, deconstruct lan-guage to reveal its emptiness and potential violence. Foote's work employs a phenomenology of language, in which he explores "the possibilities" of a found language, "not abstract, but made up of imag-ined and remembered particulars" ("What It Means to Be a Southern Writer" 23). Always interested in getting "people to reexamine and to think about each other and relationships" (Smith 27), the writer ex-plores the intent and effect of words in human community. Once Lily Dale and Will finally become aware of their weaknesses, the fragility of their marriage, and the mysteries of living, at the end of *The Young Man from Atlanta* they are careful with what they say—to one an-other and about their son Bill. More accepting of themselves and things beyond their control, the husband and wife fashion their words with a renewed respect for life itself.

In the opening scenes, *The Young Man from Atlanta* has a more theatrical look than most Horton Foote plays. Initially it is more satiric and suspenseful than Foote's usual Harrison chronicles. But as it drifts from such theatrical conventions, *Young Man*, like all of Foote's dedramatized work, discovers its subject by mostly disregarding plot. In the subtext of its seemingly aimless and finally inconclusive story is a more compelling subject: whether a couple, portrayed as "vain and selfish" in *Lily Dale* and *Cousins* (Foote, Introduction to *The Young Man from Atlanta* xi), can improve their marriage after the death of their son. They do, to a limited extent, because, as the writer says of characters in his early teleplays, they are in the process of "an acceptance of life" and "a preparation for death" (Preface viii). Such intimacy and courage in the face of death—their son's and their own—is inspired by their acceptance that finally everything, and everybody, is sacrificed to God's mysterious order.

ↄ

Note

1.   Mystery is as integral to the effect of *The Young Man from Atlanta* as its dramatic structure. The various points of view and the ambiguous ending force viewers to imagine the complexity of the human situation and reach their own conclusions. This is what Reynolds Price describes as Foote's "method...of the composer":

> His words are black notes on a white page—all but abstract signals to the minds of actor and audience, signs from which all participants (again all those at work on both sides of the stage or camera, including the audience) must make their own musical entity. (Price xi)

Young Man's dedication to the nature of mystery—in life and art—requires an audience willing to practice both insight and judgment.

Works Cited

DiGaetani, John. "Horton Foote." *A Search for a Postmodern Theater: Interviews with Contemporary Playwrights.* Westport, CT: Greenwood, 1991. 65–71.

Foote, Horton. "The Artist as Myth-Maker" (SECA lecture). Horton Foote Papers. Southern Methodist University.

———. *The Dancers. Selected One-Act Plays of Horton Foote*. Ed. Gerald C. Wood. Dallas: Southern Methodist UP, 1989. 236–64.

———. Preface. *Harrison, Texas: Eight Television Plays by Horton Foote*. New York: Harcourt, Brace, 1956. vii–ix.

———. *The One-Armed Man. Selected One-Act Plays*. 418–28.

———. *Tender Mercies*. Dir. Bruce Beresford. With Robert Duvall and Tess Harper. Antron Media/EMI, 1982.

———. "What It Means to be a Southern Writer" (SECA Lecture). Horton Foote Papers. Southern Methodist University.

———. *The Young Man from Atlanta*. Intro. Horton Foote. New York: Dutton, 1995.

Price, Reynolds. "Introduction: New Treasure." *Courtship, Valentine's Day, 1918: Three Plays from the Orphans' Home Cycle*. New York: Grove, 1987. ix–xiii.

Smith, Amanda. "Horton Foote: A Writer's Journey." *Varia* July/August 1987: 18–20, 23, 26–27.

Wood, Gerald C. "Horton Foote: An Interview." *Post Script* 10.3 (Summer 1991): 3–12.

Squeezing the Drama out of Melodrama
Plot and Counterplot in Laura Dennis
Dean Mendell

Horton Foote's dramas are uncommonly resistant to thespian virtuosity. The scripts do not leave an actor much latitude in his or her choice of how to perform a role. Robert Duvall, who played the lead in the screenplays *Tomorrow, Convicts,* and *Tender Mercies* , for which he won an Academy Award, has said, "You can't push it. You can't propel it along. You have to just let it lay there" (Freedman xxiv). This is especially true of Foote's stage plays, for they are engineered to subdue theatricality, to subdue it in unusual and intriguing ways, even in—and particularly in—plays like *Laura Dennis*, which present a society that is as lust-bloodied as a daily soap opera.

Like almost all the plays in Foote's nine play *Orphans' Home Cycle*, *Laura Dennis*, the final offering in the Signature Theatre's season of Foote plays, is a strange hybrid: a tranquil melodrama. Set in Harrison, Texas, the fictional small town where nearly all Foote's protagonists live or have lived at some point in their lives, *Laura Dennis* is soaked in the blood of two murders, one of which occurred sixteen years before the play begins, when Laura was an infant, in about 1922. To these, Foote adds a lurid third death, that of seventeen-year-old Verna Kate, who dies while giving birth to her illegitimate baby a few hours after she has married a boy who loves her but is not the baby's father.

Sex is just around the corner from death in most melodramas, so they almost always include one or two lusty affairs, if not in the foreground then in the background. The intimacy between Mrs. Dennis (the title character's mother) and her husband's cousin (the biological father of Harvey Griswold) is typical. When Mr. Dennis learned of their affair, he shot and killed his cousin—appropriately, in front of the town's movie theater. Soon after that murder and before her son Harvey was born, Mrs. Dennis abandoned Baby Laura, moving to South Dakota. Sixteen years have passed since those events. Harvey is living with an adoptive family, the Griswolds; and Laura, whose father is dead, is living in the house of Lena Abernathy, a kind woman paid by Laura's unkind uncle to free him from his responsibility to her. Such is the legacy of Harrison's many infidelities.

There are two more chunks of melodrama. One is the prospect of incest. Harvey wants to start dating Laura, since he doesn't know that she is his half-sister. (Nor is Laura aware of this blood connection, the one family secret in Harrison that is really a secret.) The second involves the circumstances of the murder of Harvey, in front of the same theater where his father was killed. Verna Kate claims that Harvey, her boyfriend, fathered her unborn baby; but Harvey, denying he is the father, insists that there were at least two other boys whose hormones had dosey-doed with Verna Kate's hormones. Finding such promiscuity unthinkable, her father, Mr. Nelson, threatens to kill Harvey, and eventually does.

But those are not the only melodramatically dysfunctional folk in Harrison. In the subplot, the audience meets Laura's cousin, Velma, a laughably pitiful drunk who is frantic because her mother, Ethel, is marrying the generically-named Seymour Mann (See More Man), a young cowboy who, in different circumstances, might have responded to her own loneliness. So frantic is Velma that she threatens suicide and must be sedated.

These are the essential elements in the soap opera that is *Laura Dennis*. Remarkably, though, *Laura Dennis* comes across as anything but soapish. Its moments of tears are just that, moments. There are no histrionics. Foote does not permit them into his play. Any actor craving a really big scene is sure to be disappointed because Foote works against everything theatrical in his characters' lives. This is especially obvious in *Laura Dennis*—which is as melodramatic as any play he has yet written but is at the same time one of his least dramatic works—because the more dramatic his story is, the more he usually turns against the conventions for creating realistic drama.

The first thing an audience may notice in the early scenes of *Laura* and many of Foote's other plays is the exposition, a mass of familial and communal history, which defies three near-taboos of playwriting—that the playwright should not use more exposition than is necessary, repeat exposition, nor unload too much exposition into the first scene to get it out of the way, a characteristic which makes the dialogue of many beginning writers seem contrived. Consider Lena Abernathy's description of Velma's past, a few minutes into the play, a passage that sounds like the beginning of a short story or novel about Velma rather than a bit of necessary exposition about a minor character in a play about Laura:

> When I first moved here Velma was fifteen, and I thought she was the loveliest, sweetest thing I'd ever seen. She had long blonde curls like Mary Pickford. That was the year they discovered oil here and the town was filled with young men working on the oil crews and her mother Ethel would have parties for them all the time.... And Velma was the life of those parties. One of the men, Charlie Deveraux, was over at her house morning, noon and night.... Her father ran him off a couple of times.... He was twenty-seven and he thought he was too old for Velma. Then Velma went to Houston and came back with her hair bobbed.... I tell you the whole town almost died because she cut off those beautiful curls.... Anyway, they soon forgot that because Velma ran off and married Charlie Deveraux and the parties stopped. (12–13)

The audience certainly does not need to know so much about Velma. A trickle of this information would float us into the main story, but this torrent is more likely to sweep us downriver, far away from that story.

Yet the narrative history of Velma is still not over. Laura is a naive and inquisitive girl, like most of Foote's fictional children and teenagers, and she continues to fire questions at Lena.

> LAURA: What happened then?
>
> LENA: After about six months she divorced him.
>
> LAURA: Did the parties start again after she had divorced him?
>
> LENA: No, because her father was sick by then, and after he died they closed up the house and moved to Houston. (12)

Velma herself continues this line of questioning some fifteen or twenty minutes later, in another scene. She shouts her mother out of bed to ask:

> VELMA: What happened to Charlie?
>
> ETHEL: Charlie who?

VELMA: Charlie Deveraux. The man I married.
ETHEL: Is that what you got me out of bed for?
VELMA: What happened to him?
ETHEL: He's dead. You knew that.
VELMA: I didn't know that.
ETHEL: You certainly did. I told you.
VELMA: Then I forgot. (19–20)

An hour or so later, the audience hears the same story yet again, this time from Laura, who explains to her friends, Pud and Annie Laurie, that she has a cousin who married at fifteen and divorced at sixteen, a cousin who had long blonde curls, like Mary Pickford.

All this exposition, it must be remembered, is spent on a secondary character. Not surprisingly, the history of Laura, her mother and father, and Harvey and his parentage, and the story of cousin murdering cousin is repeated even more often.

It would be a mistake to deny that this manner and magnitude of exposition is a weakness. After all, most people become bored when they have to listen over and over to what they already know. Repetitions can be fascinating, of course—for instance, when one character's attitude to what she is saying is used to distinguish her from another character who has said the same thing earlier or when a story told by one character has an ironic new meaning when told by another. But Foote does not use his exposition to excite his audience in either of these ways. Instead, like a chessplayer who is willing to sacrifice a little manpower to strengthen his position, he is willing to risk a little boredom so that he can drag the spotlight off plot and force it elsewhere, on the idea of family and community.

By de-emphasizing the theatrical plot, he is able to present all the tragedies that have occurred and continue to occur as commonplace familial and communal tragedies. There is nothing spectacular about them, not even the murders. Tragedy happens to everyone. The soldiers in *1918*, the sixth play in the *Orphans' Cycle*, are dying in the war while their stateside kin are dying of a virulent flu epidemic. There is another murder of cousin by cousin in the exposition of *The Death of Papa*, the final play in the *Cycle*. And Elizabeth loses her first baby in *Valentine's Day*, the fifth play in the *Cycle*, like her mother, who had twice lost babies of her own, and like Lena and Ethel, who recall their own dead babies in *Laura Dennis*.

In *Laura*, Pud's mother complains that in the days of long blonde curls, when girls were innocent, "It all seemed so simple...You fell in love, you got married, you had children" (35). But no matter what she thinks, Foote makes the audience see that life was never truly simple, was never truly happy. And the audience knows that the future will not be simple or happy either. In the last moments of the play Lena tries to console Velma, and Velma whines: "Nothing is all right. Nothing at all is all right. I try to stay sober and I get so depressed I can't stand it and I get drunk and get crazy" (47). She seeks refuge then in her memories of a halcyon past, before she had her hair bobbed, when she wore long blonde curls: "Everybody said just like Mary Pickford...sweet and innocent and...I was always very popular when I went to the dances. Even after I was married and divorced I was still very, very popular" (47).

Velma and Laura, like the characters in most of Foote's plays, want to turn the past into a refuge from the pains of the present. Lonely Laura, especially, needs to escape—to escape from knowing that "if my mother walked into this yard right now, I wouldn't know her. She would have to say Laura Dennis, I'm your mother, before I'd know who she was" (46). And she needs to escape from knowing that "I went to school with my brother for I don't know how many years and I didn't know who he was and he didn't know who I was" (46).

But how can she escape? How can anyone escape the past that has made her who she is? Foote suggests, by constantly repeating bits of familial and communal history, that people try to do so by reinventing their pasts. Laura is one of Foote's orphans, and so she more obviously than most people needs to invent a past for herself. Like Horace Robedaux, the protagonist in the *Orphans' Cycle*, she is always asking questions, trying always to arrive at some understanding of her past that goes beyond mere facts, beyond the sad plot of adultery and murder that has made her who she is.

> Do you think my mother loved my father when she married him? (11)
>
> Do you think my father was in love with my mother? (11)
>
> Did he ever mention my mother to you? (11)
>
> Why do you think he loved her? (11)

> Why do you think she's never written to me? (14)

> My father always seemed very sad to me. Did he to you? Do you think that's why he drank so much because he was sad? (15)

> Was my father rich before he killed his cousin? (23)

> I wonder what would have happened if my father hadn't killed his cousin, and if my mother hadn't fallen in love with his cousin. (36)

Needing to believe that her family was happy once upon a time, Laura is comforted when she receives a letter from her mother's friend, saying that her "mother was beautiful and was very vivacious," and that "as quiet as my father was, my mother was just the opposite—always talking, laughing and teasing." She is gratified that her mother "was a cut up," and that in fact her "father wasn't always quiet," that he too was lively in the early days of the marriage (14).

As a virtual orphan, Laura is the best representative of the need everyone has to remember a youthful time before life stopped seeming simple and delightful. Like Horace, she is not literally an orphan, of course, since her mother is alive, somewhere, but she is a clearer example of what it means to be an orphan than is anyone else in the play, including Harvey Griswold, who has had a happy childhood in his adoptive family. She is an orphan because she has been denied a childhood. Yet being an orphan does not entitle her to more pity than anyone else is entitled to. Like Horace, who had to support himself when he was twelve years old, and like his father-in-law, Henry Vaughn, and his mother's second husband, Pete Davenport, who both had to support themselves when they were children, too, Laura is just one of many sufferers in Harrison. Although she has become an orphan because of a melodramatic murder, she is still only one of innumerable victims of what life does to people. Sooner or later, everyone becomes a victim, and when that happens, one has to imagine a past that was better than the present.

So Laura asks her questions and Velma grasps at golden times before she slipped into the bottle, and everyone tells stories of her own life again and again, hoping that the past will become as golden as Velma's curls and brighten the darkness of reality. No one succeeds, however; everyone looks always in the wrong place, looks to photographs of reality, to snapshots of young and joyful mothers and fathers instead of looking for a golden past in her own imagination. The real past is not a refuge from the present, but the imagined past—or, for that matter, the imagined future—can indeed provide a satisfying refuge.

Foote's plays are in part an argument that one cannot go home again, but they are also an argument that one can go back if one learns how to make the journey. Unlike Ibsen, Foote does not insist that people be strong enough to face the past, so he does not argue that people who refuse to face facts inevitably destroy themselves. Instead he argues that every sufferer has to invent a fiction he can live with. Bragging that he is a realist who faces facts, Will Kidder speaks of his son's suicide in the opening scene of *The Young Man from Atlanta*. But that changes when he and his wife are asked to listen to other facts about their son. Rejecting the fact that he was homosexual and that his suicide had something to do with his homosexuality, they adjust their fiction in the last scene to the one fact they cannot deny, that their son has died. As to why he died, they will come up with their own reasons. Ibsen would damn this act of deception, of course, for a failure to face the truth dooms successive generations in many of his plays; but Foote just as obviously approves of it, inasmuch as it enables Will and Lily Dale to revive their dignity, giving them the strength to move on and, perhaps, make tolerable lives for themselves.

Many of Foote's sufferers, on the other hand, have to invent pasts simply because their real pasts remain frustratingly elusive, despite the gossip of community sages, whose nets trap dramatic narratives of birth and death, marriage and adultery but not the intimate histories that Laura and other orphans yearn to recover. Foote makes the past especially remote in *1918*: when Horace wants to put a headstone on his father's grave, he cannot even find out exactly where his father was buried. On the advice of a cousin, he puts the headstone on one grave and then is told by an insistent neighbor that he has made a mistake. Yet it no longer matters. Right or wrong, he has made up his mind that the headstone is exactly where it belongs. And this "fact" is all that matters, for it allows him to feel at last that he has honored his father—that is, honored the past which deserted him when his father died.

This is what Foote himself is doing, too, in nearly all the plays he has written in the last fifty years—honoring a past he has to imagine, honoring his idea of his family, in his idea of his hometown, Wharton, Texas, the Harrison of his own childhood. In *Laura Dennis*, the stoic Lena Abernathy, Laura's surrogate parent, is a fictive incarnation of the author; she observes Laura with great sympathy, but she cannot, and does not try to, help her. She will not lie to her, will not reassure her that everything is going to be all right. Laura looks to her for answers to her questions, but Lena as often as not has to say "I don't know." The facts that might help Laura, that might make her happy, are simply not available. They are not available to Foote, so they are not available to Lena or to Laura either.

In all this searching and searching for facts, Laura is very much like Melville's Ishmael, for her need to know family is as deep and unfathomed as his need to know whales. For much of *Moby-Dick*, he tries and fails to get at their secret by presenting an encyclopedia of whaling facts, chapters that are stuffed to dullness with definitions and catalogues and descriptions and explanations. Yet Melville's cetalogical chapters are useful to *Moby-Dick*, inasmuch as they make the world of whaling real to the reader and prepare Ishmael for his realization late in the book that the only way to know whales is to know them symbolically, to know them through the whale of all whales, Moby Dick—to know them, that is, not for what they are but for what he is able to see in them.

Laura chases after facts about family just as obsessively, asking Lena one question after another and quarrying lumps of new information for her efforts, information that is useless to her and boring to us. Yet this unnecessarily detailed and often repetitive information, though boring in itself, is more useful than not to the play as a whole. It shows us how characters talk about themselves and, thus, what they think of themselves, and it makes Harrison seem more real than the settings of most other playwrights. Plays are usually economical, like short stories; they include only what the audience needs to know. Foote's plays, to the contrary, like novels, include all sorts of superfluous details which help to create a sense of an entire society. This is one way in which Foote triumphs by his risky defiance of traditional strategies of exposition.

Moreover, because the mountain of facts the characters pile up on the stage is as useless to Laura as Melville's encyclopedia of facts is to Ishmael, Laura comes to see that the only way to know family is to imagine it. All the melodramatic facts she knows about the Dennis family are not sufficient to tell her the secret of what family really is, and since she has to learn that secret if she is ever to be happy, she will eventually have to leave the facts behind as Ishmael does near the end of *Moby-Dick*. Laura and all the rest of Foote's survivors end up discovering this, one way or another. For Laura, the way to escape is simply to get out of Harrison. She will take her share of an oil lease her uncle has sold, seven thousand dollars, and use it to finance her college education, away from Harrison.

Other orphans, though, never learn that they need to escape. Velma left Harrison years before but has come back to stay. She aches to belong there; she dreams of her former popularity. But the people who loved her for her girlish beauty are the same ones who will call her a whore if she ever dares go to any of the town dances without a proper escort. Laura Lee in *Night Seasons* is a prisoner of Harrison, too—a prisoner, that is, of her family and her past as is Brother Vaughn in *The Death of Papa*, a dissipated man who cannot stay away from Harrison even though the town has turned him into a murderer. "This is my home," he laments, "but I can't live in my home." He is one of the damned because he cannot give up the idea of returning: after failing repeatedly to make a life for himself in Harrison, he still cannot let go of the hope that "Maybe one day I'll be able to come back" (194).

But Laura will leave Harrison and, if she is wise, will stay away, except in her imagination, and when she goes, she will also leave behind the melodramatic narratives of her life in Harrison. Like the playwright, who left Wharton when he was sixteen and has been returning ever since to this imaginary version of Wharton, Laura, once she is safely away from the family history that has pained her all her life, may be able to create for herself the town that never in fact existed for her, in which she is a loved child of a loving family and community.

Laura Dennis is probably the most sensationally-plotted play Foote has yet written, except for the equally extreme *Habitation of Dragons*, another tale of adultery, murder, and dying children but one in which the succession of catastrophes is overwhelming because not enough is done to counter and subdue the melodramatic plot. In *Laura*, though, he attacks his plot from several angles. The brevity of his scenes—

eighteen in a play that should not run much over ninety minutes—helps to hold back the tears during the most dramatic episodes. For example, when Laura finds out who Harvey was and that he has been killed, she begins to cry, but instantly the lights fade to end the scene. (The unit set Foote calls for in his stage directions helps to speed along all such transitions.) The lights are then brought up on another potentially sensational scene: Harvey's mother crying to the condolences of family and friends. Instead of giving her a doleful, theatrical speech, however, Foote turns the conversation over to the others, who then begin to discuss Ethel's recent marriage and the oil lease Laura's uncle has been negotiating.

This foreshortening is typical of *Laura Dennis*. When Pud and Annie Laurie see Laura after Harvey's funeral, in the next scene, they talk about Laura's oil lease and their dresses and about how excited they are about the coming dance. This is a world in which people talk about sorrow and joy at the same time. Their lives are a bittersweet blend of tragedy and joy, and their conversations express that duality as nearly as is possible. Speaking about Verna Kate's death, Laura's uncle says, "It's quite a shock. I feel so for her mother and father," and then invites Laura to dinner to talk about her oil lease (32). The same shift happens earlier in the play when Velma wails to Lena and Laura that she is so depressed she "may never get out of bed ever again." Velma exits and Laura sympathizes to Lena, "She seems so unhappy." "I know," Lena says, handing her a dress pattern, then asks, matter of factly, "Do you like this one?" (28). In short, if somebody is talking about one of the tragedies that haunt Harrison, the audience can be sure that he or she is on the edge of talking about something far more commonplace.

Presented out of context, lines like these are funny, but in the play they are *not* funny, and any actor who tries to play them for laughs will disturb the balance Foote creates between tragedy and the everyday business of living. Velma is the only character that should be played for laughs—because hers is the only out-and-out tragic role in *Laura Dennis*. The possibility for her to find happiness faded away long before she makes her first entrance in the play, yet Foote saves her from being disturbingly tragic, like Maggie the Cat and Blanche and the rest of Tennessee Williams's man-hungry, post meridian belles, by encouraging us to laugh at her even though no one on stage is aware that she is funny. She alone plays to the audience; she alone is theatrical. Pathos and laughter compete with each other when she is on stage.

The town itself is funny, too. Humor, the conventional tool of playwrights who need to lighten their tragedies, helps to save Harrison from seeming lugubrious. There are no outright cheerful scenes to play against the sad scenes as in Wilder's portrait of Grover's Corners, but Foote wedges entertaining moments into many of his sad scenes, for instance, in this exchange between Pud and Laura and Annie Laurie:

PUD:	Did you hear about Verna Kate?
LAURA:	Yes.
PUD:	When did you hear about it?
LAURA:	Just now.
PUD:	Who told you?
LAURA:	My uncle.
PUD:	Isn't it terrible? I feel so bad about it. I'm sorry for every mean thing I ever said about Verna Kate.
ANNIE LAURIE	I never knew her, but I feel bad about it, too.
PUD:	Who told you about it?
ANNIE LAURIE:	You did. (32–33)

Except for Velma's tantrums, this is about as funny as anything in the play. It is good for a small laugh. But Foote does not need more to press the misery of the moment further into the background, since he relies mostly on much less conventional strategies to do so.

Foote is perhaps most daring in his flouting of the cardinal rule of playwriting: *show*, don't *tell*. It would be difficult to find a good playwright who dares to show less than Foote shows. Every major conflict occurs off-stage in *Laura Dennis*. We are told that Verna Kate is swearing that Harvey is the father-to-be of her child-to-be. Then we are told of a furious confrontation between Harvey's father and Mr. Nelson in which Mr. Nelson threatens to shoot Harvey for refusing to marry his daughter and for advertising that she is promiscuous. Then we are told that she is in a hospital, where she has given birth, married Stewart, and died. And then, as if this were not enough, as if we do not need to see anything at all, we are merely told that Mr. Nelson has murdered Harvey.

Indeed, the only dramatic scenes Foote plays on stage are a small scene between Laura and Stewart in which Stewart breaks a date with her to marry Verna Kate and three tearful but muffled scenes: one in which the Griswolds tell Harvey why he has to give up the idea of dating Laura, another in which Laura finds out that Harvey was her half-brother and that he is dead, and another in which Laura and others talk with the Griswolds after the murder. Everything else that we know, we know simply because we have overheard the gossip that devils Harrison. None of the melodrama is staged.

Most playwrights would want to excite at least a few gasps or wring a few tears out of us by staging at least some of the scenes Foote leaves out of *Laura Dennis*. Playwrights have always worked upon our sensations, even when they dramatize people who have ordinary lives like Willy Loman. So long as they are not trying to make us laugh and are not dosing us with irony, as Beckett does, they will, at various appropriate points, want to make our hearts bang in nervous anticipation or to make us cry, and the usual way to do that is to stage the most dramatic scenes and narrate only the quiet ones.

When writing is skillful and unsentimental, we react when we see characters react. If a likeable character is crying, we feel sad with him or her. But Foote does not show anyone howling in pain. There is no Blanche DuBois or Stanley Kowalski in *Laura Dennis* even though his characters are no less tortured by their lives. Velma is the only one who even raises her voice when she barks at her mother; yet we are not around when she smashes her mother's furniture.

Moreover, there is no obligatory scene in the play, not even between the central characters. No doubt, a scene in which Laura and Harvey don't know that they are half-brother and -sister while we do would be moving as might a scene in which we behold them together after they have learned that they are related. But since either scene would make Harvey's death more emotionally bruising, Foote leaves both of them out. Nor does he present a scene between the antagonists Harvey and Verna Kate or Harvey and Verna Kate's raging father. In fact, he never even puts Verna Kate or her father on stage; they are as conspicuously absent from this play as the title character is in *The Young Man from Atlanta*.

Both of these absences are risky, of course. In keeping Mr. Nelson behind the scenes, Foote denies his audience the thrill of a dramatic confrontation. Audiences would, no doubt, like to see Harvey defending himself against Mr. Nelson and the two fathers arguing and grappling in defense of their young ones. We want to be afraid for Harvey, we want the tension of climactic struggle and then catharsis, but Foote refuses to oblige us. In keeping Verna Kate behind the scenes, he doubles the risk. He takes away the possibility of catharsis through pity. Because we never see her, we cannot feel very sorry for her. So she becomes just one more victim in the routine tragedy of life.

Yet the same could be said of Velma and Stewart and Lena and the Griswolds and even Harvey and Laura. There is nothing special about their suffering. There are lonely alcoholics everywhere, and there are bereaved parents, childless widows like Lena who survive awful marriages, and lovesick adolescents like Stewart who have to live with the consequences of their reckless actions. And there are orphans and unloved children, too, in all the towns and cities of America. None of these lives is unusual. Their sufferings are melodramatic, of course, but LIFE is melodramatic!

So we do not feel especially sorry for Laura or for Harvey, our main characters. Not even for an unloved innocent like Laura, whose sadness is before us all the time. Instead, Foote makes us feel sorry for everyone. The tears for Laura which he repeatedly dams up in the audience by leaving out and cutting away from dramatic scenes seep out eventually for all the characters. In the end, he makes us want to sigh like Melville's narrator at the end of "Bartleby, the Scrivener": "Ah, Laura! Ah, Harrison! Ah, humanity!"

ᘯ

Works Cited

Foote, Horton. *Cousins and The Death of Papa*. New York: Grove, 1986.

———. *Laura Dennis*. New York: Dramatists Play Service, 1996.

Freedman, Samuel G. Introduction. *Cousins and The Death of Papa*. By Horton Foote. New York: Grove, 1986. xi–xxvi.

A Bibliography of Horton Foote's Work

The following works by Horton Foote have been produced for the stage, television, or film, though a few of the completed movies—like *The Chase* and *Hurry Sundown*—reflect little or none of his writing. Each collaboration, especially for motion pictures, has its own history which often modifies the texts and sometimes even limits Foote's personal contribution to the project. Although not a complete record, the listed productions indicate the general patterns in the staging of Foote's works.

Plays

Arrival and Departure. "Curtain raiser" for HB production of *The Road to the Graveyard.* October 15–25, 1980.

Blind Date. One-act play. Produced with *The Man Who Climbed the Pecan Trees,* The Loft Studio, Los Angeles, 1982. Dir. Peggy Feury. First New York production HB Playwrights Foundation, July, 1985, dir. Herbert Berghof, as trilogy *Harrison, Texas,* including *The Prisoner's Song* and *Blind Date.* Also Ensemble Studio Theatre, New York, May 1986, dir. Curt Dempster.

The Chase. First prod. and dir. Jose Ferrer, April 15, 1952, at The Playhouse Theatre, New York City. Starring John Hodiak, Kim Hunter, and Kim Stanley.

Daisy Speed. Dance play. Choreographed and danced by Valerie Bettis, April 1944, under title *Daisy Lee.*

Dividing the Estate. Premiere March 28, 1989, at McCarter Theatre, Princeton, New Jersey. Dir. Jamie Brown. Also produced at Great Lakes Playhouse, Cleveland, Ohio, October 11, 1990, and Roger Stevens Theatre, Winston-Salem, North Carolina, 1991, both dir. Gerald Freedman.

The Flowering of the Drama. Early play produced at Neighborhood Playhouse.

Gone with the Wind. Musical adaptation of Margaret Mitchell novel, 1970–73. Performed at Drury Lane Theatre, London, 1972–73. Music and lyrics by Harold Rome. Dallas Summer Musical, June 15, 1976.

Goodbye. Also titled *Goodbye to Richmond.* Commissioned and produced at Neighborhood Playhouse (1944), Baltimore Museum of Art and Hunter College, 1946.

The Habitation of Dragons. First produced at Pittsburgh Public Theater, September 20–October 23, 1988. Dir. Horton Foote. Starring Marco St. John, Hallie Foote, and Horton Foote, Jr.

Harrison, Texas. Title given to HB Playwrights Foundation presentation of 3 Foote one-acts: *The One-Armed Man, The Prisoner's Song,* and *Blind Date.* HB Playwrights Foundation, New York, July 9–22, 1985.

Homecoming. Produced in Washington, D.C. (1944) and later off-Broadway.

In a Coffin in Egypt. Produced 1980 at HB Playwrights Foundation. Directed by Horton Foote and Herbert Berghof. Starring Sandy Dennis.

John Turner Davis. Originally teleplay produced on Philco Television Playhouse in 1953. Staged off-Broadway at Sheridan Square Playhouse, 1956.

Land of the Astronauts. One-act play. First production Ensemble Studio Theatre, New York City, May 1988. Dir. Curt Dempster.

Laura Dennis. Produced by Signature Theatre Company, New York City, March 10–April 9, 1995. Dir. James Houghton.

The Lonely. Play with dance for Neighborhood Playhouse, co-dir. by Foote and Martha Graham, 1944.

The Man Who Climbed the Pecan Trees. First production The Loft Studio, Los Angeles, 1982, with *Blind Date*. Dir. William Traylor. Starring Peggy Feury and Albert Horton Foote. First New York production Ensemble Studio Theatre, July, 1988, dir. Curt Dempster.

The Midnight Caller. Produced off-Broadway at Sheridan Square Playhouse, 1956. Also Neighborhood Playhouse, starring Robert Duvall. Originally teleplay for Philco Television Playhouse in 1953.

Miss Lou. Produced at Neighborhood Playhouse, dir. Sanford Meisner, 1943.

Night Seasons. Produced at HB Playwrights Foundation, 1978. Premiered by American Stage Company, Teaneck, New Jersey, February 26, 1993. Dir. Horton Foote. Starring Hallie Foote and Jean Stapleton. In Signature Theater Series, November 4–December 4, 1994, dir. Horton Foote and starring Jean Stapleton and Hallie Foote.

The Old Friends. Produced at HB Playwrights Foundation, July 27–August 7, 1982.

The One-Armed Man. One-act play. Produced July, 1985, HB Playwrights Foundation, New York City, as part of *Harrison, Texas* trilogy, with *The Prisoner's Song* and *Blind Date*. Dir. Herbert Berghof.

Only the Heart. Originally titled *Mamie Borden*, produced by American Actors Company, Provincetown Playhouse, 1942–44.Dir. Mary Hunter. Starring Mildred Dunnock and June Walker. Also on Broadway, 1944.

The Orphans' Home (nine-play cycle): (1) *Roots in a Parched Ground*; (2) *Convicts*; (3) *Lily Dale*, reading at Ensemble Studio Theatre, 1977, produced Samuel Beckett Theatre, New York City, Nov. 1986. Starring Molly Ringwald; (4) *Widow Claire*, prod. Circle in the Square Theatre, New York City, 1986, dir. Michael

Lindsay-Hogg. Starring Matthew Broderick and Hallie Foote; (5) *Courtship*, prod. HB Playwrights Foundation, July 5–16, 1978, dir. Horton Foote. Also Actors Theatre, Louisville, 1984, and Dallas Contemporary American Theatre, Dallas, Texas, 1985; (6) *Valentine's Day*, prod. HB Playwrights Foundation, 1980. Also Dallas Contemporary American Theatre, February 27–April 7, 1985; (7) *1918*, prod. HB Playwrights Foundation, dir. Horton Foote. Also A.C.T. Theatre, San Francisco, California, 1991; (8) *Cousins*, prod. The Loft Theatre, Los Angeles, 1983; (9) *Death of Papa*. Premiere, Playmakers Repertory Company, Chapel Hill, North Carolina, February 8, 1997, dir. Michael Wilson. Starring Nicholas Shaw, Hallie Foote, Matthew Broderick, and Ellen Burstyn, Ray Virta, and Polly Holliday.

Out of My House. Four one-act plays produced by American Actors Company at Provincetown Playhouse: *Night after Night, Celebration, The Girls, Behold a Cry*. Also considered four-part single play. 1942. *Celebration* also produced at ANTA Theatre, New York City, 1950.

People in the Show. Produced in Washington, DC, in late 1940s. Set at New York World's Fair, May 1940.

The Prisoner's Song. One-act play. Produced July, 1985, HB Playwrights Foundation, New York City. Dir. by Herbert Berghof. With *The One-Armed Man* and *Blind Date* as *Harrison, Texas*.

The Return. Produced by King-Smith Productions, Washington, D.C., in late 40s. Early version of *In a Coffin in Egypt*.

The Road to the Graveyard. First draft early 1950. Produced at HB Playwrights Foundation, 1982, and Ensemble Studio Theatre, New York City, May 1985, dir. Curt Dempster.

The Roads to Home (trilogy of one-act plays): *A Nightingale, The Dearest of Friends*, and *Spring Dance*. First produced Manhattan Punch Line Theatre, New York City, March 25, 1982. Dir. Calvin

Skaggs. Starring Carol Fox, Rochelle Oliver, and Hallie Foote. Also Lambs Theatre, New York City, September 1992.

Roundabout. Ballet with Jerome Robbins, 1953. Produced in Broadway musical *Two for the Show.*

Talking Pictures. First produced at Asolo Theater, Sarasota, Florida, 1990. Dir. John Ulmer. Also Stages Theatre, Houston, Texas, 1991. First play in Signature Theatre Series, Sept. 23–Oct. 23, 1994, dir. Carol Goodheart.

Texas Town. First full-length play. Prod. American Actors Company, dir. Mary Hunter, 1941.

Themes and Variations. Produced by King-Smith Workshop, Washington, D.C., in late 40s.

The Traveling Lady. Produced by The Playwrights Company at The Playhouse, New York City, October 27, 1954. Dir. Vincent J. Donehue. Starring Kim Stanley and Lonny Chapman. Later produced at Alley Theatre, Houston, Texas, 1986. Also produced as teleplay with same title and film titled *Baby, the Rain Must Fall.*

The Trip to Bountiful. Prod. The Theatre Guild and Fred Coe. Dir. Vincent Donehue. Henry Miller's Theatre, New York City, November 3, 1953. Starring Lillian Gish, Jo Van Fleet, and Eva Marie Saint. Also teleplay in March, 1953. Also produced at Greenwich Mews Theatre, New York City, 1962; A.D. Players, Houston, Texas, Zachary Scott Theatre, Austin, Texas, both in 1990; Actors Theatre, Louisville, Kentucky, and New Harmony, Indiana, Theatre, 1991; Theatre Festival, Perth, Australia, 1992; TheatreFest, Upper Montclair, New Jersey, 1993; The Phoenix Theatre Company, Purchase, New York, 1993.

Two's Company. Theatre revue starring Bette Davis, 1953.

Wharton Dance. First one-act play. Written and produced by American Actors Company, 1939–40.

The Young Man from Atlanta. Produced by Signature Theatre Company, January 27–February 26, 1995. Awarded 1995 Pulitzer Prize for Drama. Also produced at Alley Theatre, Houston, Texas, 1996, dir. Peter Masterson, and starring Ralph Waite and Carlin Glinn; Goodman Theatre, Chicago, Illinois (January 1997), dir. Robert Falls, and starring Shirley Knight and Rip Torn, restaged at the Longacre Theatre, New York City (with same dir. and stars, March 1997).

Teleplays

"Alone." Original teleplay for Showtime Television, 1997, starring Hume Cronyn, James Earl Jones, Piper Laurie.

"Barn Burning." Adaptation of William Faulkner story for American Short Story series on PBS, March 17, 1980. Dir. Peter Werner. Starring Tommy Lee Jones and Diane Kagan.

"The Dancers." Philco Television Playhouse, NBC, March 7, 1954. Prod. Fred Coe, dir. Vincent J. Donehue. Starring Joanne Woodward and James Broderick.

"The Death of the Old Man ." First Person Playhouse, NBC, July 17, 1953. Prod. Fred Coe, dir. Arthur Penn. Starring Mildred Natwick and William Hanson.

"Displaced Person." Adaptation of Flannery O'Connor short story for PBS American Short Story series. Dir. Glenn Jordan. Starring Irene Worth and John Houseman. Broadcast April 14, 1980.

"Drug Store, Sunday Noon." Commissioned adaptation of Robert Hutchinson short story. Omnibus, ABC, December 16, 1956. Dir. Andrew McCullough. Starring Helen Hayes.

"The Expectant Relations." The Philco Television Playhouse, NBC, June 21, 1953. Prod. Fred Coe, dir. Vincent J. Donehue.

"Flight." Playwrights '56, NBC, February 28, 1956. Prod. Fred Coe, dir. Vincent J. Donehue. Starring Kim Stanley.

"The Gambling Heart." Dupont Show of the Week, NBC, February 23, 1964. Prod. David Susskind and Daniel Melnick, dir. Paul Bogart. Starring Tom Bosley and Estelle Parsons.

"The Habitation of Dragons." Writer's Cinema, Amblin-Steven Spielberg Production, TNT, Spring 1992. Teleplay from Foote play by same name. Dir. Michael Lindsay-Hogg, and starring Brad Davis, Jean Stapleton, Frederic Forrest, Pat Hingle, Hallie Foote, and Horton Foote, Jr.

"John Turner Davis." Goodyear Television Playhouse, NBC, November 5, 1953. Prod. Fred Coe, dir. Arthur Penn.

"Keeping On." Presented by PBS' American Playhouse, 1983. Prod. and dir. Barbara Kopple.

"Ludie Brooks." Aired on "Lamp unto My Feet," CBS, February 4, 1951. Prod. Pamela Ilott, dir. Herbert Kenwith.

"A Member of the Family." Studio One, CBS, March 25, 1957. Prod. Herbert Brodkin, dir. Norman Felton. Starring Hume Cronyn and James Broderick.

"The Midnight Caller." Philco Television Playhouse, NBC, December 13, 1953. Prod. Fred Coe, dir. Vincent J. Donehue.

"The Night of the Storm." Dupont Show of the Month, March 21, 1961. Prod. David Susskind, dir. Daniel Petrie. Starring Julie Harris, E. G. Marshall, Mildred Dunnock, Mark Connelly, Fritz Weaver, and Jo Van Fleet. Orig. title "A Golden String," also called "Roots in a Parched Ground."

"The Oil Well." Goodyear Theatre, NBC, May 17, 1953. Prod. by Fred Coe, dir. Vincent J. Donehue. Starring Dorothy Gish and E. G. Marshall.

"The Old Beginning." Goodyear Theatre, NBC, November 23, 1952. Dir. Vincent J. Donehue.

"The Old Man." Adaptation of William Faulkner story. Playhouse 90, CBS, November 20, 1958. Prod. Fred Coe, dir. John

Frankenheimer. Starring Geraldine Page and Sterling Hayden. Revised version on Hallmark Playhouse, February 9, 1997. Prod. Brent Shields, dir. John Kent Harrison. Starring Jeanne Tripplehorn and Arliss Howard.

"Only the Heart." Kraft Television Theatre, NBC, January 21, 1948.

"The Quaker Oats Show." 40 scripts for Gabby Hayes weekly television show also called "The Gabby Hayes Show." October 15, 1950–December 23, 1951.

"The Roads to Home." U.S. Steel Hour, ABC, April 26, 1955. Early teleplay different from later trilogy of one-acts with same title.

"The Rocking Chair." NBC, May 24, 1953, starring Mildred Natwick and Ian Keith (aired on series "The Doctor").

"The Shadow of Willie Greer." Philco Television Playhouse, NBC, May 30, 1954. Prod. Fred Coe, dir. Vincent Donehue. Starring Dorothy Gish, Pat Hingle, and Wright King.

"The Shape of the River." First draft March 15, 1960. Playhouse 90, CBS, May 2, 1960. Prod. Fred Coe. Starring Franchot Tone and Leif Erickson. Early versions called "Mark Twain."

"The Story of a Marriage." PBS American Playhouse five-part series based on *Courtship, On Valentine's Day*, and *1918*. April 1987.

"The Tears of My Sister." First Person Playhouse, NBC, August 14, 1953. Prod. Fred Coe, dir. Arthur Penn. Starring Kim Stanley (voice-over) and Lenka Peterson.

"Tomorrow." Playhouse 90, CBS, March 7, 1960. Prod. Herbert Brodkin, dir. Robert Mulligan. Based on William Faulkner story. Starring Kim Stanley, Richard Boone, Charles Bickford, Chill Wills, and Beulah Bondi. Also filmed under same title.

"The Travelers." The Goodyear Theatre, NBC, April 27, 1952. Prod. Fred Coe, dir. Delbert Mann. Also telecast March 7, 1954, on Philco Television Playhouse. Prod. Fred Coe, dir. Vincent Donehue.

"The Traveling Lady." Studio One, CBS, April 22, 1957. Prod. Herbert Brodkin, dir. Robert Mulligan. Starring Kim Stanley, Steven Hill, Robert Loggia, Wendy Hiller, and Mildred Dunnock. Kim Stanley won Sylvania Award for her performance. Also stage play and filmed as *Baby, the Rain Must Fall.*

"The Trip to Bountiful." Goodyear Television Playhouse, NBC, March 1, 1953. Prod. Fred Coe, dir. Vincent Donehue. Starring Lillian Gish and Eva Marie Saint.

"A Young Lady of Property." Philco Television Playhouse, NBC, April 5, 1953. Prod. Fred Coe, dir. Vincent J. Donehue. Starring Kim Stanley and Joanne Woodward.

Screenplays

Baby, the Rain Must Fall. Adaptation of Foote play *The Traveling Lady.* Prod. Alan J. Pakula, dir. by Robert Mulligan. Starring Steve McQueen and Lee Remick. Columbia Pictures, 1965.

The Chase. Late revisions to 1965 screenplay by Lillian Hellman from Foote play of same title. Prod. Sam Spiegel, dir. Arthur Penn. Starring Marlon Brando, Robert Redford, Jane Fonda, Angie Dickinson, and Robert Duvall. Horizon Pictures, 1966.

Convicts. Based on *The Orphans' Home* play of same title. Dir. Peter Masterson. Starring Robert Duvall, James Earl Jones, and Lukas Haas. Produced 1990 by Jonathan Krane and Sterling VanWagenen. MCEG-Sterling, 1990.

Courtship. From *The Orphans' Home* play of same title. Prod. Lillian V. Foote and Marcus Viscidi, dir. Howard Cummings. Starring Hallie Foote, Amanda Plummer, Rochelle Oliver, Michael Higgins, William Converse-Roberts. Indian Falls, 1986.

Hurry Sundown. Early versions commissioned by Otto Preminger. 1965–67. Foote's script not used in film though his name is retained. Released in 1967 by Paramount.

Lily Dale. Screenplay for play in *The Orphans' Home* with same title. Prod. Soisson Murphy and Walter Foote, dir. Charles Martin Smith. Not completed. Later produced and released in June 1996, for Showtime and dir. Peter Masterson. With Mary Stuart Masterson, Sam Shepard, Stockard Channing, Tim Guinee, and Jean Stapleton.

Of Mice and Men. Adaptation of Steinbeck novel. Dir. Gary Sinise. Starring John Malkovich and Gary Sinise. Released 1992 by MGM.

1918. Screenplay based on play from *The Orphans' Home* cycle with same title. Prod. Lewis Allen, Peter Newman, and Lillian Foote, dir. Ken Harrison. Starring Matthew Broderick, William Converse-Roberts, and Hallie Foote. Guadalupe Entertainment and Cinecom, 1985.

On Valentine's Day. Adaptation of Foote play *Valentine's Day* from *The Orphans' Home* cycle. Prod. Lillian V. Foote and Calvin Skaggs. Dir. Ken Harrison. Starring William Converse-Roberts, Matthew Broderick, and Hallie Foote. 1986.

The Stalking Moon. First draft completed September 14, 1967. Foote's version not used; final script completed in December 1967 by Alvin Sargent. Dir. Robert Mulligan, released 1968 by National General.

Storm Fear. Adaptation of Clinton Seeley novel. Prod. and dir. Cornel Wilde for Theodora Productions, released by United Artists, 1956.

Tender Mercies . Original screenplay. Dir. Bruce Beresford. Starring Robert Duvall, with Tess Harper, Betty Buckley, Ellen Barkin, Wilford Brimley. Academy Award winner for Best Original Screenplay, 1983–84. Writers Guild Award for Original Screenplay. Christopher Award for Best Picture. Antron Media/EMI, 1982. American entry in Cannes Film Festival, 1983. Robert Duvall won Best Actor Award for film.

To Kill a Mockingbird. Adaptation of Harper Lee novel. Prod. Alan J. Pakula, dir. Robert Mulligan. Starring Gregory Peck. Universal, 1963. Academy Award for Best Screenplay Based on Material from Another Medium. Writer's Guild of America Award for Best American Drama. American entry in 1963 Cannes Film Festival. Gregory Peck won Academy Award for Best Actor.

Tomorrow. Adaptation of William Faulkner, prod. Paul Roebling and Gilbert Pearlman, dir. Joseph Anthony. Starring Robert Duvall and Olga Bellin. Filmgroup, 1972.

The Trip to Bountiful. Based on Foote play of same title. Prod. Sterling Van Wagenen, dir. Peter Masterson. Starring Geraldine Page, John Heard, Carlin Glynn, Richard Bradford, and Rebecca DeMornay. Island Pictures, 1985. Film for which Geraldine Page won her only Academy Award. Nominated for Best Adaptation by Academy and Writers Guild.

Other Published Writing

The Chase. New York: Rinehart and Company, 1956. Novel based on play of the same title.

Emily, published in *Kansas City Review* 15.4 (Summer 1949): 263–66. Projected second play of trilogy *The Brazorians,* apparently incomplete.

"The Long, Long Trek." *Dance Observer* 11.8 (October 1944): 8–99. Foote asks artists in dance to avoid temptations of "finance capitalism" and stay true to their talent and vision.

A Selective Annotated Bibliography
of Critical Work on Horton Foote

Briley, Rebecca. *You Can Go Home Again: The Focus on Family in the Works of Horton Foote*. New York: Peter Lang, 1993. A revision of her dissertation, the only book-length study of Foote's work, and first comprehensive analysis of his published work. Focuses on father/son relationships and deals with religious implications in this work for theater, television, and film.

Broughton, Irv. "Horton Foote." *The Writer's Mind: Interviews*. Ed. Irv Broughton. Vol. 2. Fayetteville: U of Arkansas P, 1990. 3–23. Concise and thorough interview in which Foote briefly notes the role of acting in his work and compares his writing for theater and film. He describes (1) opportunities and dangers of "opening up" the physical limitations of theater when translating to film, (2) the tendency to lose dialogue in pursuit of visuals, and (3) in-process revision of film. Focuses on "the oral tradition" of South (19) and Foote's "enormous compassion for the human condition" (21).

Burkhart, Marian. "Horton Foote's Many Roads Home: An American Playwright and His Characters." *Commonweal* 115.4 (26 February 1988): 110–115. Though impressionistic, this essay accurately describes the internal struggles in Foote's otherwise ordinary characters. Burkhart also identifies the writer's demythologizing of American popular belief about identity and heroism. At the heart of the work she finds a struggle of goodness and mystery with violence and fear; the central question for Foote's work is, she says, "When so much in human nature seems to relish chaos, how do some people succeed in achieving lives orderly enough to permit a civilized society to exist?" (112).

Davis, Ronald L. "Roots in Parched Ground: An Interview with Horton Foote." *Southwest Review* 73 (Summer 1988): 298–318. A good general introduction to Foote's writing methods and history in both theater and film. Has accurate discussions of his first writing experiences, including the influence of dance, and focused analysis of most major films.

DiGaetani, John L. "Horton Foote." *A Search for a Postmodern Theater: Interviews with Contemporary Playwrights.* Westport, Connecticut: Greenwood Press, 1991. 65–71. A brief but well-focused interview in which Foote declares the need for "structure in life" and his desire "not to destroy but to construct" (67). He rejected, he says, the excesses of the 60s for his personal form of experimentation. Defines storytelling and language as central to his work and says film uses both visual and verbal concentration while theater is more verbal. He tries, Foote says, to write instinctively, without the "over-awareness" that "can stifle writing" (70).

Edgerton, Gary. "A Visit to the Imaginary Landscape of Harrison, Texas: Sketching the Film Career of Horton Foote." *Literature/Film Quarterly* 17.1 (1989): 2–12. Despite an inaccuracy or two, a very readable and useful introduction to Foote as an independent filmmaker. Surveys his career as a writer for and producer of films outside the Hollywood tradition. Sees Foote as "helping to establish a kind of filmic equivalent to regional theatre or literature for domestic filmgoers" (12).

Foote, Horton. "Horton Foote" [Interview]. *When I Was Just Your Age.* Ed. Robert Flynn and Susan Russell. Denton, Texas: University of North Texas Press, 1992. 13–24. The most personal and self-revealing of the interviews with the writer. Remembers many precious times with father, the storytelling environment, and "a deep love in our family, a great sense of kinship which always made me feel very secure" (24). While the interview focuses on his childhood memories in Wharton, Texas, Foote sketches his early career as an actor and writer for the

American Actors Company. [rptd. in *Southern Partisan* 12.3 (1992): 30–34]

——. Introduction. *Roots in a Parched Ground, Convicts, Lily Dale, The Widow Claire: The First Four Plays in The Orphans' Home Cycle.* By Horton Foote. New York: Grove Press, 1988. xi–xv. Brief but illuminating history of the composition of *The Orphans' Home*, the influence of Charles Ives, the themes of change and unreliable memory. He also notes his respect for Katherine Anne Porter, especially "Pale Horse, Pale Rider" and "Old Mortality." Ends with hope that the plays are "true to their place and time—true at least to my memory of what I was told or have seen" (xv).

——. "*Tomorrow*: The Genesis of a Screenplay." *Faulkner, Modernism and Film: Faulkner and Yoknapatawpha.* Ed. Evans Harrington and Ann J. Abadie. Jackson: UP of Mississippi, 1979. 149–162. Useful description of process of adapting Faulkner's story, though *Tomorrow and Tomorrow and Tomorrow* is more general and inclusive study. Also in *Faulkner, Modernism, and Film* is Foote essay "On First Dramatizing Faulkner" about adapting "Old Man" (49–65).

——. "Writing for Film." *Film and Literature: A Comparative Approach to Adaptation.* Ed. Wendell Aycock and Michael Schoenecke. Lubbock: Texas Tech UP, 1988. 5–20. Foote surveys his film work, emphasizing "adapting...is in some ways for me the most difficult and painful process imaginable" (7). Brief but pointed statements on each of his early film productions and a detailed explanation of restructuring of narrative in *Tomorrow*. A concise introduction to the writer's involvement in the process of filmmaking.

Freedman, Samuel G. "From the Heart of Texas." *The New York Times Magazine.* 9 February 1986, sec. 6: 30–31, 50, 61–63, 73. A seminal study of the influence of Wharton, Texas, on the writing of Foote. Mixes interview material with survey of some primary subjects and themes. Finds change, the loss of tradition and identity, and the need for dignity as the main themes of Foote's work. [variation of this essay rptd. in introduction to *Cousins, The Death of Papa: Two Plays from The Orphans' Home Cycle*. New York: Grove, 1989. xi–xxvi]

Martin, Carter. "Horton Foote's Southern Family in *Roots in a Parched Ground*." *The Texas Review* 12.1–2 (Spring–Summer 1991): 76–82. Studies the centrality of place and family in Foote's work, especially *Roots in a Parched Ground*, comparing his Harrison with the fictional places of Faulkner and other Southern writers. Unfortunately, the essay assumes Horton Foote, following all Southern writers, feels guilty for leaving the South for "the larger ideal world where people talk, dance, and love happily." His writing, Martin argues, is compensation for the "home he can never recapture nor return to" (77). More convincing is the discussion of the "myth of family" (80) in which he recognizes that though family in *Roots* can be stifling and even maddening, Foote's "dialectic is a complex, basically affirmative definition of the family" (81).

McLaughlin, Buzz. "Conversation with Horton Foote" [Interview]. *The Dramatists Guild Quarterly* 29.4 (Winter 1993): 17–27. A concise explanation of Foote's writing process, including the importance of voice, character, and revision. Also the writer's belief in personal rules and the value of creative collaboration. Foote, in passing, notes his belief in people's capacity for "tenderness and mercy" (23), "courage and endurance" (24). Comments on adaptation, including *Of Mice and Men*.

Moore, Barbara, and David G. Yellin, eds. *Horton Foote's Three Trips to Bountiful*. Dallas: Southern Methodist UP, 1993. A study, like *Tomorrow and Tomorrow and Tomorrow*, which examines the evolution of the *Bountiful* story from teleplay (Goodyear Television Playhouse, March 1, 1953) to stage (Henry Miller's Theatre, New York City, November 3, 1953) to film (Island Pictures, 1985). Includes introduction which describes production histories and interpretations of the three versions, interviews with artists (including Foote), a useful chart of changes, and an afterword by Horton Foote. The bibliography is well focused and useful for Foote research.

Porter, Laurin R. "An Interview with Horton Foote." *Studies in American Drama, 1945–Present* 6.2 (1991): 177–94. A coherent and focused discussion which focuses on *The Orphans' Home* cycle but also includes Foote's thoughts on and experiences with filmmaking. Brief survey of his early experiences with writing, comments on role in his work of visual material, acting, poetry, and music.

Price, Reynolds. "Introduction." *Courtship, Valentine's Day, 1918: Three Plays from The Orphans' Home Cycle*. New York: Grove, 1987. ix–xiii. A brief but most provocative statement on Foote's writing. Emphasizes the simplicity of its means for complex and universal ends, comparing Foote's study in *Tender Mercies* of the "dark mystery" "of human degradation and regeneration" with that of St. Augustine (xi). Describes the writer as "the supreme musician among our great American playwrights" (xi) whose language is "pruned and shaped but not visibly transformed" (xii).

Skaggs, Calvin. "Interview with Horton Foote." *The American Short Story*. Ed. Calvin Skaggs. New York: Dell, 1977. 329–36. Focusing on Foote's adaptation of Flannery O'Connor's "The Displaced Person," this interview is the most detailed and analytical discussion of his methods of adapting. Discusses his need for sympathy with the writer, the conscious sense of structure, O'Connor's unique vision. Use of personal visual material and visuals in work but not specific actors during creative process. Foote discusses at some length O'Connor's "terrible vision...so bleak...so totally without our consent" (333) and his interpretation of the main characters.

Smelstor, Marjorie. "'The World's an Orphans' Home': Horton Foote's Social and Moral History." *Southern Quarterly* 19.2 (Winter

1991): 7–16. Establishes that Foote's use of home, like that of other Southern writers, is a metaphor for identity and rootedness in the face of change and loss. Also emphasizes the primacy of storytelling, the circular and musical structures, and the poetic language of the cycle. Places *The Orphans' Home* in the context of the modern "tension between continuity and change, tradition and innovation, nineteenth-century innocence and twentieth-century experience" (14).

Smith, Amanda. "Horton Foote: A Writer's Journey." *Varia* July/August 1987: 18–20, 23, 26–27. The most readable and accurate of the popular articles on Foote's career, the involvement of his family, and his main influences and themes. Also notes his use of writing as a process of growing awareness and a hope that his work will "get people to reexamine and to think about each other and relationships" (27).

Watson, Charles S. "Beyond the Commercial Media: Horton Foote's Procession of Defeated Men." *Studies in American Drama, 1945–Present* 8.2 (1993): 175–87. Argues that Foote's willingness to examine "the broken lives of his defeated men" (175–76) and avoid happy endings in his later work indicates the writer's independence from commercial interests. Notes the possible influence of William Inge on Foote, especially darkness expressed as fear. Watson recognizes that Foote asks "self-determination" from his characters, often inspired by "a fortifying individual" (180) and requiring a clear reality principle and personal will (184). But finds Foote's "major subject" in "the parental causes" and dramatization of "the human ruins" (185) in some men's lives, which allow him to move beyond the conventions of theater and film.

Wood, Gerald C., ed. *Selected One-Act Plays of Horton Foote.* Dallas: Southern Methodist UP, 1989. The texts of 17 one-acts since the 1950s, a preface by Foote, general introduction which describes Foote's career, major subjects and themes as well brief analyses and production notes on the individual plays. Chronology and highly selective bibliography.

——. "Horton Foote: An Interview." *Post Script* 10.3 (Summer 1991): 3–12. Complements interview in *Literature/Film Quarterly*. Foote focuses on film influences and preferences, adaptation vs. original writing, theater vs. film, the radical commercialization of Hollywood. He also discusses the role of the past in his work, the importance of what he calls "texture," his female characters and mystery, and his goals as a filmmaker.

——. "Old Beginnings and Roads to Home: Horton Foote and Mythic Realism." *Christianity and Literature* 45.3–4 (Spring–Summer 1996): 359–72. Explains Foote's realism as the result of his experience with method acting, involvement with American Actors Company, and experiments with dance-in-theater. Then argues that these early impulses were modified by Foote's participation in a tradition of Southern writing which focuses on the loss of religious community for the artist. Foote's resolution in a cyclical pattern of "Going away and coming home" (368) and "myth as healing" (370), which are expressions of "the creative tension between" Foote's "public responsibility to report and his private need to believe" (370).

—— and Terry Barr. "'A Certain Kind of Writer': An Interview with Horton Foote." *Literature/Film Quarterly* 14.4 (1986): 226–37. Foote describes his methods as writer, the literary influences on his work, process of adaptation and his experiments with independent filmmaking. Some discussion of his themes, goals as writer, audiences.

Yellin, David, and Marie Connors, eds. *Tomorrow & Tomorrow & Tomorrow*. Jackson: UP of Mississippi, 1985. A study of the Faulkner story and Foote's two adaptations for television's Playhouse 90 (March 7, 1960) and the 1972 film. Includes the three versions, a textbookish but useful discussion of the three productions ("Faulkner and Foote and Chemistry," 3–31), and interviews with the artists, including Horton Foote. Also a bibliography with few Foote references.

Contributors

TERRY BARR received his Ph.D. from The University of Tennessee-Knoxville in 1986, with his dissertation examining "The Ordinary World of Horton Foote." He has published (with Gerald Wood) an interview with Horton Foote in *Literature/Film Quarterly*, articles on Jewish film and literature in *Studies in Popular Culture, The Journal of Popular Film and TV, Studies in American Culture*, and an essay for the forthcoming anthology *The Quiet Voices: Rabbis in the Black Civil Rights Era* (The University of Alabama Press, 1997). Associate Professor of English and Film Studies at Presbyterian College in Clinton, South Carolina, he lives in Greenville, South Carolina, with his wife and two daughters.

CRYSTAL BRIAN is a native of Texas with degrees from Baylor University (B.A.) and the University of California (M.F.A. and Ph.D.). A former theatre critic for the *L.A. Weekly*, she is a professional director in Los Angeles, having earned awards for her productions of Horton Foote's plays, *The Habitation of Dragons* and *Laura Dennis*. She is currently an Associate Professor of Theatre Arts at Whittier College and is completing a Horton Foote biography entitled *The Roads to Home*.

REBECCA LUTTRELL BRILEY is the author of *You Can Go Home Again: The Focus on Family in the Works of Horton Foote* (Peter Lang, 1993) and *River of Earth: Mythic Consciousness in the Works of James Still* (Appalachian Heritage, 1981). She teaches at Jefferson Community College, Louisville, Kentucky.

MARION D. CASTLEBERRY has worked as an educator and professional director for twenty-five years. A graduate of Louisiana State University, he wrote his dissertation on the significance of family to Horton Foote's theory and practice. His other research interests include modern and contemporary American drama and performance theory.

KIMBALL KING has edited a casebook on Sam Shepard for the Garland casebooks on modern dramatists and serves as general editor for this series. He has also published book-length studies on modern English, Irish, and American drama and is Professor of English at the University of North Carolina at Chapel Hill.

S. DIXON MCDOWELL is an Associate Professor and Chair of Radio, Television and Film at The University of Southern Mississippi. He has written an award-winning original screenplay and produced numerous short films and video programs. Professor McDowell is currently in post-production on *Horton Foote: Regional Voice—Universal Vision*, a feature-length documentary about the life and work of Horton Foote.

DEAN MENDELL holds the Ph.D. in English from Washington University in St. Louis, where he won the A.E. Hotchner Playwriting Award. His academic interests include American literature and twentieth-century poetry and drama. He currently teaches writing and literature at Touro College in New York City.

LAURIN PORTER is an Associate Professor of English at the University of Texas—Arlington, where she teaches drama, twentieth-century American literature and women's studies. She is the author of *The Banished Prince: Time, Memory, and Ritual in the Late Plays of Eugene O'Neill* (1988) and numerous articles on modern and contemporary drama. Her interview with Foote appears in *Studies in Modern American Drama, 1945–Present* (1991).

SUSAN UNDERWOOD is an Assistant Professor of English at Carson-Newman College where she teaches twentieth-century American literature, multicultural literature, and poetry. She earned an MFA in creative writing from the University of North Carolina at Greensboro and the Ph.D. from Florida State University. She has published scholarly articles, poetry, and fiction in a variety of edited collections, journals, and anthologies.

GERALD C. WOOD has written essays on literature and film for various journals including the *Keats-Shelley Journal, Byron Journal*, and *Markham Review* as well as *Recasting: Gone with the Wind in American Culture* (Florida, 1983) and *Handbook of American Film Genres* (Greenwood, 1988). In addition to interviews with Horton Foote for *Literature/Film Quarterly* (with Terry Barr) and *Post Script*, he has published a critical essay on Foote for *Christianity and Literature* and edited *Selected One-Act Plays of Horton Foote* (SMU, 1989). He is a Professor of English and Chair of the English Department at Carson-Newman College.

TIM WRIGHT teaches as an Assistant Professor in the School of Cinema, Television and Theatre Arts at Regent University in Virginia Beach, Virginia, where he earned his Ph.D. in Communication Studies. He continues to freelance as a professional actor and writer while pursuing his ongoing research on the works of Horton Foote and other contemporary American writers and filmmakers. He currently lives in Norfolk, Virginia, with his wife and four children.

Index

A

Agee, James 49
Allen, Lewis 139
American Actors Company 1, 2, 7,
    24–26, 30–32, 205–7, 217, 221
Anthony, Joseph 25, 53, 146

B

Beresford, Bruce 142, 146, 148
Berghof, Herbert 9, 203–6
Bergman, Ingmar 138
Bettis, Valerie 25, 31, 32
Broderick, Matthew 143

C

Chayefsky, Paddy 36, 37
Chekhov, Anton 2, 6, 49, 71, 82, 83,
    99, 103, 110, 129, 141, 142
Chodorow, Nancy 168, 169, 174
Christian Science 20, 97, 134, 170
Coe, Fred 36–39, 43–46, 51, 163,
    207–11
Conkle, E. P. 4, 25

D

Degas, Edgar 74
DeMille, Agnes 25, 32
Donehue, Vincent J. 39, 44, 45, 207–
    11
Duvall, Robert 53, 140, 142, 143,
    145, 189, 205, 211–13

E

expressionism 67, 68

F

Faulkner, William 2, 8, 49–56, 58, 63,
    112, 133, 208–10, 213, 217,
    218, 221
Foote, Albert Horton (father) 15, 16,
    22, 89, 163
Foote, Hallie (daughter) 40, 132
Foote, Harriet Gautier (mother) 14,
    16, 20, 23, 29–30, 40, 89, 163
Foote, Horton
  awards
    Academy Award 1, 8, 9, 137
    Christopher Award 9
    Compostela Award 10
    Ensemble Studio Theatre
        Founders Award 9
    Independent Film Award 9
    Lucille Lortel Award 1, 11
    Luminas Award 9
    Outer Critics Circle Award 11
    Pulitzer Prize 1, 11, 137, 180
    William Inge Lifetime Achieve-
        ment Award 10
    Writers Guild of America Award
        1, 8–11
  works
    Alone 11, 208
    Arrival and Departure 9, 203
    Baby, the Rain Must Fall 8, 144,
        145, 173, 207, 211
    Barn Burning (adaptation) 9, 54,
        60, 63, 208
    Blind Date 9, 164, 203–6
    Chase, The 2, 8, 139, 149, 167,
        203, 211, 213

DATE DUE

GAYLORD

PRINTED IN U.S.A.